D1104289

Manufacturing Powerlessness in the Black Diaspora

Manufacturing Powerlessness in the Black Diaspora

Inner-City Youth and the New Global Frontier

Charles Green

ALTAMIRA
P R E S S

A Division of
ROWMAN & LITTLEFIELD PUBLISHERS, INC.
Walnut Creek • Lanham • New York • Oxford

ALTAMIRA PRESS
A Division of Rowman & Littlefield Publishers, Inc.
1630 North Main Street, #367
Walnut Creek, CA 94596
http://www.altamirapress.com

Rowman & Littlefield Publishers, Inc.
4720 Boston Way
Lanham, MD 20706

12 Hid's Copse Road
Cumnor Hill, Oxford OX2 9JJ, England

British Library Cataloguing in Publication Information Available

Library of Congress Cataloging-in-Publication Data

Green, Charles (Charles St. Clair)
    Manufacturing powerlessness in the black diaspora : inner-city youth and the
new global frontier / Charles Green.
        p. cm.
    Includes bibliographical references and index.
    ISBN 0-7425-0268-6 (alk. paper) — ISBN 0-7425-0269-4 (pbk. : alk. paper)
    1. Urban youth—United States.   2. Urban youth—Caribbean area.   3. Urban youth
Africa, East.   4. African diaspora.   5. Inner cities.   6. Globalization—Social aspects.
I. Title.

HQ796.G723   2001
306.76—dc21   00-065065

Printed in the United States of America

∞™ The paper used in this publication meets the minimum requirements of American
National Standard for Information Sciences—Permanence of Paper for Printed Library
Materials, ANSI/NISO Z39.48-1992.

In Memory of Mummy,
the peacemaker and my inspiration
and for Nia and Chenza,
the future

Contents

List of Tables

Preface

Contrary to popular belief, the problems of contemporary urban life are not monopolized by black people; rather, they are the shared experiences of poor and working-class people around the globe. In the case of black people, because of exploitation and the history of racism they have endured and continue to endure, they have been victimized and labeled the source of the problem. What to do about the black problem became, in Winthrop Jordan's terms, the white man's burden. Europeans have borne this burden throughout the periods of enslavement and colonialism with little, if any, change upon entering the twenty-first century.

Manufacturing Powerlessness bridges my scholarly interest in development, political empowerment, race and ethnic relations, international migration, and diasporic studies. It is the culmination of a decade-long quest for answers to questions concerning the plight of urban blacks across regional borders with the hope of identifying relevant policy solutions. Specifically, these questions probe the nature of persistent powerlessness in the black diaspora, the interface of historic racism and the new globalization in understanding powerlessness and the urban crisis, and the similarities and differences of powerlessness and the urban crisis between blacks from developed and developing regions.

Insufficient attention has been directed to those structural and sociocultural forces that operate to keep black people in their immiserated state wherever they happen to be on the globe. Stated differently, there is a need for critical examination of those forces that contribute to the manufacture or reproduction of urban powerlessness on the African continent and in the diaspora. Most visible among these forces are economic and cultural globalization, the system of white supremacy, inept leaders, and, too often, ineffective government-sponsored social policies. Few analysts would disagree that the most vulnerable subpopulations happen to be youth, women, and small children.[1] Contributing to youths' vulnerability is their lack of marketable skills and, as well, their unpreparedness to assume full responsibility for their personal needs.

It is not the case that the powerless quietly accept their condition. Quite to the contrary, they continue to resist their condition in various ways. We see, for example, the rise of hip-hop and the rap genre, the escalation of informal economic activities, crime and violence, and at times, direct protest. But because the powerless are politically fragmented, their effective mobilization is at best tenuous. Studies are needed that seek a better understanding of the urban condition by exploring the similarities and differences of problems across cultural borders. These studies will be helpful in countering the claim that solutions to problems can be found in the same shopping bag. Efforts by international agencies to assist the governments of developing nations in finding immediate solutions for problems in their urban areas are very often misguided. These agencies operate under the assumption that if problems are similarly manifested, then a similar set of strategies can be applied to resolve them. Such an approach represents a departure from basic sociological wisdom about societal relativism that underscores the importance of conducting analysis through a socially specific lens.

In the early 1990s, the debate among leading American sociologists and other social scientists on the urban question had reached its zenith. Liberals and conservatives were visible in framing that debate, and, unsurprisingly, the liberal voices were painstakingly careful not to disturb the status quo. In 1987, William Julius Wilson's highly acclaimed book, *The Truly Disadvantaged,* described the problem of the "urban underclass" and proposed a nonracially based corrective policy.[2] Critics on the left attributed the book's warm reception to its middle-of-the-road, nonthreatening approach to the American capitalist establishment. Also mentioned was conservatives' appreciation for the courage demonstrated by a prominent black scholar to question certain cultural values of inner-city black life, which they believed the black community and its liberal supporters have denied. Wilson's book was not a pioneering effort. Earlier works dealt with this subject and they varied in their ideological approach to the problem and its resolution. Among them were Kenneth Clark's *Dark Ghetto* (1968), Douglas Glasgow's *The Black Underclass* (1980), followed by Ken Auletta's *The Underclass* (1982), Paul E. Peterson's *The New Urban Reality* (1985), Roger Starr's *The Rise and Fall of New York City* (1985), and my own work, coauthored with Basil Wilson, *The Struggle for Black Empowerment in New York City* (1989).[3] As these studies proliferated, the system of global capitalism, whereby capital moves about the globe freely responsible only to itself, and the new information age were already transforming the global village.

America, and certainly the world, is a different place since the end of World War II. The most important concern now is how to prepare nations and citizens to meet the demands of the new global frontier. The problem of the inner cities has not disappeared. What has changed is the system's response to it. This response is choreographed by the imperatives of the globalized economy. We have seen in the United States and other developed states, for example, a contraction of resources to poor and working-class people and a get-tough approach to crime. Policymakers across the United States have chosen to deal with the urban poor and the issue of crime through the allocation of more resources to construct prisons and hire more police officers in the central cities. The lid on liberalism was tightly secured with the introduction of radical welfare reform in 1996 and the enforcement of workfare regulations. Ostensibly, the American approach is working so well that Tony Blair, the British liberal Labour Party Prime Minister, announced that he will adopt a similar measure to affect Britain's welfare-state crisis.

Other imperatives of globalization and the new information age ensure that a serious commitment to addressing urban social problems continues to elude us. In that respect, globalization and the new information age dictate expediency and demand quick fixes to social problems. Time, we hear, translates to money. With the development of the Internet, information is neatly packaged for us: With a simple click on the keyboard, we can access reams of data and be on our way. Paradoxically, despite the availability of information and the immersion of people in it, an aura of anti-intellectualism engulfs us. It was C. Wright Mills who reminded us that the problem of the ordinary man is not the absence of information—rather it is his inability to use and synthesize the wealth of information that surrounds him.[4] Who has the time to devote to serious introspection and the rigors of empirical investigation? For many Internet users today, it is far easier to surf for information than to gather in-depth data. Users access information with little attention to matters of authenticity or accurate interpretation. I frequently refer to this generation as the "take it and run generation."

The problem of the black urban poor still snarls, but it has run its course of public attention. In the current social Darwinist environment, the less fortunate must either shape up or perish. Black leaders and activists must understand and confront this latest structural dynamic. By the start of the 1990s, I had already begun to conceptualize the problem in comparative global terms. It occurred to me that in spite of the world's economic restructuring, studies on the black urban crisis in America maintained their domestic focus. I recall a discussion on this subject with my colleague Erol Ricketts, who was a fellow at the Washington, D.C.-based Urban Institute, which sponsors a number of research projects on the inner cities and the black underclass. He concurred that a cross-cultural comparative dimension would contribute to a broadened understanding of the urban black problem. But, for the moment at least, it appeared that black scholars were not particularly interested in treading that path and that funded research would continue to reflect the domestic and not global condition. My interest in exploring the global dimensions of the problem prompted the 1997 publication of *Globalization and Survival in the Black Diaspora: The New Urban Challenge,* which links the problem of powerlessness to globalization. A leading argument in that volume is that the urban crisis is not the misfortune of blacks from any one region of the world but is now global. The diaspora was represented by black populations in the urban centers from five regions including the source of the diaspora, Africa. Considered alongside Africa were Latin America, the Caribbean, North America, and Europe. The background of the crisis in specific territories within each of the regions was described and analyzed, and recommendations about corrective policies were advanced.[5]

In many respects, then, *Manufacturing Powerlessness* represents a continuation of the aforementioned compendium. It takes the argument a step further by analyzing the crisis and globalization in terms of the access to or lack of power in poor and working-class urban dwellers. Powerlessness is a debilitating condition that affects blacks not only in the developing world but in highly industrialized societies whose material base is considerably stronger. Thus, a comparison of the crisis and the reproduction of power are compared for blacks from North America (the United States), the Caribbean, and East Africa.

My earlier book discussed at length the problems associated with youth. Universally, youth are regarded as society's future, but being an extremely vulnerable segment of the population, they are easy prey. Preparing today's youth is insurance that tomorrow will produce an empowered people who are better equipped to introduce change and improve the cultural and material conditions of black people throughout the world. An important premise according to Godfrey St. Bernard is that the needs and aspirations of this subpopulation should be carefully understood and met, or, where necessary, altered so as to be congruent with a given nation's goals. Another premise is that the economic viability of the region should hinge on the sustainability and effectiveness of efforts that facilitate the social development of youth and integrate them into developmental initiatives that are cognizant of domestic and global forces.[6] Although he was addressing the Caribbean region, St. Bernard's comment is relevant for policy engineers outside that region. Finding the answers to these empirical questions is the major thrust of this book.

For all of these reasons, concern about the current and future situation of youth is continued in this book. Comparing urban youths' perception of the crisis and the epistemiologic underpinnings of the urban problem across regions will lead us toward an improved understanding about the relevant solutions.

Jerry Mander and Edward Goldstein's latest work, *The Case against Globalization,* underscores the fraudulent claim of the proponents of globalization that all of the world's people will benefit and will be able to row their rising boats in unison.[7] Even if that were the case, in light of the history of white supremacy worldwide, there would be little reason to anticipate that the plight of blacks would be significantly altered. In a globalizing age, similarities in terms of behaviors and cultural patterns are not difficult to detect. Specific to black people, in the current racially based climate, such notions as all blacks look alike or behave and respond similarly appear to have gained wider acceptance among nonblacks. Some view this as a convenient rationale for not taking black people or their problems seriously. If differences are in fact observed, it would support the proposition that a common approach to the problems that confront urban blacks in the diaspora is misguided. Moreover, it would buttress the need for policy solutions that are sensitive to the respective societies and cultures in which they reside.

To conclude, if the fate of urban blacks in an era of uncontrollable globalization is to be properly charted as we prepare for tomorrow, it will require that black folk and their leaders become more enlightened about their immediate environment and the world around them. Such a world view will help increase their awareness of the circumstances that challenge other blacks in the diaspora and at the same time encourage them to forge strong working alliances. Forging alliances on the basis of common and distinct experiences will not only help strengthen their sense of unity, it will also serve as a mechanism to challenge the ideal of a global culture and restore the sense of commitment to national pride and identity, particularly among the youth who are the future.

It is hoped that the chapters in this book will appeal to urban residents, advocates for youth, grassroots activists, scholars, and nongovernmental bodies that are already in the struggle, and in that process contribute to the larger cause of democracy and empowerment for all of the world's oppressed people.

NOTES

1. Ruth Sidel, *Women & Children Last* (New York: Viking, 1986).

2. William J. Wilson, *The Truly Disadvantaged* (Chicago: University of Chicago Press, 1987).

3. Kenneth B. Clark, *Dark Ghetto* (New York: Harper & Row, 1965); Douglas Glasgow, *The Black Underclass* (New York: Vintage, 1981); followed by Ken Auletta, *The Underclass* (1982); Paul E. Peterson (ed.), *The New Urban Reality* (Washington, D.C.: The Brookings Institution, 1985); Roger Starr, *The Rise and Fall of New York City* (1985); and Charles Green and Basil Wilson, *The Struggle for Black Empowerment in New York City* (New York: Praeger, 1989).

4. C. Wright Mills, *The Sociological Imagination* (New York: Oxford University Press, 1959).

5. Charles Green (ed.), *Globalization and Survival in the Black Diaspora: The New Urban Challenge* (Albany, N.Y.: SUNY Press, 1997).

6. Godfrey St. Bernard, "Labour Market Challenges and Contemporary Youth in Caribbean Societies" (Unpublished paper presented at the 23rd Conference of the Caribbean Studies Association, St. John's, Antigua, 1998), 2.

7. Jerry Mander and Edward Goldsmith (eds.), *The Case Against the Global Economy* (San Francisco: The Sierra Club, 1997).

Acknowledgments

Behind any book stands the author but also a number of other people. This book is not an exception to that rule. There are many people to whom I would like to express my sincere gratitude for the parts they played in this production.

For their technical support with the various computer runs and general research assistance, I thank Farrukh Hakeem, Godwin Bernard, Elena Cervallos, Joong Oh, Jamie Burg, and Sebastian Canon. Not to be forgotten is the late Thereza Mswia, who volunteered to translate the survey questionnaire from English into "Kiswahili" for the Tanzanian sample. The surveys in the United States could not have been conducted without the special assistance of Lorenzo Merritt, Walter Beach, Ronald Timmons, James Lacy, and the late Beulah Lucien. Assisting in the city of Dar es Salaam were William J. Mallya, Angela K. Ishengoma, and Jan Jasper. In Nairobi were Lydia Nymbura Ndung'u and also Mary Kinyanjui of the Institute of Development Studies, University of Nairobi. For their commitment and support in gathering the data for St. Thomas, I am indebted to Doris Baptiste and Dione E. Phillips from the University of the Virgin Islands. Also, Lio Remy, Brian Smart, and Rhoda Reddock who assisted in Trinidad and Tobago. I cannot forget the staff at Small Projects Assistance Team (SPAT) as well as Jean Finucane in Dominica. Barbara Matthews of Marion House, Kenyon Pierre, and Adrian Fraser were invaluable to me in St. Vincent and the Grenadines.

Others were vital as readers of early chapter drafts and as scholarly mentors with whom I was able to bounce around wild ideas and theories. Among them were Aubrey Bonnett, Joe Lugalla, Kinuthia Macharia, Marcia Sutherland, Naomi Kroeger, John H. Stanfield II, Janet Domingo, Trevor Purcell, Obika Gray, Clarence Lusane, Joyce Toney, Bert Thomas, Trevor Grant, and my colleagues from the Department of Sociology at the University of Dar es Salaam, especially Patrick Masanja, Chris Comoro, and C. K. Omari. A special thanks is extended to my students in the Ph.D. Program at the CUNY Graduate Center from the fall

1997 and 1999 semesters for their patience as I tested out some of the ideas and themes presented in this book.

Finally, I am grateful to the PSC-CUNY Research Award Program for the generous support provided this research and to New College of the University of South Florida, where I spent three semesters, for the support of research assistants.

In my haste it is possible that I might have overlooked some persons. If I have, let them be assured of my gratitude.

1

Globalization, Powerlessness, and the Urban Crisis: An Introduction

Philip McMichael could not have been more correct when he asserted in his recent work that the world is a fairly well-integrated place both economically and politically and that everything we experience in our daily lives can be credited to the process of globalization.[1] Given the scope of globalization, it is unimaginable that any of the world's 6 billion people could manage to eschew its far-reaching tentacles.

As we shall see, globalization is dictated by the interests of a very few players, namely the Group of 7 (G-7: United States, France, Germany, Italy, Canada, United Kingdom, and Japan) and the Organization for Economic Cooperation and Development (OECD)[2] nations who control the world's economy while obfuscating the demands of the least-organized states. Powerlessness—or the inability of groups to influence those critical political and economic decisions that shape their lives—is a necessary condition of the globalization process. Youth, a vulnerable subgroup in most societies around the world, tend to express their frustration through rebellious behavior: committing crimes and acts of violence, dropping out of school, joining the drug subculture, and so on. As cultural dislocation in developing societies occurs, the indigenous practices and values of the dislocated are replaced by new technologies and foreign mass media. But while indigenous culture has been forced to the sidelines, a full eclipse of societal-specific cultures is not manifested.

The world today is a highly integrated place, and various diasporic peoples are beginning to find their place in the rapidly changing world economy. Unmistakably, this has not been the case for people of color, particularly those of African descent, who have been dehumanized and oppressed on the African continent and in the diaspora.[3] To imply that blacks are unique in their victimization would be historically incorrect. That blacks have suffered in unique ways because of their race cannot be denied.

Globalization, or the increasing movement and exchange of capital, commerce, communications, and culture worldwide, is the central economic phenomenon of our day. When considered in relation to the historic plight of black people, it is nothing more than a continuation of the age-old practice of oppression, but now there is a new twist. We would be remiss to interpret globalization strictly in terms of its economic effects—its cultural and political implications are equally disruptive for the present and future state of blacks and non-blacks the world over. A framework is needed to provide a more concrete understanding of the problem of urban black diasporans. Such a framework would show the relationship of globalization to persistent powerlessness, cultural dislocation, and urbanization.

Economics and culture notwithstanding, a critique of globalization is most informative when the extent to which group power is encouraged or delimited is brought into the analysis. Drawing the connection between globalization and the powerless state of urban black diasporans is the major thrust of this study, as outlined in this opening chapter.

THE STATE OF POWERLESSNESS

We open our discussion with the concept of power. Throughout the course of history we have acknowledged the importance of power and the extent to which we are prepared to engage in struggle to achieve it. The general acceptance of power as one of society's scarce social rewards is contradicted by the quest of groups and individuals in society to control it. The sharing of power, which would seem to be the logical choice, is one of man's most formidable problems.

Earlier writings by Max Weber[4] on organizations and bureaucracy help us to put into perspective the nature of power and its various manifestations. We come to understand, for example, that authority, which is one articulation of power, is legitimate power as in the case of police officers who are sanctioned by society to make arrests and carry out the order of the law. On the other hand, power can be coerced. With coercive power, the intent is unambiguous: Power is illegitimately acquired in order to sustain a system of class inequality between empowered elites and their subordinates that serves the interests of the elites.

Other left-leaning writers have made the connection between capital and power. Prominent among them is Karl Marx. Marxian analysis places economics and the small elite that controls it at the base or substructure of society.[5] Maintaining power over the proletariat was the chief objective of the capitalist class. Class consciousness and the restructuring of roles would occur, Marx predicted, once the proletariat arrived at a subjective awareness of their oppressed state. Marx clearly outlined for us that mobilizing for change a people conditioned to accept the status quo is not an easy task.

In his stirring work *The Power Elite,* C. Wright Mills drew a strong link between capital and power. According to Mills:

> The power elite is composed of men whose positions enable them to transcend the ordinary environments of ordinary men and women. They are in positions to make decisions without having major consequences. They are in command of the major hierarchies and organizations of modern society. They rule the big corporations. They run the machinery of the state. They direct the military establishment.[6]

Frantz Fanon's work, particularly *The Wretched of the Earth,* offers an incisive examination of oppression, powerlessness, and colonization on a global scale. He considers powerlessness the effect of the dehumanizing condition of colonial rule. Because the powerless were not willing to accept their subjugated state, the colonial elite had to rely on force and violence to control their wretched masses.[7]

In *The Pedagogy of the Oppressed,* Paulo Freire offers what could be described as one of the most provocative analyses of powerlessness and its victims worldwide. According to Freire, because their oppression has been so internalized and conditioned, it is extremely difficult for the oppressed to see themselves as people or as members of an oppressed class. He adds, "This does not necessarily mean that the oppressed are unaware that they are downtrodden. But their perception of themselves as opposites of oppression is impaired by their submersion in the reality of oppression."[8]

Pierre Bourdieu's work on culture and power relations is an important footnote to this discussion, given the attention we direct to culture and cultural globalization in this book. Since the 1970s, Pierre Bourdieu has become a major theoretical voice in the study of cultural production and cultural practices. Combining rigorous empirical analysis with a highly elaborate theoretical frame, his central concern is the role of culture in the reproduction of social structures—or the way in which unequal power relations, unrecognized as such and thus accepted as legitimate, are embedded in the systems of classification used to describe and discuss everyday life.

In his article, "Distinction," Bourdieu argues that systems of domination find expression in virtually all areas of cultural practice and symbolic exchange, including preferences in dress, sports, food, music, literature, art, and so on. Because these forms are linked to the global economy, consciously or not, they fulfill a social function of legitimating social differences and thus contribute to the process of social reproduction. For Bourdieu, power is diffuse and symbolic and frequently concealed in broadly accepted and often unquestioned ways of perceiving and describing the world. This diffuse or symbolic power is closely intertwined with, but not reducible to, economic and political power, and thus serves as a legitimating function.[9]

From this, we can posit that the powerless are people whose historically oppressed state inhibits their participation in those critical decisions that directly affect their daily lives. The implication here is that oppression is not aberrant or a condition that occurs by chance—rather, it is produced and reproduced because it serves the economic interests of those who constitute the ruling elite.

Intentional or not, the inability of the state and its respective agencies to respond effectively to the social erosion occurring in the major urban districts of core and developing regions is a guarantee that powerlessness will be reproduced for future generations. In many respects, this process could be viewed as analogous to a manufacturing plant whose raison d'etre is to produce a commodity without regard to its immediate or long-term effects. The plant's managers are preoccupied with meeting the projected production level, thereby ensuring profits and upholding the company's commitment to stockholders.

So, too, is the manufacture of powerlessness wherever it occurs. The manufacture of powerlessness is carried out for a single purpose: to preserve the interests and hegemony of those in power. The youth, it will be argued, who reside in the central cities of developing countries and metropolitan centers around the world, are at particular risk. The future of any society rests with the generation perched at the threshold of maturity. Thus the production and reproduction—the manufacturing—of powerlessness among the youth ensures the continued subjugation of an entire group of people, denying them the possibility of becoming fully integrated into the decision-making process.

Manufacturing is a highly charged term. For more than just a few readers of this book it may imply conspiracy, an idea that is followed up in the next chapter. What makes conspiracy theories—so often viewed with disdain—difficult to reject is that, in many respects, they bear the possibility of truth. Many African Americans discounted the sole gunman theory following the assassination of Dr. Martin Luther King Jr. in Memphis, Tennessee, in 1968. They were convinced that his death was part of a larger plot by the white power structure to derail what was perceived to be a potentially threatening black radical movement. Shortly after the death of convicted assassin James Earl Ray in 1999, a federal court ruled that there was in fact a conspiracy to kill King. However, there is no indication that efforts will be made to reopen the case.

The history of virulent racism in this country has caused conspiracy theories to flourish, or certainly to ebb and flow, in response to current social conditions insofar as the black community is concerned. Elsewhere in the diaspora, where blacks are the majority and control the political state, allegations of conspiracy tend to be relegated to the state or its major functionaries. As we will discuss, many of these leaders, due to personal greed and quest for power, are known to conspire with foreign interests at the expense of their people's human development needs.

Using the manufacturing plant metaphor could also be criticized as unrealistic in that it doesn't allow for the fact that many youths do manage to escape the clutches of this operation. However, our central point is that for a growing lot of young people, escape is not an option. Their continued entrapment and the state's indifference or inability to address their needs is the situation we now face in developed and developing societies around the world.[10]

A variety of structural forces have been identified as contributors to this state of affairs. Among them are the processes of economic and cultural globalization, forced international and internal migration, the system of institutionalized racism, the subordinate relationship between the state and capital, and the omnipresence of inept, visionless leaders. The interaction between these forces, societies, and cultures cannot be separated from the experiences and behavioral responses of urban folk in the regions and territories in the diaspora. A principal product of economic globalization has been cultural homogenization—or cultural colonialism, a term preferred by some observers.[11] The argument is that differences in terms of the development and structure of powerlessness among urban sufferers exist and require particular attention. However, this argument is steadily losing ground. It is not uncommon today to hear Americans, black and white, talk about the social and cultural patterns they observe while traveling throughout poor and working-class black urban areas in the United States, Europe, the Caribbean, and Africa. Frequently they describe patterns in the urban areas of one region as identical or nearly identical to those found elsewhere.

Recently, a friend from Brooklyn—a 20-year permanent resident of the United States—visited his native Barbados, stopping over in London on his return home. In describing his trip, he said he was captivated by the similarities he saw between black people living in his Bedford-Stuyvesant New York City neighborhood, blacks in his native city of Bridgetown, Barbados, and in the black community in London. He saw similarities in their patterns of dress, in television and music preferences, in living conditions, and in social problems including family dislocation, chronic unemployment, and crime and violence among the youth.

What I find so intriguing as I ponder this and other accounts is the secondary importance these observers seem to assign to societal and cultural differences across regions. In my friend's case, it was as if the societies he had observed formed a single chain across the world distinguished only by name and location.

Orlando Patterson dealt extensively with this subject in an article in which he questioned the claim held by many that all blacks constitute a distinct undifferentiated group of people. Patterson's work presents an opposite viewpoint with overwhelming evidence of diversity rather than uniformity. He argued, "Historically, there have been tremendous differences in the conditions of blacks and in their responses to these varying conditions."[12] The common black experience of slavery took on many forms in the New World, resulting in varying responses by those in bondage and their slaveholders. But the tendency to undifferentiate black people and the black experience, I have come to realize, is consistent with today's media hype and the scholarly discourse directed to the theme of globalization and the new global order.

GLOBALIZATION AND THE NEW GLOBAL ORDER

Before we proceed, it is important to clarify the meaning of *the new global order*. Assuming commerce and cultural exchange between nations is the core of this idea, using the adjective *new* to describe the current restructuring of states to accommodate the globalization initiative is somewhat misleading. Early expeditions by the Dutch, Portuguese, Spaniards, and other Europeans were imperialistic and very much bound to trade and the creation of new trade routes for commerce.[13] Jerry Mander argues in a special issue of *The Nation* that the new global order is new more in scale than concept or form and offers new freedoms of mobility and investment to corporations and banks.[14] Piore and Sabel[15] suggest that we should view globalization as part of the new system of flexible specialization. As consumer markets become more differentiated, the old industrialized system of mass production becomes obsolete. Moreover, it has been offered as an economic system of interdependence designed to ignore and defy the prerogatives of nations, even the most powerful.[16]

To be competitive today, a firm must be able to produce small batches of different goods for diverse customers. Globalization contributes to this process by enabling firms to produce a vast range of products in multiple countries simultaneously.[17]

The digital and electronic transfer of information via satellite, telecommunications, fax, and modem has created an instantaneous and interconnected world of finance that was unimaginable only a few decades ago. Just as industrial technology directed money away from land and into the factory system, information technology has propelled investment away from manufacturing and into global speculation. Earlier, goods that were produced in one country by its own labor force were exported for trade. Today, border issues have eased, allowing production anywhere outside a given country and finance capital to move around the world instantaneously. As one observer put it, "Ours is a world of 24-hour trading in which billions of dollars are sent around the globe for an 18-cent phone connection."[18] Moreover, the integration of global markets for money, finance, and technology, and the predominance in these markets of transnational enterprises based in the North have far-reaching implications for the world economy.[19]

William Greider's use of the machine metaphor to describe the power and drive of global capital and the global industrial revolution is instructive. He quickly points out that "the metaphor offers a simplified way to visualize what is dauntingly complex and abstract and impossibly diffuse, that is, the drama of a free-running economic system that is reordering the world."[20] These economic practices have had a significant effect on the expansion of the diaspora. As residents scramble to adapt to a constantly changing economic climate, they are forced outward in search of work. The maquiladora assembly factories established in various parts of the developing world do not come close to solving their unemployment woes. As a result, unskilled workers are forced into the status of undocumented aliens wherever laborers are believed to be in demand. Unfortunately, their hopes and aspirations are often deferred. Some critics of economic and cultural globalization find it disingenuous that the benefits, chiefly in the form of profits, are unmistakably skewed in favor of the powerful minority of transnational corporations and away from (in political critic Noam Chomsky's terms) *the restless many*.[21] Chomsky would agree that globalization is simply a euphemism for imperial domination that advances the false credo that when capital is allowed to move about the world freely, all of humanity will benefit via employment and the availability of more consumer products.

A timely example of this is seen in the operation of international trade and one of its principal agencies, the General Agreement of Tariffs and Trade (GATT), currently recognized as the World Trade Organization (WTO), and dominated by the major developed nations. The 1995–1996 Uruguay Round expanded GATT's powers to include eliminating barriers to the rapidly growing trade in such areas as banking, insurance, information, the media, and in professional services such as law, medicine, tourism, accounting, and advertising. According to Martin Khor, director of the Third World Network, this undeniably gives the major GATT players the ability to define as "free trade" investment in hospitals (among other things) in the South and their eventual privatization, not to mention the export of rare forest products and herbs.[22]

Commenting on the long-term consequences of the global economy, Chomsky foresees the strengthening of the international state that will ultimately lead to an international executive office. The international state or "de facto world government" will have its own institutions like the International Monetary Fund (IMF), the World Bank, and trading structures like GATT, and will be the property of the G-7.[23] For Chomsky, a "democratic deficit" is created by the populations and nations having less influence and who stand outside this orbit of decision making.[24] With the launching of negotiations for a Multilateral Agreement on Investment (MAI) through the OECD in 1995, MAI became the most far-reaching investment liberalization agreement ever written. It is more sweeping than the North American Free Trade Agreement (NAFTA) or GATT in its assertion of basic rights for investors and corporations. It mandates that member states allow the entry and establishment of any foreign company or institution in all sectors and that foreign investors are to be treated at least as well as any local investor. Under MAI, laws that may have an unintended discriminatory effect may be nullified. Fortunately for many exploited nations, MAI was foiled in 1999 as the result of mounting criticism and international grassroots protest.

Much of the information on globalization and the new global order that bombards the media airwaves pertains to economic matters such as the investment activities of transnational corporations and trade agreements. Needless to say, making sense of this is a low priority for the ordinary citizen who is struggling to make ends meet. A consequence of the popularity currently assigned to the economic component is that the cultural component to globalization is over-looked or, at best, misunderstood. Keohane and Nye (2000) recognize this and offer a useful definition of social-cultural globalism. This globalism involves the movement of ideas, information, images, and people who carry ideas and infor-mation with them. Social-cultural globalism affects the consciousness of indi-viduals and their attitudes toward culture, politics, and personal identity. By ne-cessity, they act in tandem with other globalisms, namely economic globalism.[25] Once we arrive at the basic sociological axiom that culture is everything, the im-portance of both economics and culture to the globalization process will be more fully appreciated.

Like their domestic counterparts, globalized markets and investments require fair-minded, properly socialized, and well-informed consumers to ensure that corporate entities are competitive and achieve even higher levels of profitability. Properly socialized consumers are responsive to the latest fashions, trends, and ideas. Through the careful orchestration of information and telecommunications technology, corporate elites will be capable of penetrating even larger consumer markets and attaining unimagined profits.

It is important to note that while the major cast of players competes for their share of—or more accurately, their domination of—the global marketplace, cul-tural dimensions from entertainment media to sneakers, designer jeans, and ham-burgers are unmistakably American influenced and dominated.[26] For example, the Japanese may monopolize the electronics industry through the manufacture of television sets, radios, and VCRs, but the accompanying images and voices are chiefly American. Barber found that although indigenous language MTV pro-gramming is available in more than 71 countries, or nearly a quarter of a billion households, young people around the world are not singing Japan's number one pop tune. They prefer American (English language) music.[27]

As we witness the rapid unraveling of the cultural side to globalization, we are better able to appreciate the new meaning behind the often-used term, "It's a small world." Ecologist and culture critic Helena Norberg-Hodge notes:

> Almost everywhere you go in today's global village, you will find multilane high-ways, concrete cities, and a cultural landscape featuring gray business suits, fast-food chains, Hollywood films, and cellular phones. In the remotest corner of the planet, Barbie and Madonna are familiar icons, and the Marlboro Man and Rambo define the male ideal. From Cleveland to Cairo to Caracas, "Baywatch" (and "Fresh Prince of Bel Air") are entertainment and CNN is news.[28]

Benjamin Barber's application of a "McWorld" is instructive. For Barber, Mc-World is quintessentially American in form and style: "Music, videos, theater, books, and theme parks—the new channels of a commercial civilization, in which malls are the public squares and suburbs the neighborhoodless neighborhoods—are all constructed as image exports creating a common world taste around logos, advertising slogans, stars, songs, brand names, jingles, and trademarks."[29] Barber extends his argument with the idea of McWorld as the future world that will demand integration and uniformity and mesmerize people everywhere with fast computers and fast foods. Nations will become even more compressed into one homogeneous global theme park through technology and entertainment. He bemoans that "the planet is falling precipitously apart and coming reluctantly together at the very same moment."[30]

In their comparison of urban societies across several continents, Gilbert and Gugler (1993) also found that people are beginning to resemble each other not solely in styles of dress but in patterns of food consumption and other behaviors. Commonly observed hotels (Holiday Inn, Grand Hyatt, Hilton), shopping malls and superstores, accounting firms, banks, and food chains (Kentucky Fried Chicken, Pizza Hut) offer convincing evidence of this trend.[31]

And so in the literature we see a growing concern with cultural globalization and the impact that the increased penetration of ideas, values, and the latest trends from the North present for the indigenous cultures of the South. I believe that Jerry Mander (1996) aptly sums up the long-term effects of cultural globalization here:

The guiding principles of the new economic structures assume that all countries, even those whose cultures have been as diverse as Indonesia, Japan, Kenya, Sweden, and Brazil must row their rising boats in unison. The net effect is global monoculture or the homogenization of lifestyles and level of technological immersion with the corresponding dismemberment of local traditions and self-sufficient economies.[32]

As global capital rapidly rearranges the world's diverse societies, and simultaneously unites them, its impact on the masses takes on new dimensions. So argues William Grieder in his work, *One World Ready or Not.* The enormity of it all is overwhelming, and as a result, people are beginning to feel a sense of smallness and helplessness.[33] Writing for *The New York Times* on the subject of America's role in the global culture, columnist Barbara Crossette draws our attention to an important observation about globalization, both as a concept and as a phenomenon, that corroborates Grieder's argument. According to Crossette, "The social and cultural effects are borne out by the people of the world to the extent that the shrinking world everyone was so proud of a decade ago has become a cultural strangler."[34] She goes on to say, "It wraps up all the fears of somehow losing control to foreigners, felt as much by Americans who hate the United Nations and immigrants as it is by Indians or Filipinos who feel threatened by the International Monetary Fund, Kentucky Fried Chicken, Joe Camel, or Time Warner."[35]

It would appear that few, if any, aspects of the human experience can claim immunity from the current homogenizing trend and the likelihood of being compressed under some common umbrella or interpretation. The spate of corporate downsizings, consolidations, and mergers on a world scale is just another manifestation of the shrinking global environment, an idea that also emerges from Sassan's discussion of the global city.[36]

The relationship between urban dislocation throughout the world—manifested by high unemployment, homelessness, crime, and the drug subculture—and the process of globalization has been established.[37] This destabilization has been in motion for some time and is felt as harshly in the developed North—where present day globalization originated—as it is in the developing South. Unequivocally, this is the situation in the United States where the deindustrialization of its urban cities flourishes as the leading transnational corporations exercise their right to outpost industry and manufacturing jobs to the suburban fringes and externally to developing regions. This allows them to take advantage of these areas' cheaper non-unionized labor and other fringe benefits that usually attract foreign-based capital.[38] There is little doubt that the end of the Cold War accelerated the process of economic and cultural globalization and that this situation has delivered a devastating blow to poor and working-class people who are clustered in the cities and towns around the globe.

In the last analysis, Jerry Mander's claim that the new global order is new only in scale buttresses the argument put forth by the late Guyanese scholar Walter Rodney in his seminal work, *How Europe Underdeveloped Africa*. From Rodney's analysis we can determine that what is currently referred to as the new global order has existed at least since the fifteenth century. At that time, Europeans' skillful application of technology enabled them to sail the high seas to exploit and extract cultural and material riches from ancient Africa, Asia, and other parts of the world. From that period to the present, Europeans have enjoyed uninterrupted global hegemony.[39] Having reached a general understanding about the economic and cultural sides to globalization, and considering the related issue of homogenization, let us return to the matter of the urban problem in the black diaspora.

In what appears to be a shrinking global environment, it is little wonder that some people would begin to trivialize the social and cultural problems prevalent in most urban areas in the black diaspora and perceive them as undifferentiated. If we determine that the problems that unfold in these areas are similar, then simple logic dictates that the solutions, too, should overlap. International financial institutions that have come forward with loan packages to tackle many of these same problems in the less-developed states have complied with this logic. They have been criticized by progressive groups for seeking common definitions to problems and for anticipating similar outcomes.[40]

The universal antidote for poverty and the plethora of social problems in the developing world is defined by such terms as privatization and neoliberalism under the panoply of the free-market system. Like globalization, neoliberalism is not new but became the buzzword of the 1990s. The neoliberal agenda that emerged at the latter stage of the Cold War was conceived as another combative strategy by capital and its multinationals during the course of that war. It has also been suggested that neoliberalism represented a replacement for the defunct Bretton Woods model dating back to 1944 that heralded the twin engines of modernization and development: the IMF and the World Bank.[41] Importantly, neoliberalism is grounded in neoclassic economics, which views an open economic approach with a limited role for the state as the ultimate development policy for struggling Third World nations.

Helena Norberg-Hodge reminds us that the difference between the economies of the North and the South are critical to understand. Projects that appear to work smoothly in the North are not guaranteed to work in less-developed economies of the South. This holds true even if we are discussing a policy or a project that originates and is implemented in the South. Norberg-Hodge explains:

> Introducing microloans for small scale enterprise may actually contribute to the destruction of local, nonmonetized economies and create dependence on a highly volatile and inequitable global economy where factors such as currency devaluation can prove disastrous. Pulling a thousand people away from sure subsistence in a land-based economy into an urban context where they compete for a hundred new jobs is not a net gain in employment: nine hundred people have, in effect, become unemployed.[42]

While the controversial Africa Trade and Development Bill passed by Congress in May, 2000 reduces certain barriers to U.S. markets, especially in textiles, and creates new export opportunities for some African capitalists, the authors of the bill failed to address the questions of the health, safety, and well-being of African societies, particularly the poor. The trade bill says nothing about how the investment in infrastructure by U.S. transnationals exporting billions in capital in the form of debt service payments to financial institutions would help Africans ravaged by the AIDS epidemic. In effect, the bill requires that African countries follow the strict policies of the IMF and the World Bank—the same policies that have brought disaster to the export-led growth-model success stories of Latin America and Asia.[43]

Meanwhile, elites charged with running these governments have little to contribute to this discourse. Bankrupt of ideas and vision, they are frequently more preoccupied with the contradicting issues of deficit reduction while supporting the buildup of corporate wealth and greed than with identifying real causes and solutions to their urban problems. Contributing to this, in the case of post-colonial black leaders including those on the African continent, is their inability to disentangle themselves from the colonized mentality of inferiority and their perception as being a powerless minority on their own territories. Needless to say, this post-colonial mentality affects their ability to lead while ensuring the perpetuation of powerlessness of the masses.

As the discussion so far indicates, the evidence in support of a world culture thesis is compelling. Nevertheless, there are some who caution the proponents of the "homogenization thesis" to recognize that, despite glaring similarities, important differences prevail among societies that have much to do with their position in the world economy and overall cultural orientation.[44] This is the position we will argue in our comparison of the urban situation in the black diaspora.

THE BLACK DIASPORA

Thus far, we have used but not defined *black diaspora*. Like other diaspora—Jewish, Irish, Asian, Indian, and Chinese—the black or African diaspora refers to the dispersion of peoples from their homeland on the African continent to other regions and hemispheres in the modern world. The term is chiefly rooted in the Jewish tradition and is supplemented with the Hebrew words "galut" (meaning exile) and "tephuztzot" (meaning scattering or dispersal).[45] Between the mid-1950s and the mid-1960s, black scholars and writers increasingly began to use diaspora as a concept. It is not coincidental that this occurred at the very period when African and Caribbean states were winning independence from their European colonizers. Writing on this subject, Shepperson suggests that, "Relieved of the imposing presence of the Europeans, the former subjects were overcome by feelings of ease and freedom to begin to analyze their victimization from the perspective of a people dispersed across the globe."[46]

Returning to the Hebrew interpretation of diaspora cited above, Bonnett and Watson (1990), Laporte (1990), and Segal (1995) remind us that black migration throughout the world predated their capture on African soil and eventual enslavement. In fact, Van Sertima argues that blacks' dispersal and scattering from African shores took them in many directions, including what is now America, long before the arrival of Christopher Columbus.[47] All agree, though, that involuntary migration through enslavement by Europeans best explains the formation of the black diaspora and distinguishes it from other diaspora. Therefore, as many from the left would agree, the interface between the black diaspora and globalization began centuries ago as black labor was coerced for the exportation and later production of raw materials to various parts of the new world, mainly for the benefit of capital. To reiterate a point made earlier, these economic practices have had a significant effect on the expansion of the diaspora by uprooting scores of people from the Third World to migrate outward in search of work and livelihood for themselves and their families. The immediate source of the contemporary diaspora is no longer Africa but rather from various poles outside the continent or wherever blacks happen to be.

Throughout their analyses, students of diasporic studies compare groups' successes and hardships at home and in the societies they settled. Indicative of this are the histories of the Jews in Europe and also the nineteenth- and early-twentieth-century Irish in New York City. Late-twentieth-century American Jews, albeit targets of anti-Semitism, and the Irish, whose whiteness was once called into question by nativists, are regarded as assimilated into the American mainstream. Both groups have amalgamated with dominant white ethnics, and the son of Irish immigrants rose to become president of the United States in 1960.[48] But the situation is far more complicated for diasporic blacks. Whether our examination is situated in the societies and regions where they constitute a majority of the population (in the Caribbean and Africa) or where they are a minority (in the United States and Europe), a consistent pattern of a people enveloped in crisis emerges.[49] Blacks' situation in the United States is such that, despite their status as the largest racial minority and the second oldest on American soil behind Native Americans, the descendants of slaves cannot claim the privilege of assimilation. Bonnett and Watson inform:

> No other group besides blacks had Jim Crow laws passed against them. No other group had to struggle against unspeakable odds, for basic civil rights which others enjoyed; no other group had to live with the reality that the highest Court in the land supported and fully sanctioned a post-slavery slavery by handing down rulings which officially institutionalized and legitimized educational apartheid, essentially establishing the pre-Civil War value of white supremacy and domination. In effect, for black Americans, a form of mortification analogous to slavery persisted, with official support, for a hundred years after the Civil War.[50]

Laporte admits that the problem with the concept of diaspora for blacks rests with its amorphousness stemming from centuries of enslavement and cultural annihilation. Thus, we find that the term has different meanings and implications among blacks. Fundamental to this is the problem associated with the concept of home or homeland. For blacks in the diaspora, Laporte says, "the concept may refer to different places, real or imagined, in their trek across the continent and passage across the ocean to the city or locality of their present abode." This problem, one might add, is not casually visible among other diasporans. Laporte further explains:

> It may well be their official country of origin or birth, adopted country of settlement or nationality, or their intermediate country of passage; for others it may well refer to a set of conditions or a state of being, a condition or state to be strived for, emulated, or constructed, or a place of destination to which they hope to (re)migrate and (re)settle and prosper or retire.[51]

In the final analysis, diaspora is a critical analytic concept because it helps us put into perspective the historical antecedents of the black condition throughout the modern world. It speaks to the system of virulent racism, the Middle Passage, slavery, and colonialism. As well, diaspora highlights our awareness of the exploits of economic globalization. The preponderance of blacks in some of the least desirable conditions in urban centers on and outside the African homeland enables us to understand that—albeit different in many respects from the system of slavery—what links economic globalization to that earlier system is human exploitation and also its reliance on involuntary migration.

URBANIZATION

Urbanization is not a recent process. It would appear so, given the international media attention it has received with respect to overcrowding and social problems. People have always gravitated to the urban centers where they have greater access to basic necessities, commerce, and culture. At certain junctures and conjunctures—for example, the advent of capitalism and economic and cultural globalization—the rippling effect of urbanization is evident. Much of the world's population today is urbanized, residing in large and mid-size cities and suburban areas. The United Nations Population Growth (UNPG) projections indicate that the level of urbanization for the world as a whole is expected to increase to 50 percent by the year 2005 and 65 percent by the year 2025. That is to say, more than three-fifths of the world's population will live in urban areas.[52]

But the growth factor has had the greatest impact in the less-developed regions of the world. While the projected growth rate for the developed regions is 61 percent, for the less-developed regions the projection is 83 percent.[53] Moreover, by the year 2010 there will be 33 mega cities—cities with more than 5 million inhabitants—and 21 of them will be in less-developed countries. Of the 26 urban agglomerations expected to have 10 million or more inhabitants by 2010, 21 will be in developing countries. Of these, 14 will be located in Asia; five will be in the Latin Americas; and two will be in Africa.[54]

But the issue is not just increased migration to the urban metropolitan centers. It is also about poverty. Badash (1996) observed that urbanization around the world has accompanied a heightened incidence of poverty. He cited UNPG data that estimated that more than half of the world's poor will be concentrated in places defined as urban areas by the end of the 1990s and that about 90 percent of poor households in Latin America, 40 percent in Africa, and 45 percent in Asia will be in urban-based areas. Evidently these estimates were quite accurate, as UNPG's current calculations for the world's urban poor and those living in Latin America, Africa and Asia have increased.[55]

Table 1.1 below is a glance at the global urban picture for the major regions of North America, Africa, the Caribbean, and Asia between 1950 and 1990, with projections into the twenty-first century. Although the greatest figures are reported for North America, the regions to watch are East Africa, followed by Asia and the Caribbean.

Table 1.1 Urbanization Trends in Selected Regions of the World, 1950–2025 (as a percent of the overall population)

North America			East Africa			Asia			Caribbean		
1950	1990	2025	1950	1990	2025	1950	1990	2025	1950	1990	2025
63.9	75.4	83.3	5.30	19.40	39.5	7.40	31.9	52.4	35.4	59.4	72.31

Source: UN Secretariat, World Urbanization Prospects: The 1996 Revision Annex Tables.

In the developed societies of United States, Canada, Britain, and France, blacks have achieved critical mass with concentration in the inner cities. Their migration to cities and towns in the United States was the result of internal capital expansion and exploitation. In Britain and France it was much more a case of colonial—and in the post-independence period, former colonial—subjects immigrating to the mainland with the hope of finding a better life for themselves and their families. For a significant portion of the developing world, increased urbanization by blacks has been the byproduct of foreign capital expansion that has taken the form of offshore assembly operations and light manufacturing in those regions. It has also been energized by the decline in living conditions, including low-wage jobs in rural areas, land displacement, and the fall in crop production that has heightened the demand for food importation and substitution policies. The trek to the urban areas has become the means to survival for a growing number of people.[56]

THE CASUALTIES OF GLOBALIZATION AND URBANIZATION

As we have noted, in many developing as well as developed countries, women and children are extremely vulnerable to the sudden and constant fluctuations of the economy and consequently are the greatest casualties.[57] This is so because a disproportionate number of the world's 6 billion people are under 25. For practical purposes, the United Nations has defined youth as that age group between 15 and 24 years,[58] but as the Kenyan sociologist Charles Nzioka informs, the concept of youth remains polemical and lacks universal acceptance. This is because the concept is extremely flexible and tends to vary with the physical, social, cultural, political, and economic features of a society or a community.[59]

The United Nations designated 1985 the International Year of Youth to recognize that young people comprised approximately 45 percent of the world's population and that the future of humanity depended on their direct participation in all important aspects of economic, political, scientific, and cultural development of the nation in which they lived. Fifteen years later, in 2000, the effect of that UN proclamation on the condition of the world's youth is still debated. This situation presents a major contradiction for societies seeking to become developed, and unequivocally for more affluent nations that are vociferous in their commitment to preserve and support the next generation.

Arguably, Americans epitomize this contradiction more so than other Westerners due to their preoccupation with preserving a youthful appearance. Americans' relentless quest for the proverbial fountain of youth is aided by medical science and the major pharmaceutical companies. For those who can afford to join expensive health spas, undergo cosmetic surgery, or sport the latest in designer apparel, the opportunity to look younger *and* add a few more years to their lives is readily available.

Needless to say, this has led to a redefinition of who and what is considered "youth" in contemporary society. It has also meant that as adults hasten toward a more youthful appearance, a number of problems have presented for youth and adolescents. When parents and adults in general begin to overidentify with the youth culture, those norms, roles, and values that have traditionally marked the boundaries separating youth and adulthood become blurred.

An important consequence of this is the confusion it triggers among young people. A study issued by the U.S. Department of Health and Human Services captured the problem of contradicted values between youth and adults. According to that study, the problem of increased marijuana and drug use by young people could in part be explained by the finding that a significant proportion of the youth surveyed reported that their parents—baby boomers and youth of the 1960s hippie generation—also used drugs of some kind and were passive about their children's use.[60]

Aspects of the adult–youth dialectic can be found in the urban ghettos where it is difficult to distinguish between teenage males—and, to a lesser degree, females—and their 21- to 24-year-old counterparts. In the not-so-distant past, the latter age group was defined as adults in the fullest sense of the term with the expectation that they had completed secondary school and acquired some basic work-related skills, were employed, and were likely to be married with a family. Today, that age group resembles their younger counterparts in many respects. Although in most black urban areas this situation appears to be inspired more by economic hardship than by a quest for the fountain of youth, the various age groups are linked by a common appreciation for "hip-hop"[61] clothing and their wavering maturity level. They hang out together, belong to the same gangs, are without marketable skills, and are very likely to have fathered or mothered one child or more outside of marriage.

As viewed by most American social scientists, youth and adolescence is an intrinsically perilous, unstable, and rebellious stage in the human developmental cycle. This is rooted in the science (or pseudoscience) of biological determinism in the nineteenth century. In his book, *The Scapegoat Generation*, Mike A. Males excerpts nineteenth-century psychologist G. Stanley Hall's exposé on teenagehood:

> The momentum of heredity often seems insufficient to enable the child to achieve the great revolution and come to complete maturity, so that every step of the upward way is strewn with wreckage of body, mind, and morals. There is not only arrest, but perversion at every stage and hoodlumism, juvenile crime, and secret vice. . . . Home, school, and church fail to recognize its nature and needs, perhaps most of all, its perils.[62]

According to Males, modern psychology and other human behavior disciplines resurrect this extreme notion of youth when it is in their interest to do so. It is functional to scapegoat youth for the widespread problems of the day rather than to confront "the complex interactions of individual biology, personality, cultural preference, political expediency, and social dysfunction."[63] Importantly Males adds, "To assert that impoverished (inner-city) youth tend to be more violent is to deny the condition of poverty that engenders it while advancing the notion of violence as innate to poorer youth—let alone to all youth."[64]

It is little wonder that social scientists in Western societies outside the United States—with leading examples being Britain, France, and Germany[65]—faced with mounting urban problems are responding similarly by scapegoating their youth. What is so critical about Males' analysis is his recognition of the interplay of macro forces in explaining the crisis of contemporary urban youth. It draws upon the earlier work by sociologist Robert K. Merton whose paradigm on deviance correctly linked crime and other antisocial behaviors to one's predisposition to accept or reject socially defined means and goals.[66] Parenthetically, Merton's identification of the innovator has relevance here. The innovator accepts society's goals and material values but rejects the socially prescribed means for achieving them. In the global information age, the roles of television and the advertising industry are pivotal for the creation of innovators. Increasingly, desperate youth throughout the diaspora are enticed by an infinite array of ubiquitous consumer products displayed on every entertainment medium with the subliminal message that to not possess these things is to be an outcast.

Princeton University scholar and well-known writer in the field of criminal justice, John DiIulio, is pessimistic about the future of juveniles, who he sees as the "demographic crime bomb and as super-predators." Although the nation's overall crime rate is reported to have stabilized, DiIulio believes that the juvenile crime rate will continue to rise. The new breed "juveniles–predators," to use his phrase, are less fearful of the stigma of arrest, the pains of imprisonment, or the pangs of conscience. He sees this new breed as radically impulsive, brutal, and remorseless. As long as more young men and especially young black men continue to be reared in an environment of failure and despair, he argues, violent crimes will continue to increase. There is no available evidence to suggest that the pathologies are under control. In true DiIulioan style, which is to introduce the idea of society's shortcomings, he gives us his simple remedy: lock them up.[67]

DiIulio introduces evidence that shows that the number of juveniles in the population, and especially the number of minority juveniles, is increasing faster than the general population. Between 1985 and 1994, juvenile arrests for murder increased 150 percent, while arrests for aggravated assault and weapons charges doubled—and this was occurring at a time when the adult crime rate was leveling off.[68]

Anchoring studies by Males, Merton, and others, the current study rejects the views of biological determinism and victim blaming. These views informed earlier works by psychologist Stanley Hall and more recent works by John DiIulio and company and have emerged as the great explainers for the problems currently afflicting youth. By defining today's inner-city youth as a vulnerable subpopulation, we are adopting the structural approach to urban social problems. That approach targets economic and cultural globalization as well as failed domestic social policies for the trauma inflicted on this critical generation that sits at the edge of maturity, and importantly, that embodies the future of the race. Importantly, it incorporates the argument put forth by Buvinic and Morrison (2000) and others that globalization has accompanied an explosion of transcontinental media networks that have transplanted Hollywood images of violence around the globe. It has also expanded trade in death industries such as firearms and drugs. The consequence of this is that it has reinforced the culture of violence, particularly for children who are media's chief targets.[69]

Examining the economy of the United States in which markets have become more lean and where race has never mattered more, the material condition of people in the inner-city ghettos has worsened. There, black youth are considered to be out of control. Unemployed, lacking marketable skills, and under the watchful eye of a mainly white suburban police force—perceived as foreign agents—feelings of entrapment, frustration, and a sense of hopelessness about the future are to be expected for any number of these young urbanites.[70] The consequences are particularly threatening to young people in the developing regions of East Africa and the Caribbean, where structural adjustment policies and the penetration of foreign mass culture is a foregone conclusion. This is especially true in the Caribbean region where crime and violence, youth unemployment, school rejection, and increased involvement by young people in the illicit drug subculture have exploded. In time, the concept of underclass was adopted to identify this subpopulation. Not since anthropologist Oscar Lewis' introduction of the phrase "culture of poverty" in the 1960s has a single term created as much controversy among American scholars and journalists as has *urban underclass*. The term is broadly defined and has come to be associated with long-term welfare recipients, unwed teen mothers, the homeless, the surplus labor force, school dropouts, street criminals, hustlers, and the drug subculture located chiefly in the nation's urban cities. This cohort disproportionately comprises African American and Latino males who lack skills, education, technical preparation, and other labor prerequisites of post-industrial society. Described as an essentially marginalized mass, entrenched frustration and feelings of hopelessness have been noted as pervasive among this population.

In his widely read study, *Streetwise*, Elijah Anderson points out the irony that many of the Northton (pseudonym for the studied community) residents, who made up the so-called underclass and were among the unemployed, the underskilled, and the poorly educated, had high school diplomas. Moreover, he added that they were intelligent but demoralized by institutionalized racism and that this condition immobilizes its victims and precludes them from negotiating the wider system of employment and society in general.[71] Various scholars have argued against the continued use of the term "urban underclass." Probably the most compelling of these arguments was posed by sociologist Herbert Gans, whose contempt for the term rests chiefly with what he considers its pejorative intent wherein the poor are blamed for their unwillingness to adhere to the cherished American work ethic. He argues that the current definition has become a stereotype because it sees the underclass as essentially black and Hispanic. Furthermore, the underclass is often used as a causal term, with the risk that the only solution will be to mount a direct attack on the cause itself—that is, the troubled masses themselves.[72]

When Swedish social scientist Gunnar Myrdal introduced the word *underclass,* he intended it as a purely economic concept to describe the jobless and the chronically unemployed. His concern was not with introducing behavioral change but with reforming an insensitive economy. On the other hand, when Oscar Lewis introduced the idea of a culture of poverty, impoverishment and the poor were perceived as self-perpetuating. That is to say that some poor people would get so used to poverty that they would be incapable of adapting to change even when improved conditions offered the probability of escaping from poverty. But it was Lewis's definition that captured the imagination of American policy makers, journalists, and some scholars at that critical juncture and helped shape current thinking about the underclass. According to Gans, the current use of the word underclass represents a shift in public opinion away from Myrdal's economic causal argument. The economic argument has been strategically replaced by a set of behavioral patterns as the criteria for membership in the underclass. Whether one accepts Gans' view of the underclass as victims, which he offers as a rationale for dropping the term, or the mainstream position of behavioral deviance, the overarching reality is that we are faced with a growing constituency of people located along the margins of society who are without the necessary economic and political clout to shape the decisions that affect their lives. Therefore, rather than invoke an "underclass," in the current study the politically conscious term "urban powerless" will be used where possible. It is felt that this term best captures the real issue: That people, due to lack of skills and educational preparation in postindustrial society, are becoming superfluous and are at greater risk of joining the ranks of school dropouts, street hustlers, criminals, and drug addicts. Moreover the term urban powerless captures their entrapment and lack of conscious awareness about the true nature of their situation and inability to participate in decisions that would bring about the necessary change.

THE COMPARATIVE APPROACH TO THE BLACK DIASPORA

For this study, we selected territories in which blacks constitute a demographic majority or are a significant proportion of the overall population. A more detailed justification for the selected study sites is offered in appendix A. To underscore the scope of the crisis that challenges urban-bound blacks, we chose territories that are experiencing urban social dislocation. The small-island versus large-island debate stirred among Caribbean scholars and diplomats in the immediate post-independence period could be credited, in part, for the limited attention given smaller island states in the scholarly literature and in the international media. Thus larger or more cosmopolitan island states such Jamaica and Barbados have drawn greater attention compared with tiny islands such as Dominica and Grenada. From the Caribbean, therefore, Trinidad and Tobago was selected as were two Eastern Caribbean states, Dominica and St. Vincent and the Grenadines, and one U.S. territory, St. Thomas, Virgin Islands.

On the African continent as well we find that certain subregions have received greater attention than others due to the geopolitical or material interests of foreign powers. An example is Africa's western and southern regions, which have been more visible than its eastern region. In Africa, therefore, we examine two eastern states, Kenya and Tanzania. These states were selected because of their similar political histories, their divergent post-independence developmental patterns, and currently, their corresponding levels of social and cultural dislocation in their urban areas.

Crisis in America's inner cities, where blacks predominate, predates that which is taking place in other parts of the world. In light of the pervasiveness of social dislocation in the nation's inner cities, five U.S. cities were selected arbitrarily as part of the study sample. Other considerations in their selection included the fact that the United States holds unofficial status as the popular culture capital of the world and, importantly, African Americans' status as a key social and political role model for blacks living outside the United States. In this instance, the U.S. sample will serve as a backdrop or yardstick to compare the pace and the scope of the crisis taking place elsewhere. Such an approach, it was felt, would encourage a more systematic examination of the similarities and differences between and among the regions and territories. Precisely, it was felt that the selection of the countries in this study would bring to light two critical themes. First, in the global economy, all societies, irrespective of size or obscurity, are thrust into the arena as players. The second theme has to do with the pace of the urban crisis and the expectation that for societies with a higher human development index, the pace of the urban crisis will be more rapid.

By using the comparative model, differences and similarities among urban blacks from the selected regions are more effectively assessed. Several factors were deemed important for this comparison and were explored using a survey-type questionnaire that was administered to urban youth in the age category 14–24 in 1994. Among them were their degree of social integration or involvement in social activities in their community, powerlessness, personal dysfunction (e.g., criminal activity, drug use), their perception of the problems surrounding them, and their outlook for the future. Three additional factors were considered that were believed to be linked to the crisis. They were not assessed using the survey instrument but rather through a series of interviews with public officials and the use of secondary sources.

First among them was the quality of economic and cultural development. This refers not merely to the economic status of the society—most commonly measured in terms of per capita GNP/GDP—but to the value base that constitutes the political economy and its willingness to meet the basic needs of the citizenry. Essential, therefore, is the ability of the economic order to sustain a sense of hope for the future among the masses.

Proponents of modernization have equated that model of development with the commitment to adopt Western tastes, beliefs, and culture.[73] But according to critics, among the daunting principles behind this model is the vilification of traditional ways as backward, irrational, and even brutish in some cases, with the view that a positive first step toward modernity is to jettison traditional ways.[74]

I have always felt tremendous appreciation for Walter Rodney's definition of development, which I consider one of the most direct counterchallenges to modernistic rhetoric. Among his arguments is that underdevelopment has little merit, as one cannot infer the absence of development among a people. In his view, "Every people have developed in one way or another and to a greater or lesser extent." Another of his profound beliefs is that the development of a given society should be tied directly to its ability to provide its subjects with the sense of material well-being, freedom, and the opportunity to be creative and self-disciplined.[75]

At a cursory level, one need only examine the course of sociocultural structuring of any advanced modern industrial society today to fully appreciate the modernist–traditionalist dialectic. This point is particularly timely for a growing number of Americans whose hue and cry is for a return to the basics. They are overcome by the feeling that a cultural crisis exists and that it is directly related to the erosion of basic norms, values, and institutions. This sense of cultural uneasiness and tension is echoed in the calls to strengthen family values,[76] to restore a sense of order and morality to the nation's public schools, and to restrict what some perceive as an uncontrollable mass media. It is interesting to note that these calls resonate not solely from the conservative right but increasingly from the liberal camp as well. This point is substantiated by the accusations from conservative Republicans that liberal Democrats have hijacked their platform and are sounding more like conservatives than liberals. Nationally, but most vividly in the urban areas, the need by residents to develop parallel or substitute arrangements as alternatives to the inept and mistrusted institutions that surround them has not always been successful. In many respects, this has only served to deepen the crisis. What is so typical about these platitudes concerning morality and justice is that the role of the market is left completely outside the orbit of critique. Former prime minister of Jamaica, the late Michael Manley, captured this spectacle of sensationalism and contradiction in one of his many commentaries. On this occasion he was espousing his views on the criticism made by the United States and other Western powers about the struggle for self-rule in then-occupied South Africa. Manley said, "We are told that in South Africa the choice is between stability and communism. That is a lie. The only choice is between justice and profit."[77]

On the other hand, in the case of less-developed societies, one might expect to find a conspicuous reliance on traditional ways concomitant with encroaching modernist practices. These traditional arrangements have served as buffers against economic hardship but also against potentially rebellious, recalcitrant youth and the destabilization of families. But as the pace of modernity shifts into a higher gear—a scenario perceived to be inevitable and so has remained unchallenged—traditional culture is rapidly losing ground.

The second factor in the urban crisis is the influence of foreign mass culture on the society. For much of the developing world, the presence of foreign culture is profound, if for no other reason than the inadequacy of their own communications technology. It is easier and less costly for these states to turn to existing systems and infrastructures from abroad, mainly the West. This factor is related to the preceding factor to the extent that as these societies become more dependent for information and entertainment from outside their borders, indigenous cultural forms and values slowly begin to lose their importance and eventually atrophy. A number of studies have supported this, demonstrating that as the television airwaves in most developing societies have increased the amount of external programming, new forms of violence and aggressive behavior have also surfaced.[78]

The third factor in the crisis concerns the migration–urbanization process and the emergence of urban ghettos with its most formidable form, the "hyper-ghetto."[79] In the United States, the system of racism and residential apartheid is[80] causally linked to the formation of poor black ghettos and the problem of the urban powerless. Although migration, where it is not propelled by race, is a shared experience across the diaspora, the matter of race requires a different application. Certainly this is so in the case of the Caribbean and Africa. For one thing, blacks constitute majorities in the countries of these two regions. Second, their migrations to the cities and towns was chiefly the effect of their class position and the economic developments taking place in the larger society and the world.

CONCLUSION

Earlier in this chapter, we referenced a Caribbean American immigrant who had observed in his travels that blacks in the diaspora have more than just race in common. Connecting them are a variety of sociocultural patterns and nuances that appear to be distinctively African American. However, this should not gainsay the influence of the African heritage on African Americans and the influence, albeit not quite as strong, of other black diasporans. The latter point is seen in the growing appreciation by African Americans for steel pan, reggae music, foods, and other Caribbean cultural forms. The mainstream success of Alex

Haley's *Roots* fostered a renewed interest by black people (mainly in the West) to come closer to their African heritage but also to appreciate and develop in Smart's terms, those "amazing connections" between themselves and others in the diaspora.[81]

Beyond material cultural linkages, other aspects, such as social problems, are becoming trivialized with the assumption that their solutions can be compartmentalized. For this reason the argument was posed that, while many of the problems we come to observe among urban blacks in the diaspora may be similarly manifested, the forces giving rise to them impact the victims differently. In turn, the policies to remedy these problems will have to reflect the structural peculiarities of the societies.

The next three chapters are devoted to a description and an analysis of the urban situation in the United States, the Caribbean, and East Africa and their connectedness to the larger question of globalization and powerlessness. Primary data gathered from surveys of youth from each of the three regions are integrated and discussed in the respective chapters. The use of primary data was considered as a supplement to the secondary sources. Importantly, these findings would broaden our understanding about the plight of the future generation from their own perspective, not to mention the opportunity to procure firsthand information about the differences among youth in the diaspora and the pace of the crisis. From this discussion we might expect to find sharp commonalities between the United States and the Caribbean respondents along several survey items due to their geographic proximity, the role of transmigrants in bridging the two regions, and the role of mass media.

Intraregional differences are equally significant. For the Caribbean, represented by four states, it would be important to consider for each state the stage of politico-economic development and interface with the major global players as well as the extent of mass cultural penetration from abroad. This same interpretation would apply to the other region in this study, East Africa. In the case of the two states, Tanzania and Kenya, examined there, post-independence political divisions have contributed to their respective developmental problems and hence what we now entertain as the "urban crisis" in each country.

Chapter 5, "The Urban Problem: A Comparative View" is devoted to a comparison of the findings from the survey that was administered to urban youth from the United States, the Caribbean, and East Africa. This cross-cultural analysis will address the issue of similarities and differences of the urban condition in the diaspora but also will provide the basis to argue for societal-specific solutions.

Chapter 6 propounds that in an atmosphere in which the state is morally bankrupt and local leaders are without vision, the prospects for meaningful change and the empowerment of the people are undermined. Data that substantiate this thesis are offered for the three study regions. In addition, the impact of the crisis on nongovernmental and community-based organizations—considered by many observers to be the only thread of hope for real change—are explored.

Behind all of the uncertainties, a glimmer of optimism appears in chapter 7: that a transformation can indeed take place and that empowerment can be manufactured. Toward that objective, and incorporating findings from the survey reported in chapter 5, the chapter suggests general policy solutions that are culturally sensitive and relevant to the regions in question.

It is hoped that this book will encourage readers to eschew the cultural homogenization trap and support solutions to urban problems that are culturally relevant to the concerns of the people in the diaspora. With an eye on this objective, we now shift our attention to the first region for examination: the United States and its urban black belt.

NOTES

1. Philip McMichael, *Development and Social Change: A Global Perspective* (Thousand Oaks, Calif.: Pine Forge Press, 1996).

2. The Organization for Economic Cooperation and Development (OECD) bloc comprises the 26 richest countries in the world: Australia, Austria, Belgium, Canada, Czech Republic, Denmark, Finland, France, Germany, Greece, Ireland, Iceland, Italy, Japan, Luxembourg, Netherlands, New Zealand, Norway, Portugal, Spain, Sweden, Switzerland, United Kingdom, United States, Turkey, and Mexico. These countries contain roughly 16 percent of the world's population but control two-thirds of its merchandise (or tradable goods).

3. Marcia Sutherland, *Black Authenticity: A Psychology for Liberating People of African Descent* (Chicago, Ill.: Third World Press, 1997). Chancellor Williams, *The Destruction of Black Civilization* (Chicago, Ill.: Third World Press, 1987). Cheikh Anta Diop, *The African Origin of Civilization: Myth or Reality*, ed./trans. Mercer Cook (New York: Hill, 1974). Ivan Van Sertima and Runoko Rashidi, eds., *African Presence in Early Asia*, Revised Edition (New Brunswick: Transaction,1988). W. E. B. DuBois, *The Souls of Black Folk* (New York: The Library of America, 1990/first published in 1903).

4. See various works by Max Weber including his *The Theory of Social and Economic Organization*, trans. A.M. Henderson and T. Parsons (New York: Free Press, 1947).

5. Karl Marx, *The Grundrisse*, trans. Martin Nicolaus (New York: Vintage, 1973).

6. C. Wright Mills, *The Power Elite* (New York: Oxford University Press, 1956). Quoted in W. Kornblum's *Sociology in a Changing World*, 5th ed. (New York: Harcourt Brace), 655.

7. Frantz Fanon, *The Wretched of the Earth* (New York: Grove Press, 1968).

8. Paulo Freire, *The Pedagogy of the Oppressed* (New York: Continuum, 1983), 30.

9. Pierre Bourdieu, *The Field of Cultural Production*, ed. Randal Johnson (New York: Columbia University Press, 1993). See Nicholas Garnham, "Bourdieu's Distinction" in *Sociological Review*, 34 (May 1986), 423–433.

10. See Kwando Kinshasa, "Crisis and Lifestyles of Inner-City Bloods: Youth Culture as a Response to the Urban Environment," in Charles Green (ed.), *Globalization and Survival in the Black Diaspora: the New Urban Challenge* (Albany, N.Y.: SUNY Press, 1997), 289–307. Elijah Anderson, *Streetwise: Race, Class and Change in an Urban Community* (Chicago, Ill.: University of Chicago Press, 1990). Claire E. Alexander, *The Art of Being*

Black: The Creation of Black British Youth Identities (Clarendon, U.K.: Clarendon Press, 1996). Stephen Small, "Racism, Black People and the City in Britain," in Green, *Globalization and Survival in the Black Diaspora*, 357–379. Obika Gray, "Power and Identity Among the Urban Poor of Jamaica," in Green, *Globalization and Survival in the Black Diaspora*, 199–227. Raquel Z. Rivera, "Rap in Puerto Rico: Reflections from the Margins," in Green, *Globalization and Survival in the Black Diaspora*, 109–129.

11. See cultural homogenization, or "cultural colonialism," the term preferred by some observers. For example, Elizabeth A. Brown, "Music Television Turns 10," in *The Christian Science Monitor* (August 6, 1991), 10–11.

12. Orlando Patterson, "Toward a Future That Has No Past: Reflections on the Fate of Blacks in the Americas," in *Public Interest* (Vol. 27, 1972) 25–26; See also: Mary C. Waters, *Black Identities: West Indian Immigrant Dreams And American Realities* (Cambridge, Mass.: Harvard University Press, 1999, Chapters 2 and 3).

13. Walter Rodney, *How Europe Underdeveloped Africa* (London, U.K.: Bogle–L'Ouverture/Washington, D.C.: Howard University Press, 1972).

14. Jerry Mander, "The Dark Side of Globalization," in *The Nation* (July 15/22, 1996), 10. Also, Mander and Edward Goldsmith (eds.), *The Case Against the Global Economy* (San Francisco, Calif.: The Sierra Club, 1996).

15. Michael J. Piore and Charles F. Sabel, *The Second Industrial Divide: Possibilities for Survival* (New York: Basic Books, 1984).

16. William Greider, *One World Ready or Not: The Manic Logic of Global Capitalism* (New York: Simon & Schuster, 1997), 17.

17. Edna Bonacich, Lucie Cheng, Norma Chinchilla, Nora Hamilton, and Paul Ong (eds.), *Global Production: The Apparel Industry in the Pacific Rim* (Philadelphia, Pa.: Temple University Press, 1994), 8.

18. Jerry Harris, "Globalization and the Technological Transformation of Capitalism," in *Race & Class* (Vol. 40, No. 2/3, October–March 1998–1999), 22.

19. Harris, "Globalization and the Technological Transformation of Capitalism"; Greider, *One World Ready or Not*.

20. Greider, *One World Ready or Not*, 11–26.

21. This is carefully detailed by Noam Chomsky in *The Prosperous Few and the Restless Many* (Berkeley, California: Odonian Press, 1995, first section); see also: Robert O. Keohane and Joseph S. Nye Jr.'s article that discusses the widening gap between rich and poor, "Globalization: What's New? What's Not? (And So What?)," (*Foreign Policy*, Spring 200, 104–119.)

22. Martin Khor, "Colonialism Redux," in *The Nation* (July 15/22, 1996), 18.

23. Following the June 1997 meetings held in Denver, Colorado, this summit is now being called the "G–8." At that summit, Russia was included for the first time as a full participant at all deliberations.

24. Chomsky, *The Prosperous Few*, page 7. See also: Benjamin R. Barber, *Jihad vs. McWorld: How Globalism and Tribalism Are Reshaping the World* (New York: Ballantine Books, 1996), 13.

25. Robert O. Keohane and Joseph S. Nye Jr., "Globalization: What's New? What's Not? (And So What?)," (*Foreign Policy*, Spring 2000, 107).

26. World Bank, 1997; Barber, *Jihad*; George Ritzer, *The McDonaldization of Society* (Thousand Oaks, Calif.: Pine Forge, 1996); Mike Mason, *Development and Disorder: A History of the Third World Since 1945* (Toronto, Canada: Between the Lines Press, 1997), 17–19.

27. See Barber, *Jihad*, 105.

28. Helena Norberg-Hodge, "Break Up the Monoculture" in *The Nation* (July 15/22, 1996), 20; CNN currently broadcasts to 200 countries and is listened to by one-half billion people.

29. See Barber, *Jihad*, 15.

30. See Barber, *Jihad*, 4.

31. Alan Gilbert and Josef Gugler, *Cities, Poverty, and Development: Urbanization in the Third World* (New York: Oxford University Press, 1993, 29–32).

32. Mander, "The Dark Side of Globalization," 10.

33. Greider, *One World Ready or Not,* 15.

34. Barbara Crossette, "Un-American Ugly Americans," in *The New York Times* (Section 4, May 11, 1997), 1, 5.

35. Crossette, "Un-American Ugly Americans," 5.

36. Saskia Sassan, *The Global City* (Princeton, New Jersey: Princeton University Press, 1991). See also: Sarah Anderson and John Cavanagh, *The Top 200: The Rise of Global Corporate Power* (Washington, D.C.: Institute for Policy Studies (September 25, 1996); Holly Sklar, *Chaos or Community? Seeking Solutions, Not Scapegoats for Bad Economics* (Boston, Mass.: South End Press, 1995, particularly chapter 4, "Full of Unemployment").

37. Sassan., *The Global City*; Norberg-Hodge, "Break Up the Monoculture"; Mander, "The Dark Side of Globalization"; Green, *Globalization and Survival in the Black Diaspora.*

38. William J. Wilson, *The Truly Disadvantaged: The Inner-City, the Underclass, and Public Policy.* (Chicago, Ill.: University of Chicago Press, 1987); also Wilson, *When Work Disappears,* 1996.

39. Rodney, *How Europe Underdeveloped Africa*; Mason, *Development and Disorder.*

40. See J. Wagaoa's article, "Beyond the International Monetary Fund Package in Tanzania," in C.K. Omari (ed.), *Tanzania: Persistent Principles Amidst Crisis* (Arusha, Tanzania: ELCT, 1989), 224–254; *The IMF, World Bank and Africa* (London, U.K.: Institute for Africa Alternatives (monograph), 1987.

41. In *21st Century Policy Review* (Vol. 2, No. 1–2, Spring 1994), see Hilbourne Watson's editorial introduction, p. 1; also: L. Dietz and Emilio Pantojas-Garcia, "Neoliberal Policies and Caribbean Development: From the CBI to the North American Free Trade Agreement," 18–25.

42. Helena Norberg-Hodge, "Shifting Direction: From Global Dependence to Local Interdependence," in Mander and Goldsmith, *The Case Against the Global Economy,* 393–406. Meryl James-Bryan points out some of these same contradictions in her report, "Entrepreneurial Development in Trinidad and Tobago: A Continuing Challenge" (a report on Youth Training and Employment Partnership Programme (YTEEP) delivered in Kingston, Jamaica (August 30, 1992); YTEEP, LTD brochure 1995, P.O.S., Trinidad and Tobago.

43. Horace Campbell, "U.S. Partnership or Domination of Africa: Reflections on the Discussions over the Africa Growth and Opportunity Bill" (International Committee of the Black Radical Congress, February 10, 1999), 4.

44. Gilbert and Gugler, *Cities, Poverty, and Development: Urbanization in the Third World;* Mike Featherstone, "Global Culture: An Introduction," in *Global Culture: Nationalism, Globalization and Modernity* (London: Sage Publications, 1990), 1–14; Anthony D. Smith, "Towards a Global Culture?" in Featherstone (ed.), *Global Culture,* 171–190; Norberg-Hodge, *The Case Against the Global Economy,* 20.

45. This is an old term that dates back to the Bible. In Joseph E. Harris (ed.), *Global Dimensions of the African Diaspora* (Washington, D.C.: Howard University Press, 1982). See: essays by George Shepperson, "African Diaspora: Concept and Context," pp. 51, 46–47; Elliott P. Skinner, "The Dialectic between Diaspora and Homelands," 17; Oruno D. Lara, "African Diaspora: Conceptual Framework, Problems and Methodological Approaches," 58. See also: Ronald Segal, *The Black Diaspora* (New York: Farrar, Straus & Giroux, 1995 especially sections 1 and 3); Ruth Simms-Hamilton, "Toward a Paradigm for African Diaspora Studies," African Diaspora Research Project (Michigan State University, East Lansing, Mich., 1988); Edward Blyden, *Christianity, Islam and the Negro Race* (Edinburgh: Oxford University Press, 1967), 114–120.

46. Shepperson, "African Diaspora," 46.

47. Aubrey Bonnett and G. Llewellyn Watson (eds.), *Emerging Perspectives on the Black Diaspora* (Lanham, Md.: University Press of America, 1990); Roy Simon Bryce-Laporte, "On the Black Diaspora and Its Study" (Foreword to Bonnett and Watson, *Emerging Perspectives on the Black Diaspora*; Ronald Segal, *The Black Diaspora: Five Centuries of the Black Experience Outside Africa* (New York: Farrar, Straus and Giroux, 1995).

48. Alan Dershowitz notes that assimilation by Jews has occurred to such a degree that the Jewish religion and its future are threatened. See his book, *The Vanishing American Jew: In Search of Jewish Identity for the Next Century* (Boston, Mass.: Little, Brown & Co., 1997). This is also noted by Ari Shavit in "The Vanishing Jews," in *The New York Times Magazine*, June 8, 1997, 52–54. Stephen Steinberg also addresses this in *The Ethnic Myth* (Boston, Mass.: Beacon, 1989) (see chapter 2).

49. Green, *Globalization and Survival in the Black Diaspora*; Sutherland, *Black Authenticity* (see chapters 1 and 3).

50. Bonnett and Watson, *Emerging Perspectives on the Black Diaspora*; also suggested by Benjamin Ringer, *We the People, and Others* (New York: Travistock, 1983); Andrew Hacker, *Two Nations* (New York: Ballantine, 1992).

51. Bryce-Laporte, "On the Black Diaspora and Its Study," xvii.

52. The United Nations, *United Nations Population Newsletter* (December 1990, No. 50), 7–16.

53. *United Nations Population Newsletter,* December 1990.

54. *United Nations Population Newsletter,* December 1990.

55. See Akhtar A. Badshah, *Our Urban Future* (New York and London: Zed Books, 1996) 2.

56. See Introduction to Green, *Globalization and Survival in the Black Diaspora.*

57. See *Human Development Report* (UNDP, 1995). This year's publication was devoted to reporting on gender issues and inequality. *Poverty Reduction and Human Resource Development in the Caribbean* (World Bank Report, No.15342 LAC, May 1996); United Nations/UNICEF Press Release of April 21, 1997, "650 Million Women and Children Live in Abject Poverty"; Philip L. Kilbride and Janet C. Kilbride, *Changing Family Life in East Africa* (Nairobi, Kenya: Gideon and Were Press, 1990); Vânia Penha-Lopes, "An Unsavory Union: Poverty, Racism, and the Murders of Street Youth in Brazil," in Green, *Globalization and Survival in the Black Diaspora,* 149–171; Ben Wattenberg, "The Population Explosion Is Over," in *The New York Times Magazine* (Nov. 23, 1997), 63.

58. G. A. Bennars, "African Youth in the 1980s Documentation," in *Basic Education Resource Centre Bulletin* (Vol. 12, 1985).

59. Charles B. K. Nzioka, "The Youth Unemployment Problem in Kenya," in C. K. Omari and L. P. Shaidi (eds.), *Social Problems in Eastern Africa* (Dar es Salaam: University of Dar es Salaam Press, 1991), 55–56.

60. Refer to Meredith Bagby, *Annual Reports of the United States of America*, 1997 (section on drugs/substance abuse).

61. Kevin Arlyck distinguishes between hip-hop and rap. See Arlyck's article, "By All Means Necessary: Resisting and Rappin' in Black Urban America," in Green, *Globalization and Survival in the Black Diaspora*, 269–289.

62. Mike A. Males, *The Scapegoat Generation: America's War on Adolescents* (Monroe, Maine: Common Courage Press, 1996) 220.

63. *The Scapegoat Generation,* 219.

64. *The Scapegoat Generation*, 222.

65. See Green, *Globalization and Survival in the Black Diaspora* (section on Europe).

66. Robert K. Merton, "Social Structure and Anomie," *American Sociological Review*, 3, 1938, 672–682.

67. John DiIulio with William Bennett and John P. Walters, *Body Count* (New York: Simon & Schuster, 1996). See James Traub's excellent review article on *Body Count* entitled, "The Criminals of Tomorrow," in *The New Yorker* (Nov. 4, 1996), 50–65.

68. James Traub, "The Criminals of Tomorrow," 50–65.

69. Mayra Buvinic and Andrew R. Morrison, "Living in a More Violent World," (*Foreign Policy*, Spring 2000, 58–71).

70. Cornel West, *Race Matters* (Boston, Mass.: Beacon Press, 1993); C. K. Omari, *Tanzania*; Charles Green, "Identity and Adaptation in the 1990s: Caribbean Immigrant Youth in New York City" in *Wadabagei: A Journal of Caribbeans in the Diaspora* (Winter/Spring 1998); Green, "Powerlessness and the City: Comparing the Black Urban Crisis in the U.S. Black Belt and the Caribbean" (a paper presented at The Annual Conference of the British Sociological Association, Leicester, England, (April 10–13, 1996).

71. Anderson, *Streetwise.*

72. Herbert Gans, *People, Plans and Practice* (New York: Columbia University Press, 1991), 239, 333–337; also, Gans, "Deconstructing the Underclass," in Paula S. Rothenberg (ed.), *Race, Class, & Gender in the United States* (New York: St. Martin's Press, 1992).

73. Offering a lucid critique of the modernists' position are: W. W. Rostow, *The Stages of Economic Growth* (Cambridge: Cambridge University Press, 1960); Thomas Sowell, "Second Thoughts About the Third World" in *Harper* (November 1983), 34–42; Peter L. Berger, *The Capitalist Revolution* (New York: Basic Books, 1986).

74. Rodney, *How Europe Underdeveloped Africa*; also, Andrew Webster, *Introduction to the Sociology of Development* (London, U.K.: Macmillan,1984); Mason, *Development and Disorder*; Norberg-Hodge, *The Case Against the Global Economy.*

75. See Walter Rodney's definition of development in *How Europe Underdeveloped Africa*, pages 3 and 13; also, Julius K. Nyerere, "Freedom and Development" (originally a policy statement presented in October 1968) in *Man And Development* (London: Oxford University Press, 1974), 25–39.

76. See Barbara Dafoe Whitehead's article, "Dan Quayle Was Right," in *Atlantic Monthly*, April 1993.

77. A collection of Manley's most memorable comments and speeches that was aired in March 1997 on the Howard University Radio Station, Washington, D.C.

78. Barber, in *Jihad*, cites a number of works in his chapter 7, "Television and MTV: Mc-World's Noisy Soul," for example, in Marie Winn's *Plug In-Drug* (New York: Grossman Publishers, 1977); Frank Mankiewicz and Joel Swerdlow, *Remote Control: Television and the Manipulation of American Life* (New York: Ballantine Books, 1979); Jerry Mander, *Four Arguments for the Elimination of Television* (Brighten: Harvester Press, 1980); "Television's Most Violent: It's Payback Time" in *The New York Times Commentary* (Sunday, Jan. 18, 1998), 7; Michael Parenti, *Make–Believe Media: The Politics of Entertainment* (New York.: St. Martin's Press, 1992). A recent report by UCLA. found that while violence has declined on network television series, it has proliferated in a raft of new reality-based "shockumentaries" featuring footage of people jumping to their deaths off burning buildings, cop shootouts and wild beasts tearing their jungle brethren to bloody shreds. *Report by the UCLA. Center for Communication Policy*, 1996–1997, page 7; Mayra Buvinic and Andrew R. Morrison, "Living In A More Violent World," *Foreign Policy* (Spring 2000, 58–77).

79. The notion of "hyperghetto" is taken up by Löic J. D. Wacquant in "The Ghetto, the State, and the New Capitalist Economy," in *Dissent* (Fall 1989); also in Wacquant's "The Rise of Advanced Marginality: Notes on Its Nature and Implications" in *ACTA SOCIO-LOGICA* (Vol. 39, 1996), 121–139.

80. On residential apartheid, see Douglas Massey and Nancy Denton, *American Apartheid: Segregation and the Making of the Underclass* (Cambridge: Harvard University Press, 1993); Andrew Hacker, *Two Nations*, 35–37.

81. Ian I. Smart. *Amazing Connections: Kemet To Hispanophone Africana Literature*, Washington, D.C. and P.O.S. (Trinidad: Original World Press, 1996).

2

The Saga of Crisis in the U.S. Black Belt[1]

The United States is the logical location to begin our comparison of the urban crisis in the black diaspora. Trailing Nigeria and Brazil, the United States has the third-highest concentration of persons of African descent within its borders. Given the developing-nation status of both Nigeria and Brazil, it is understandable that most blacks outside the United States would consider African Americans privileged, or at least the most fortunate blacks in the world. Several other reasons could be cited for this with the most obvious being America's status as the richest nation on the globe and its hegemonic role in what is frequently referred to as "world culture."[2] More than 50 years after the end of World War II, America's military might is undisputed. Having lagged in the immediate post-Cold War period, many economic analysts are satisfied that the U.S. economy has finally bounced back into first place. Aiding America's comeback is the precarious state of the Asian tigers. The economic crisis that has crippled Thailand, South Korea, and Indonesia and threatens the rest of Asia promises that America's chief rival, Japan, whose economy has been locked in recession for quite some time now, will sever its competitive edge.

In this chapter it will be important for us to challenge the myth of African American privilege. We will argue that African Americans have managed to acquire and enjoy certain material benefits by virtue of their residence in America. We also will argue that, besieged by racism and the usual vagaries of market capital, African Americans remain in relative terms a powerless and impoverished people. Given the strategic role of the United States, the global economic order, and, too, its self-proclaimed status as the democratic citadel of the world, it would be important to explore the effects of globalization on African Americans compared with blacks elsewhere in the diaspora. Two such impacts are considered in this chapter. One is the movement of industrial and manufacturing jobs from the urban centers outward to the developing world and select regions of the country. The other is heightened white racism.

The black urban condition and blacks' response, whether we consider the protest for civil rights, coping strategies, or self-destruction, has been telecast to the world. In the eyes of the white power structure, the African American urban condition has become a prototype of black urban life globally. It is not surprising to find that many African Americans perceive themselves as cultural trendsetters for other blacks around the world. For these reasons, in this study the African American urban condition is used as a backdrop against which others in the diaspora are compared and analyzed.

For African Americans, the escalation of globalization has simply meant the exacerbation of historic racial and economic inequality. The fact that black people are disproportionately isolated in the inner cities all across America at the very time when work is disappearing and that these same cities, once the gateway to the American capitalist enterprise, are in decline is not coincidental. It is borne out of the historic relationship between racism and capital, a relationship that Eric Williams so carefully analyzed for us in the classic work, *Capitalism and Slavery*. The strategic integration of slavery into the economy enabled the poor, warfatigued, and recently independent nation of America to excel in the production of cotton during the agricultural phase of its development. It was then able to make the leap forward into the industrial phase at a pace that would eventually outshine its European competitors.[3]

To discuss the structural forces of racism and capital and their impact on America's black population is to not discuss a uniquely African American phenomenon. Blacks outside the United States were no less dismembered by the forces of racism, enslavement, and capitalists' insatiable thirst to accumulate profits. The differences, however, are to be found in terms of their specific histories and experiences under colonialism, their present majority–minority mix, and the nature of cultural development in the outposted regions and territories.

AMERICAN CULTURE AND BLACK CIVIL SOCIETY

An interesting feature of ethnic America is its pluralistic structure, although one should be careful not to overstate pluralism as an idea that is embraced by all Americans. Steinberg's[4] view, which is supported by leading scholarly critics of American race relations, recognizes that the ignominious origins of ethnic and race relations in the society have not been effectively redressed. Consequently, the prospects for a meaningful expression of ethnic and racial pluralism are at best elusive, and groups' quest for some form of ethnic expression is often vague and symbolic in nature. A more realistic pattern of race and ethnic relations in America is that of disparate groups competing for upward mobility through the processes of integration and assimilation.

The American version of ethnic pluralism—in which groups see the opportunity to sustain aspects of their own cultures while enjoining American ways—has historically drawn immigrants to its shores. It has drawn scores of tourists to the cities where the experiences of specific ethnic groups have been celebrated. They seek out New York City's Little Italy, the Chinatowns of New York and San Francisco, and German-ethnicized towns like Milwaukee that are famous for their breweries.[5] As well, they seek out the Amish villages of Pennsylvania and the great national parks, once the Native Americans' homelands, stolen as they were corralled and cast off to reservations.[6] Harlem, dubbed the black capital of the world, stands out as another must-see attraction for many international and domestic visitors to New York City. They travel along the famed 125th Street to see the Apollo Theatre and the old Saint Theresa Hotel, which once lodged prominent black artists who were not welcome at the downtown hotels during the 1930s and 1940s. The trail also covers landmark churches, nightclubs, and residences of famous intellectuals, artisans, and activists dating back to the Harlem-Renaissance period.[7] Its glorious past notwithstanding, Harlem and its people have been altered dramatically—those same tourists can't help but see the poverty and indignity the residents endure today.

African American culture has been promoted and commercialized internationally in the form of MTV music, entertainment, lifestyles, language, cuisine, and dress codes for all to appreciate. Civil rights legal scholar Derrick Bell points out that neither America nor the world for that matter could survive without African American culture.[8] On the other hand, achievements by blacks in fields outside of entertainment and sports such as the sciences and medicine are seldom, if ever, reported. Among the few exceptions is General Colin Powell, the first black Chairman of the Joint Chiefs of Staff. His valor and loyalty to the "red, white, and blue" guided his successful military offensive in the invasion of Panama in December 1989 and his leadership in the Persian Gulf War. Overall, it would be inaccurate to suggest that African American culture is one-dimensional or that other blacks are linked to their North American brothers and sisters solely by culture and entertainment. Internationally, blacks have identified with African Americans' legacy of political activism and leadership in the struggle for civil and human rights during the 1950s and 1960s. Names like Martin Luther King, Jr., Elijah Muhammed, Malcolm X, Stokely Carmichael, and Huey Newton—along with their respective organizations: SCLC, The Nation of Islam, SNCC, and the Black Panthers—emerged during this period. The first Pan African Congress in Paris in 1919, and more recently, the struggle to free Nelson Mandela and liberate South Africa, found African Americans out on the frontlines. These celebrated individuals, organizations, and movements had a tremendous appeal to the oppressed members of the global black community and served to advance the role of African Americans as "political catalyst."[9]

Notwithstanding the legacy of cause and activism, in the last 15 years the material aspects of African American cultural life have captured the imagination of blacks (and nonblacks) living outside the United States.[10] What immediately comes to mind are superstar Michael Jackson, hip-hop style and the rap genre, videos and films that portray life in the "hood," and urban blacks' lifestyles and dress codes. It is all too common to see a No. 23 jersey (representing the retired Chicago Bulls superstar Michael Jordan) on the backs of youth in some of the least-expected corners of the black diaspora. The magnetic pull of communications technology has ensured that these expressions of mass culture leave an indelible mark on blacks outside the United States and that they become intricately woven into their cultural existence. To discuss African American culture as highly influential in the diaspora is not to imply that blacks are necessarily in control of that culture. Bourdieu enlightens us that various fields are hierarchically organized, for example, political, economic, cultural, educational, and so on. Each field has its own laws and is sufficiently autonomous. Agents who occupy diverse positions in a given field compete for control of the interests or resources specific to the field in question. Agents bring various skills and talents to the field, which allow them to enter and play the "game" to their advantage.[11]

MIGRATION AND THE CHANGING URBAN LANDSCAPE

The role of migration is fundamental to the urbanization process and the emergence of poor ghettos, barrios, and shanties. Push and pull forces, which are central to migration theory,[12] are extremely helpful in explaining the movements of people between countries and within geographic boundaries of a given state or region. The demand for skilled and unskilled labor in Country A will serve as the pull factor. Push factors respond during periods of slack economic growth in which high unemployment rates or an oversupply of idle labor are evident. During such periods, for example, Country B will sound the alarm and encourage or "push" its excess labor to Country A, where the demand is. This push and pull process also takes place within regions or areas of a given country. Many developing countries have come to rely heavily on the migration of their citizens to foreign countries as a method to control their population size and resultant labor surplus. It is also a way to deal with their inability to satisfy the material needs of citizens. Push and pull forces have been operational in the history of the U.S. migration policy, both domestic and international. In the case of the post-bellum South, blacks were pushed off the land with the introduction of mechanization and other technological advances. These changes demanded fewer and fewer unskilled hands. Also guiding this process was the prevalence of deep-seated racial intolerance for the former slaves and their descendants.

Despite two centuries as chattel on the cotton plantations of the American South and their continued rural existence in the immediate post-bellum period, blacks are viewed today as a historically urban people. This myth provides the basis for their stigmatization as "America's urban problem," which in turn has been reinforced by media reports of inner-city violence, drive-by shootings, and immorality.[13] It is interesting to see how this view is also reinforced during political campaigns when candidates and their retinue of media personnel pound the ghetto pavements as a show of commitment to the poor when the real aim is to attract votes. Such was the case in 1976 and 1980 when presidential hopefuls Jimmy Carter and Ronald Reagan walked through the rubble of Charlotte Street in New York's depressed South Bronx community shaking hands and making typical election promises that were not kept.[14] We also witnessed this in August 1996 at the Democratic National Convention in Chicago when CNN took an international viewing audience literally steps from the convention headquarters to interview poor black residents and their community leaders at the Henry Honer Houses, one of Chicago's most depressed housing projects.

To set the historic record straight, prior to 1950 the majority of American blacks were nonurbanized. In 1940, 77 percent of black Americans still lived in southern states with 40 percent in the rural South and 37 percent in southern urban areas. Nicholas Lemann documents that: At the earliest development of mechanized cotton farming in the South, around 1910 through 1970, approximately six and a half million black Americans headed up North. By that time "urban" had become a euphemism for black.[15]

Prompting this migration prior to World War I was mechanization intended to meet the needs of capital in the agrarian sector. The watershed occurred with Eli Whitney's invention of the cotton gin in the nineteenth century, and in the 1940s, Howell Hopson's cotton harvester. Both inventions impacted the growth of the crop and the size of the labor force needed to tend it. These technological advances demanded fewer and fewer unskilled cotton pickers. Migration was also steered by the pervasive racial intolerance for the former victims of bondage and their offspring. The outbreak of World War I in 1914 and America's entry into the war greatly affected migratory trends as the demand for labor at industrial sites increased in order to fill the void left by European immigrants whose ocean voyages were interrupted. Following the war, the pace of black migration North accelerated even though their participation in the industrial labor sector began to wane. Contributing to this was the resumption of European migration following the war and the preferential treatment given them over black labor. Lemann notes: "Black migration became one of the largest and most rapid mass internal movements of people in history—perhaps the greatest not caused by the immediate threat of execution or starvation. In sheer numbers it outranks the migration of any other ethnic group—Italians or Jews or Poles—to this country."[16]

URBANIZATION AND ADAPTATION

Learning to adjust to urban life was not easy for the streams of newcomers whose cultural orientation was strictly rural based. But the promise of steady work and the opportunity to escape the South's apartheid system far outweighed the uncertainties of urban life that awaited them in the North. The trek north was devastating for families, and in many cases entire families did not travel at the same time.[17] Migration penetrated southern cities such as Atlanta and Richmond but the thrust of it was directed to the cities of the Northeast and the Midwest such as New York, Philadelphia, Washington, D.C., Boston, and Chicago.[18] Where the black experience in these and other cities has been captured in writing, enacted on stage, and put into lyrics and sung, it is the black experience in New York, specifically Harlem, that has received the greatest attention.[19]

During the process of transplanting the black community, the black church—the single most influential institution of black civil society during and after slavery—was challenged to make an adjustment.[20] As a fundamental part of this challenge, the church had to compete with newer institutions in an increasingly complex urban environment that included political clubs, trade union organizations, and pool halls. It was not much longer before the newcomers came to the realization that the unshackling of the chains of southern apartheid, which they believed had become undone by moving north, was nothing more than an illusion. One difference they found at this historical juncture was that up North they were not separated on rural farms as sharecroppers; instead they were huddled together in large numbers in tenements and row houses in the urban ghettos of major industrial cities. Ironically, proximity to each other would be to their advantage at a later date in their mobilization for civil rights and justice.[21]

For certain, the segregation of urban life for the newcomers, which was buttressed by white racism, could not be denied. Fortunately, their southern past had prepared them for this aspect of their migration. The church managed to meet most of its challenges and go about its business of saving souls and providing support to families and needy individuals. The ghetto of old, through the 1950s, was imbued with a communal spirit that was grounded in the African cultural tradition, which Hillary Rodham Clinton wove into the title of her book, *It Takes a Village*.[22] It was this communal spirit and strength that served as an instrument of collective solidarity and mobilization for the members of black civil society. At that time, providing guidance and direction to a child was not limited to the biological parents but was the responsibility of everyone in the neighborhood. In fact, it is not uncommon to hear African Americans of the baby boom generation recount their early socialization on the urban streets of New York City, Chicago, Baltimore and elsewhere when it was understood that any adult on the residential block was a force to be reckoned with if they misbehaved and that it would be double trouble later on when their parents learned about it. It was a period when black civil society that included the church, the black press, lodges and social clubs, political groups, and businesses and professional services were very much in place. Finally, it was also a time when, despite virulent racism and the occasional violation of blacks as strike breakers at industrial work sites, the demand for semiskilled and unskilled work was still relatively high.[23]

At the same time that black Harlemites and those from Chicago, Detroit, Boston, and other urban constituencies were learning to adapt, strong winds of change and social dislocation were gusting in the background. Unlike a hurricane or other climatic disturbance whose winds wreak havoc but are followed by a period of calm, the winds that arrived by the mid-1960s were unrelenting. This in turn prompted newer and emboldened coping strategies by urban residents. Unfortunately, these strategies have thus far proven incapable of controlling the direction of the storm or improving the quality of life for inner-city black residents in terms of meaningful employment, functional primary and secondary schools, or the struggle for racial justice.

URBAN DISLOCATION

In much the same way that technological development and the shifting needs of capital were responsible for the demographic shift that led to the rise of black urban America, so too were these structural forces responsible for its decline. The creation of scapegoats was central to this process. Instead of placing the responsibility for the decline of the nation's inner cities where it rightfully belongs—a plethora of insensitive urban policies amidst capital flight—the concept of a "black urban underclass" was invented by leading social scientists, policy engineers, and legislators and eventually was publicized by journalists. In the opening chapter of this book it was mentioned that the problem most progressives have with the concept of an underclass is its pejorative connotation that charges the victims with being the source of their misery and thereby sees them as responsible for changing their condition.[24] So-called underclass tracts [25] were identified in the black and Latino communities where the nation's industrial and manufacturing centers were once located. They now serve as depressing reminders of a once glorious era.[26]

Compared to the 1930s and the 1940s, the contemporary ghetto is discussed as a "hyperghetto." In this instance, physical decay, violence, family disruption, and chronic unemployment have demolished the ghetto of old. Wacquant (1994) summarized the causes of hyperghettoization as involving a nexus of economic and political factors. Among the causes cited are (1) the shift from the factory-oriented "Fordist" system and the deindustrialization by capital flight; (2) residential apartheid; (3) the retreat of the welfare state in principle in favor of welfare capitalism; and (4) planned shrinkage of public services and institutions in the ghetto.[27]

Demographic shifts cannot be left out of this description. Many depressed inner-city areas were once inhabited by ethnic whites who were the descendants of the earlier European immigration streams who worked in the industrial factories. At the time of the economic upswing following World War II, the G.I. Bill and the Federal Housing Authority were offering inexpensive mortgages for first-time homeowners. This encouraged many urbanites to join the suburbanization movement, and the role of the federal government in this was instrumental. In communion with business (construction firms, banks, and the auto industry), the government sold the suburban package to middle- and working-class Americans as the great opportunity to own their piece of the American dream and to experience American freedom and democracy at work firsthand.[28] Through this policy, America would become the beacon of hope and opportunity and at the same time guarantee the corporate elite abundant profits. Importantly, this period, which Paul Blumberg carefully details in *Inequality In An Age of Decline,* occurred just prior to the start of the Cold War and provided the building blocks for post-war America.[29] It was a period when convergence theorists dominated much of the debate on stratification and inequality in American society and set out to convince poor and working-class Americans that the heyday of the class divide was over and that the great fusion was about to take place between their interests and those of more fortunate Americans. To hasten this process and once and for all disarm leftist ideologues, that acerbic episode in the history of America better known as the "red purge" commenced and by all accounts was successful.[30]

So white veterans alongside middle- and working-class residents from the urban areas joined the outbound migration movement to the suburbs. Later on (specifically during the 1960s) but at a much slower pace, middle-class blacks living in the cities would follow.[31] The impact this out migration had on the urban areas was significant. In the black community, black doctors, lawyers, teachers and other professionals—who resided within the general community, served a black clientele, and provided role models for the community's youth—were departing with no one to fill the vacuum.[32]

Another impact of the flight by urbanites to the suburbs was that poorer and working-class residents were left behind. Consequently, the tax base of these areas would eventually decline. This is corroborated by Peterson's data, which demonstrated that poor blacks replaced whites who chose to move to the suburbs, small towns, and the Sun Belt region. By 1980, 58 percent of all blacks in the United States lived in the central cities of metropolitan areas, compared to 25 percent of all whites. Seventy-seven percent of blacks lived in the metropolitan areas of the Snow Belt (the Northeast and Midwest cities) compared to only 28 percent of whites.[33] Table 2.1 shows the black population growth patterns for five selected metropolitan areas between 1950 and 1990. (See appendix A for a description of the sample selection.) While population growth for all cities has been significant, the data show that since 1970 there has been some tapering off, possibly explained by blacks' return migration south and the explosion of Latino migration in all urban areas. It should be noted that the black urban migration was not strictly an African American migration by those seeking work or the perceived opportunities associated with big-city life. Other blacks, chiefly those from the small island states of the Caribbean, have had a long history of immigration to U.S. cities, with New York assimilating the greatest share of West Indian immigration. Passage in 1965 of the liberal Hart-Celler Immigration Act, which reduced the restrictions on former British subjects from the Caribbean, is credited with the influx of blacks

Table 2.1 Black Population Growth In Select U.S. Cities, 1950–1990 (percents)

	1950	*1970*	*1990*
Los Angeles	10.7	17.9	14.0
Newark	17.2	54.2	58.5
New York	9.8	21.1	28.7
Richmond	31.7	42.0	55.2
Washington, D.C.	35.4	71.1	65.8

Source: Compiled from U.S. Bureau of the Census Population Data.

from that part of the hemisphere and their eventual development into a critical mass for the first time in the city's history. Exact figures for the Caribbean-born population have varied from 500,000 (which is several times the size of the average West Indian island) to well above that margin.[34]

A precise figure for undocumented immigrants is not available, but it has been suggested that including them would significantly alter the estimated population size of African Caribbeans living in New York City. What is so essential to understand about the influx of the newer black immigrants is that they do not represent the middle and upper classes in their respective countries as was the case with earlier waves of immigrants. That they do not arrive with substantial savings lessens their ability to offset the weakened tax base of the inner-city districts of Bedford-Stuyvesant, East Flatbush, and Crown-Heights in New York's most populous borough, Brooklyn, where they tend to settle. Not to be overlooked is their arrival at the period of major transformation of the American economy.

In the United States today, the fastest growing sectors of the economy are business services, recreation services, nonbanking financial services, social services, and brokerage services. Manufacturing jobs, once the major employment sector, have shrunk from absorbing 33 percent of the labor force in the 1950s to about 17 percent presently. Since 1992 a rising share of new jobs have paid more than average in the U.S. manufacturing sector. For example, 25 percent of the new jobs in 1995 paid at least 30 percent more than the national average which was $29,420.[35] So far in 2000 we continue to hear that mid- to upper-range service sector jobs are paying higher salaries. But when one considers the distribution factor of the new jobs, we find that growth has been uneven. The metropolitan areas of the Sun Belt cities such as Atlanta, Phoenix, Dallas, and Las Vegas have experienced significant growth, whereas in the major metropolitan areas of states such as California, New York, New Jersey, Connecticut, and Pennsylvania, job growth is dragging.

A key factor then for understanding the urban crisis is the flight of industrial and manufacturing jobs from the central cities outward to the Sun Belt region and to the Third World. William Julius Wilson cites the case of the once highly regarded black belt neighborhood of Washington Park on Chicago's south side: "A majority of adults had jobs in 1950; by 1990, only 1 in 3 worked in a typical week." He cites another case, on the west side of Chicago, in the black community of North Lawndale: "Since 1960, nearly half of its housing stock has disappeared, the remaining units are run down or dilapidated. The two large factories that buttressed the neighborhood's economy were the Hawthorne Plant of Western Electric and International Harvester. Together, they accounted for over 57,000 employees. Beginning in the 1960s through 1984, the companies slowly moved out."[36] Consequently, Washington Park and North Lawndale have become "hyperghettos," a scenario that has been replicated in other major cities across the nation.

Since President Clinton took office in 1993, the economy has spun off 10.1 million new jobs at a rate of 245,000 a month, even faster than under the Reagan administration. The Bureau of Labor Statistics reports in 2000 that the labor market is at its tightest in seven years. At the start of 1997, national unemployment plummeted to 4.9 percent from a peak of 7.7 percent in June 1992. But the relevant question to probe is how this growth has affected the urban sufferers. For starters, one must interpret these statistics carefully. While the national unemployment was plummeting to 4.9 percent, New York City, the nation's largest urban center, registered at 10.3 percent. Currently at 5.1 percent, New York is still above the national rate of approximately 4.3 percent.[37] One has to understand that the national figure represents an average and that not every hamlet, village, and city is enjoying 4.3 percent unemployment. Citing national averages is a common practice and often misleading for the general public. Unemployment data do not include "discouraged workers" or frustrated people who have ceased searching for work. But looking at it from the perspective of those who stand to benefit most, this is a convenient way to camouflage the true state of affairs.

It should also be pointed out that two-thirds of the jobs created under President Clinton have been lower-paying jobs that do not provide employee health benefits. New manufacturing jobs, which have been steadily declining, only accounted for 14 percent of the total jobs created in 1996. For 2000, that figure is a mere 12 percent.[38] The greatest share of job growth between 1989 and 1995 took place at the high and low ends of the pay scale with the greatest gains occurring in high-paying occupations requiring abundant skill and education. That explains one journalist's cynical outlook on the jobs bonanza in her *New York Times* column: "For all this demand for workers, many Americans can still only dream of a better job. They simply do not have the education or the skills to qualify for good jobs."[39]

Despite all of the celebration around the robust U.S. economy and the Clinton administration's role, millions of low-skilled inner-city workers remain jobless or stuck in low-paying dead-end jobs without health benefits. According to *The Multi-City Study of Urban Inequality*, these people are unable to secure the kind of employment that might provide them with better chances for success. The great debate that actually led to the urban inequality study was the need to determine whether this was due to skill and spatial mismatches or to persistent racial barriers. Preliminary findings suggest that space and skills gaps create major obstacles to the advancement of inner-city workers, but they reveal only one part of the larger picture. Unsurprisingly, it is racial barriers that continue to have the greatest influence on the job prospects of this community. Many employers continue to believe that blacks and Latinos are best suited for the lowest-paying menial jobs because they need work and are willing to put up with more. Moreover, Harry Holzer's investigation, *What Employers Want,* found that employers deliberately chose locations for firms that are inaccessible for blacks and that they tend to prefer immigrants over blacks even when the newcomers had fewer skills and lived farther away from the work site.[40]

With black youth unemployment in the inner cities persisting in double digits, it is difficult to counter Wilson's claim that many of the problems that plague these neighborhoods such as crime, family dislocation, drug trafficking, and so on are directly related to the "disappearance of work." In fact 65.9 percent from the U.S. sample of our youth survey (representing New York City, Newark, Washington, D.C., Central Los Angeles, and Richmond, Virginia) indicated that they were not employed (see appendix D). While many of these young people were not actively seeking employment, for those who were, the unavailability of jobs in and outside their neighborhoods was a real problem. When jobs are scarce, people tend to lose their feeling of connectedness to work in the formal economy; they no longer expect work to be a regular and regulating force in their lives. When these youth grow up in inner-city environments where the idea of work as a central experience of adult life is weakened, they develop no real attachments to the labor force.[41] Criminal offenses of various types have been a clear outcome of youth frustration.

Almost two million people are currently locked up in American prisons and jails. Problematic is that one in every four black men in America are in some way connected to the criminal justice system—or what some activists choose to call the criminal "injustice" system. This translates to more than 70 percent of America's imprisoned population as persons of color. Drug offenses, it should be mentioned, account for a significant proportion of these arrests.[42] Examining the data from the mid-1990s, there were 21,597 murders reported nationally in 1995, 7 percent fewer than in 1994 and 13 percent below the 1991 level. But 49 percent of the victims were black. Persons incarcerated in federal and state prisons in 1995 reached a record high of 1.3 million. This represents a 6 percent increase over 1994. Fifty-two percent of those are African American.[43] These data strengthen the argument that there is a connection between institutional racism at the turn of the twentieth century and the globalization of capital.

We now learn that the national crime rate is declining precipitously. Violent crimes in large cities dropped by 8 percent in 1995, paving the way for a 3 percent drop nationwide. In 1995, the FBI's annual survey of crime indicated the lowest murder rate in a decade and the lowest overall rate of violent crime since 1989. The number of reported crimes of all types according to the FBI survey was down 1 percent from the previous year.[44] Eight cities were highlighted in that report: Chicago, Dallas, Houston, Los Angeles, New York, Philadelphia, Phoenix, and San Diego. The relevant question to probe is: Is crime really declining in the central cities or is it the result of aggressive policing and more arrests? For certain, because the social and economic conditions that lead to crime remain unaddressed, a revolving door of crime is predicted.

Family disruption, especially in terms of the growth of female-headed households that function at or below the poverty level, is a national problem that has reached alarming proportions in the black community. In 1990, 56.2 percent of black households were headed by females, compared to 17.3 percent for whites. Approximately 59.7 percent of these black families are located in the inner cities versus 28.1 percent of white families.[45]

A majority of the youth from our survey (43.7 percent) reported living in households with a single mother at the head while 36 percent reported living with both parents.

Presently, one in four children are born into poverty, which places the United States well behind other major industrialized nations of the world. In 1970, the infant mortality rate for the United States was 20 for every 1,000 live births, which ranked it thirteenth among other developed OECD countries.[46] The U.S. lag in infant mortality continued well into the 1980s and only turned around in 1991, when it was reported at seven per 1,000 where it presently stands.[47] Contributing to this latter statistic are the ignominious health conditions in the poor urban centers that skew the data. [48] Those without Medicaid or other health insurance must rely on the hospital emergency room as their primary care facility. On any given day or evening, emergency rooms that were previously occupied by those requiring immediate care are filled to capacity. Poor immigrants are especially visible among those awaiting treatment. In New York City this problem is acute in light of the downsizing of hospital staffs, deteriorating physical plants, and outdated equipment. The current city administration is aggressively exploring privatization of key city-owned hospitals as the response to its fiscal woes. Privatization would solve the city's fiscal woes, but it is highly unlikely to attract corporate executives with moderate appetites for profits and a magnanimous attitude toward the poor.[49]

The state of education at inner-city schools is not much better than the state of health care. Compared to wealthier suburban districts, most of the urban schools are overcrowded, with deteriorating physical infrastructures, low teacher morale, and limited, inferior equipment and supplies. Students are not learning, and consequently, many reject high school altogether for a more profitable life on the streets. The disparity between urban and suburban public school districts is related to the method used to fund school districts[50] and to the demographic shifts in urban areas. This has led to the out migration of higher-tax-paying residents and an increased proportion of lower-salaried working-class and poorer residents, many of whom are dependent on some form of public assistance.

A serious disparity appears when one considers the growth of poor black female-headed households, high infant mortality rates and poor health care in the black communities, and the deterioration of urban inner-city schools. The top one-fifth of all families currently brings home 44.6 percent of the total income of the United States compared to 4.4 percent earned by the bottom fifth. From 1979 to 1994, the top 5 percent of American earners saw their incomes grow by 45 percent, compared to the lowest 20 percent of earners, who saw their incomes drop by 13.5 percent in real terms. Those in the middle of the income distribution also received proportionately less of the nation's income. The middle 60 percent of households received only 53 percent of the aggregate household income in 1968. By 1994, that figure had declined to 48 percent.[51]

Powerlessness, as earlier defined, can be understood both as a cause and an effect of an individual's or group's absence from the decision-making process. Crime, family disruption, unemployment, and inadequate health care and education all underscore the problem of powerlessness and the crisis that challenges black people in America's inner cities.

THE CASE OF URBAN POWERLESSNESS

Efforts to address powerlessness in the black community as manufactured is routinely dismissed as conspiratorial. Conspiracy theories have been enigmatic in America and thus have received limited support even in progressive liberal circles. Liberals may analyze powerlessness from the perspective of race but mainly as the absence of group self-help initiatives and specific government inputs. For sure, conservatives are unlikely to analyze race from the structuralist perspective, which might just lead them to see it as necessary for the normal operation of the capitalist state.[52] Marxists and the left may critique black powerlessness from the structuralist perspective, but as Charles Mills points out, in their efforts to unite classes, they reject the significance of race and posit a universe comprised of abstract, colorless individuals.[53]

But a recent sequence of events has fostered renewed interest in the black community for the conspiracy argument in explaining persistent black powerlessness. This includes the Personal Responsibility and Work Opportunity Reconciliation Act (welfare reform) signed into law by President Clinton on August 23, 1996 and the unrelenting assault on affirmative action. California is leading this latest round with the introduction of Proposition 209, better known as the California Civil Rights Initiative. The clearest example in terms of events that helped to rekindle the conspiracy theory was the publication of a three-part series entitled "Dark Alliance: The Story Behind the Crack Explosion" that appeared in the August 18, 1996 *San Jose Mercury News*. Let us quickly glance at each of these.

When it was legislated under the landmark Social Security Act of 1935, the Aid for Families with Dependent Children (currently known by the acronym AFDC) program was not intended as a permanent government handout but rather as a form of temporary relief to widowed mothers and their dependent children. By the 1960s, the program expanded exponentially in terms of numbers of beneficiaries and the size of the federal disbursement.[54] With the atrophy of jobs, the cutback of day care support for working mothers, and the increasing rates of divorce, separation, and abandonment, the welfare rolls swelled. Not only were these causes contrary to those conceived by the program's creators, the racial composition of the newer beneficiaries was nonwhite. That significant reform—which had been building since the Nixon administration in the 1970s—would occur was assured. Just when the reform would take place was less certain.

Citing some demographic data would be helpful here. In 1994 there were 4.5 million children on AFDC. Blacks constituted 34.2 percent and whites (non-Hispanic) 39.9 percent; however, blacks were disproportionately represented, as they were only 12.4 percent of the nation's population.[55] While it is difficult to disagree with the view of the public assistance program as ineffective and dependency-oriented, in the absence of work training and jobs at adequate wages, the thought of pulling the plug on the scores of families, mostly children, is immoral. Moreover a criticism from the nation's black community and its sympathizers is that the new welfare reform policy is fraught with racism. The new reform measure sets the lifetime limit for aid at five years. Federal block grant funds are provided to the states to use as they see fit to aid the poor. After two years of receiving benefits (and depending on the age of a mother's youngest child), work is required or benefits will be terminated. Estimates by the Congressional Budget Office that by the year 2004 between 2.5 and 3.5 million children could be affected by time limits is a chilling forecast.[56]

The assistance package, though inadequate, does offer a cushion that includes medical benefits, but this draconian measure offers no answers as to how families, once terminated, will survive. With the buildup of domestic economic crises and pressure from largely conservative middle-class voters to end welfare as it had come to be known and enforce workfare nationally, the Clinton administration felt compelled to act. In true election year form, the administration was convinced that action on this important issue would improve its standing among the Republican electorate and strengthen Mr. Clinton's position with Democrats who favor a get-tough approach to welfare by enforcing the value of work, not handouts.

The argument could be posed that affirmative action, to a greater extent than public assistance, is viewed as a contradiction to the American value structure. Drawing from the social Darwinist ideology that came to embody the American ethos, any form of government aid was seen as a threat to the normal work ethic and the spirit of laissez-faire capitalism. It will be recalled that AFDC was seen initially as temporary relief, and the fact that mostly white mothers and their dependent children were the chief beneficiaries at that historical juncture aided its passage. Nevertheless, the program was universal and not racially or ethnically specific. Affirmative action, on the other hand, according to Nathan Glazer in his seminal work, *Affirmative Discrimination*, wrongly rewards select groups on the basis of their past discrimination—whether or not that is still the case—and ultimately reinforces the class-based system by pitting selected groups against non-selected groups.[57]

Since Glazer's 1978 treatise, the venom has flowed throughout society but observably so from "angry white men" who believe that their interests are at greatest risk by the unfair advantage accorded racial minorities and women in the professional and educational arenas via quotas and timetables. Glazer's position is classic in the sense that all American groups are viewed as having experienced some form of discrimination, for example, the Irish, Italians, Poles, and Jews, and that they too should qualify under the quota protection. This leads to another classic argument—that whites should not be forced to pay reparations to blacks for the misdeeds of their slave-owning ancestors.[58] What is noteworthy is that when most whites think of affirmative action, they think "black," as in black people, and not the fact that white women in large numbers have benefited from these very policies.

Another salient point is that blacks at the lower end of the socioeconomic spectrum have benefited least of all from affirmative action measures, compared to those from the middle class, who have the skills and education to move into the affirmed positions. This unfortunately has been the case following the gains made during the civil rights era. As middle-class blacks continued to stride upward, striding in the opposite direction were poorer blacks, who constitute roughly one-third (10 million people) of African Americans, and this phenomenon according to Jervis Anderson has become "one of the greatest contradictions in Black America."[59] Moreover, in spite of affirmative action, black unemployment levels nationwide, and profoundly so in the poor urban areas, have always remained higher than those of whites with perhaps one exception: during the period of enslavement when blacks were forced to work.[60]

The California Civil Rights Initiative amends the state constitution to prohibit state agencies and local governments from using race or gender as a basis for hiring, for educational policies, and for contracting. President Clinton had hoped to ease the controversy last year when he promised to rework federal affirmative action programs. He used the motto "Mend It, Don't End It," but it appeared that California had voted by a 55 to 45 margin essentially to "End It."[61] Civil rights groups filed suit after the election to prevent the measure from becoming law and vowed to organize politically to defend their programs. Considering California's position as a bellwether of retrogressive politics, it comes as no surprise to learn that other states are following California's example in their efforts to destabilize affirmative action.

Many well-known activists in black communities across the nation view this as the final phase of an organized plan to dismantle affirmative action and further disempower that group perceived to be its chief beneficiary. Once that occurs, the increased powerlessness of the black middle class is certain to follow. This will undoubtedly affect those at the bottom in the urban areas as it will erode the prospects of assistance from more fortunate blacks to their communities. It also will extinguish for some ghetto residents the small spark of hope and aspiration that they will one day find a way up and out. In many respects this turn of events and the despair it generates in the black community is reminiscent of the eve of the withdrawal of the federal troops from the South in 1877 that led to the end of Reconstruction. If the fate of affirmative action appears destined for termination, President Clinton's "Mend It, Don't End It" statement will have to be viewed as no more than political window dressing.

Finally, we have Gary Webb's ground-breaking report alleging a 1980s Central Intelligence Agency conspiracy to continue to support the Nicaraguan Democratic Force (or Contras) in their war against communism and the Nicaraguan Sandinista government—in defiance of Congressional legislation to discontinue that policy. The deadly drug "crack," a more affordable derivative of cocaine, was allegedly sold to the Crips and Bloods street gangs of Los Angeles and filtered its way into the hands of youths throughout the nation's urban areas. The millions in profits from these sales were passed on to the CIA's contra guerrillas in the form of weapons and other items. These allegations have been flatly denied by the CIA but if proven otherwise, they will explain the exponential rise of senseless violent crime on the urban streets. Webb writes:

> While the war is barely a memory today, black America is still dealing with its poisonous side effects. Urban neighborhoods are grappling with legions of homeless crack addicts. Thousands of young black men are serving long prison sentences for selling cocaine—a drug that was virtually unobtainable in black neighborhoods before members of the CIA's army started bringing it into South Central (Los Angeles) in the 1980s at bargain-basement prices.[62]

These same signals were sounded earlier in 1974 when passage of the Freedom of Information Act made possible the release of the FBI files labeled Cointelpro, or the Counter Intelligence Program. That operation was responsible for the infiltration and decimation of militant black groups such as the Black Panthers and the Student Non-Violent Coordinating Committee (SNCC) but also for white anti-war and Socialist Workers Party activities. Allegations that a chemical war was being waged against the black community with the feds' introduction of cocaine and heroin into their neighborhoods also surfaced at that time.[63] We will have to see if the response by the community that pushed for Congressional hearings and a formal investigation into the matter will swell into a larger movement for change. As of this writing, at least one black member of Congress, Maxine Waters of California, has demonstrated resilience around this issue and managed to keep it in the public eye.[64] Whether or not one is inclined to support the conspiracy theory as an explanation for the plight of inner-city blacks, these examples inform us about the extent of blacks' mistrust for the system and why their feelings of hope about their future in the system continues to wane.

Police brutality in the black community is a long-standing problem that has been consistently avoided at the highest levels of government. The brutality issue seemed to reach a crescendo in March of 1992 when, unbeknownst to those involved, a young white man trying out a new video camera videotaped 56 blows by Los Angeles police officers to the body of motorist Rodney King as other officers stood by. According to Gerald Horne (1997), that the incident had been videotaped was not sufficient to convince a suburban jury (that had no African Americans) to issue a conviction. The officers' counsel achieved this result in part by decontextualizing the video of the beating, showing the jury each static frame, as opposed to a continuous showing.[65] The tide of allegations against the police created an important twist in the summer of 1996 when Amnesty International, the renowned human rights watch group, went to New York City—the nation's largest city with the largest concentration of African Americans—to investigate the situation there. Their report corroborated the findings of an earlier investigation during the summer of 1984 headed by Rep. John Conyers (D-Detroit) that New York City's police officers were out of control.[66] By all accounts what would have to be considered the most despicable case of police misconduct in recent New York City history occurred in August 1997, when Haitian immigrant Abner Louima, who was in police custody allegedly for resisting arrest, was beaten and sodomized with a toilet plunger by the arresting officer while others watched. All of this took place in the bathroom of a Brooklyn police precinct. According to the victim's medical team, it is likely that he will incur permanent bodily injuries.

On the heels of this was the case of Amadou Diallo. Also an immigrant, from the West African state of Guinea, Diallo was approached by four police officers from the special street crime task force unit in the early morning hours of February 4, 1999, for questioning in an unsolved rape case in the Bronx. It was alleged that the victim reached into his pocket for a weapon, but it was later discovered that he was unarmed. What ensued was 41 shots fired off by the police with 19 riddling the body of Diallo. One year later: All four officers were acquitted of all charges of negligent conduct.

It is not surprising that youth from our survey, which covered five U.S. cities, responded that they mistrust the police. While 71 percent agreed that the police should protect the community, 67.6 percent felt that the police do not treat people equally and that they would not receive a fair trial if arrested. Judging from their responses about the police, it was surprising that 81 percent of the youth respondents believed that adults care about them. But that was quickly contradicted by their response to the question about the government and whether they felt the government could do more to help them—86.7 agreed with that question. In the case of the police and the government it is adults who are in positions of authority. Responses to these survey items bring us closer to the confusion and powerlessness that surround the future generation.

Blacks are not alone in their mistrust of the political system and the view that the police and the criminal justice system are severely prejudiced against them. To the far right, white rural and working-class militias bearing names like Patriots and The Freemen have proliferated. The event that is said to have catapulted them to action and national attention occurred in 1992 when federal agents seized fugitive Randy Weaver's farmhouse in Ruby Ridge, Idaho, killing his wife and son. These militias are distinct from anything that preceded them, largely because their aggression is not directed to Communists (who were a clear and convenient political scapegoat during the Cold War), other leftists, or racial minorities. Their aggression is aimed at the American government, which they consider treasonous and whose laws and enforcement agencies they perceive as violating citizens' constitutional rights. This does not gainsay the racist mentality of many militia members. In recent years they have resorted to bombing government buildings such as the federal complex at Oklahoma City in April 1995, in which 168 innocent men, women, and children lost their lives and 500 were injured. Bombings and murders have occurred at clinics where legalized abortions are performed, and there have been other reported forms of violence including harassment and threats made by government officials.[67] Recent allegations against the U.S. Internal Revenue Service by militias about undue harassment and corruption that was supported by testimony of former IRS employees and victims lends a certain degree of credibility to the militants' charges, while at the same time damaging the government's own credibility.

Pulling together all of the information presented thus far, one finds that the interplay of powerlessness, frustration, and hopelessness becomes that much clearer. These sentiments are said to be especially evident among the youth whose sense of the future is tied to immediate social rewards,[68] the security of the gang, or even impending parenthood.[69] Consciously or not, a readily available means for avoiding their distress is the media. While the youth in our survey are marginally linked to social clubs and formal activities, 42 percent indicated that they spend at least 2-4 hours watching TV. (See: Appendix D.) Compared to their white peers, black American youth watch more television and respond more positively to marketing stimuli than their white counterparts. Because of their low status in society, black youth are particularly vulnerable to the messages that are sent out to them about what to buy, why they should buy, and who they could be if they buy.[70] The profusion of Tommy Hilfiger designer outerwear, Girbaud jeans, and Nike sneakers has caused one observer to refer to them as "walking shopping malls."[71]

Some researchers seem to suggest that urban residents have learned to accept their powerless state as an act of fate. Others believe that the poor's disdain for the welfare system, their lack of desire to find jobs at livable wages, the rap genre, violence, and illicit behaviors should not be overlooked as rejections of their powerless state. A *New Yorker* magazine survey[72] of 1,200 African Americans nationally, found that 58 percent of blacks (including 66 percent from lower classes, 57 percent working class, 58 percent middle class, and 50 percent upper-middle class) feel that conditions are worsening for them in the United States. Jennifer L. Hochschild's 1995 study, "Facing Up to the American Dream," found that better-off blacks are more pessimistic about the future than their poorer counterparts. One key explanation that she offers for this is that middle-class blacks' proximity to the American dream has increased their awareness about institutionalized racism and consequently has fostered their disillusionment and cynicism.[73] These and similar research findings have led various writers to view hopelessness and even "nihilism" among urban youth in the inner cities as natural outcomes.[74] But another view is captured in Katherine Newman's book, *No Shame in My Game: The Working Poor in the Inner City*. She found the durability of the work ethic among the study sample of residents from the beleaguered districts of central and west Harlem.[75] In *The Uptown Kids: Struggle and Hope in the Projects*, Williams and Kornblum bring out something that we somehow manage to overlook: behind the most serious odds, strength and hope often find a way to seep through.[76] Youth from our survey expressed this same outlook of hope when asked: "Where do you see yourself two to five years from now? Do you feel that youth are capable of changing their situation? Do you feel that youth have control over their social environment?" While it is not an easy task to determine the truth behind their positive responses, it does nevertheless offer a thread of hope (see appendix D).

CONCLUSION

The coincidence of globalization and social disorganization in black life in the developing world but also in developed economies such as the United States has engendered a number of interesting responses. One critical response is the tendency to view black problems as essentially the same but, importantly, as having a common set of policy solutions. Despite this trend, it is our argument that different articulations of the urban crisis are to be found. Central to this view is that as global structural forces collide with the various cultures they encounter, unique dimensions of the urban crisis are being revealed. Sociologist Orlando Patterson seemed to be alluding to this very argument in his article, "Toward a Future That Has No Past: The Fate of Blacks in the Americas," which he prepared more than two decades ago. He associated the differences among blacks in the Americas with their differing cultural experiences and developmental paths that resulted from the legacy of enslavement and colonialism.[77]

Our decision to advance America's urban black belt as a prototype of the urban crisis is consistent with the finding about the impact of American culture in general but specifically the impact that African American culture has had and continues to have in the diaspora. Yet this is not to deny the influence that blacks outside the United States may also pose. Ongoing research by University of Wisconsin political scientist Obika Gray points out that African American culture notwithstanding, Jamaican popular culture in the form of reggae music has become transnationalized. This underscores the ability of black culture—emanating from a small developing island nation—to influence the world. Its appeal to blacks globally has much to do with its groundings in resistance and liberation.[78]

So it is against this backdrop that answers to questions about similarities and differences of the urban crisis in the diaspora and the nature of the solutions that will be required to address them will be explored. It is to the problem of urbanization and crisis in the contemporary Caribbean that we now turn.

NOTES

1. The term "black belt" has been commonly used in the literature to reference the concentration of blacks in the old South. Löic Wacquant is one among several writers who uses the term to refer to urban-based blacks. It is used both as a geographic designation and a demographic identification for U.S. blacks (see J. D. Wacquant, "The Ghetto, the State and the New Capitalist Economy," in Philip Kasinitz (ed.), *Metropolis: Center and Symbol of Our Times* (New York: New York University Press, 1995), 413–450; also, "Redrawing the Urban Color Line: The State of the Ghetto in the 1980's." in Craig Calhoun and George Ritzer (eds.), *Social Problems* (New York: McGraw-Hill, 1992).

2. Poverty Reduction and Human Resource Development in the Caribbean. The World Bank (Report No. 15342 LAC), 1996; also, Benjamin R. Barber, *Jihad vs. McWorld: How Globalism and Tribalism Are Reshaping the World* (New York: Ballantine Books, 1996); George Ritzer, *The McDonaldization of Society* (Thousand Oaks, Calif.: Pine Forge Press, 1996) (especially chapter 1).

3. Stephen Steinberg, *The Ethnic Myth* (Boston, Mass.: Beacon Press, 1989) (chapter 1).

4. Steinberg, *The Ethnic Myth*; also, Benjamin Ringer, *We the People, and Others* (New York: Travistock, 1983); Howard Zinn, *A People's History of the United States* (New York: Harper Perennial, 1990).

5. Thomas Sowell, *Migrations and Cultures: A World View* (New York Basic Books, 1996).

6. See Howard Zinn, *A People's History of the United States*; Steinberg, *The Ethnic Myth*; Ringer, *We the People, and Others*.

7. Frank Bruni, "At Harlem Churches, Flocks of Tourists," in *The New York Times*, (Sunday, Nov. 24, 1996, Metro Section, 37).

8. Derrick Bell, *Faces at the Bottom of the Well: The Permanence of Racism* (New York: Basic Books, 1982).

9. Anna Grimshaw (ed.), *The C.L.R. James Reader* (Oxford, U.K.: Blackwell, 1992); Tony Thomas and John Riddell, *Black Power in the Caribbean: The 1970 Upsurge in Trinidad* (New York: Pathfinder, 1971); Connie Sutton and S. Maiesky, "Migration and West Indian Racial and Ethnic Consciousness," in H. Safa and B. M. DuToit (eds.), *Migration and Development* (Hague: Moton & Co., 1975); Susan Craig, "Background to the 1970 Confrontation in Trinidad and Tobago," in Susan Craig (ed.), *Contemporary Caribbean: A Sociological Reader* (Vol. 2, Port of Spain, Trinidad and Tobago: Susan Craig Publisher, 1982, 385–425.

10. See Tony Chapelle. "Soul For Sale: Companies Are Taking Black Culture and Consumers To the Bank" in *Emerge* (January 1998), 42–48.

11. Pierre Bourdieu, *The Field of Cultural Production* (ed. Randal Johnson) (New York: Columbia University Press, 1993).

12. Alejandro Portes and Rubén G. Rumbault, *Immigrant America* (Berkeley, Calif.: University of California Press, 1990); also, Aristide R. Zolberg, "The Next Waves: Migration Theory for a Changing World," in *IMR* (Vol. 23, No. 5, Fall 1989), 403–431.

13. David Kotolowitz's description of life in one of Chicago's depressed public housing complexes and surrounding area is profound. See his *There Are No Children Here* (New York: Anchor Books, 1991).

14. Charles Green, *Elitism v. Democracy in Community Organization: The Agonies of a South Bronx Group* (Bristol, Ind.: Wyndham Hall Press, 1987).

15. Nicholas Lemann, *The Promised Land: The Great Black Migration and How It Changed America* (New York: Alfred A. Knopf, 1991), 61.

16. Lemann, *The Promised Land,* 6.

17. See Jacqueline Jones, "Southern Diaspora: Origins of the Northern Underclass," in Michael B. Katz (ed.), *The Underclass Debate: A View from History*, (Princeton, N.J.: Princeton University Press, 1993), 27–55; also, Jones, *The Dispossessed* (New York: Basic Books, 1992); also, Jones, *A Labor of Love, A Labor of Sorrow* (New York: Basic Books, 1985).

18. See Jacqueline Jones in Katz, *The Underclass Debate.*

19. Gilbert Osofsky, *Harlem, The Making of a Ghetto* (New York: Harper and Row, 1971), 17.

20. Charles Green and Basil Wilson, *The Struggle for Black Empowerment in New York City* (New York: McGraw-Hill, 1992), 61; also, Green, "The Black Church in the Struggle for Housing and Neighborhood Revitalization," in John H. Stanfield (ed.), *Research in Social Policy: Social Justice Philanthropy* (Greenwich, Conn.: JAI Press, 1997) 81–97; Green, "Genocide, Victimization, and America's Inner-Cities," in Charles B. Strozier and Michael Flynn (eds.), *Genocide, War, and Human Survival* (Lanham, Md.: Rowman & Littlefield, 1996).

21. See Green and Wilson, *The Struggle for Black Empowerment in New York City*; also, the following works by Frances Fox Piven and Richard Cloward: *Regulating the Poor: The Functions of Public Welfare* (New York: Vintage, 1971); *The Politics of Turmoil: Essays on Poverty, Race and the Urban Crisis* (New York: Vintage, 1972); *Poor People's Movements: Why They Succeed and How They Fail* (New York: Vintage, 1979).

22. Hillary Rodham Clinton, *It Takes a Village: and Other Lessons Children Teach Us* (New York: Simon and Schuster, 1996).

23. John H. Ehrenreich, *The Altruistic Imagination: A History of Social Work and Social Policy in the United States* (Ithaca, New York: Cornell University Press, 1985) (See chapter 3 and especially pages 98–100 for a splendid analysis of the black condition during the construction of the welfare state and the New Deal that was essentially an "Old Deal" for black people.) Also, August Meier and Elliott Rudwick, *Black Detroit and the Rise of the UAW* (New York: Oxford University Press, 1979).

24. Wacquant, "The Ghetto, the State and the New Capitalist Economy"; Stephen Steinberg, "The Underclass: A Case of Color Blindness," in *New Politics* (1, 1987) 42–60; Katz, *The Underclass Debate*; Holly Sklar, *Chaos or Community? Seeking Solutions, Not Scapegoats for Bad Economics* (Boston, Mass.: South End Press, 1995), 70–72; Douglas Massey and Nancy Denton, *American Apartheid: Segregation and the Making of the*

Underclass (Cambridge: Harvard University Press, 1993); See Herbert Gans, "Deconstructing the Underclass," in Paula S. Rothenberg (ed.), *Race, Class, & Gender in the United States* (New York: St. Martin's Press, 1992); Joel A. Devine and James D. Wright, *The Greatest of Evils: Urban Poverty and the American Underclass* (Hawthorne, New York: Aldine de Gruyter, 1993).

25. Erol Ricketts and Isabel Sawhill, "Defining and Measuring the Underclass: A Report" (Washington, D.C.: The Urban Institute, 1986).

26. Lemann, *The Promised Land*; Green and Wilson, *The Struggle for Black Empowerment in New York City*.

27. Wacquant, "The Ghetto, the State and the New Capitalist Economy;" also, Wacquant "The Rise of Advanced Marginality: Notes on Its Nature and Implications," *ACTA SOCIOLOGICA* (Vol. 39, 1996) 121–139; also, Kenneth B. Clark, *Dark Ghetto* (New York: Harper & Row, 1965). See also: Barry Bluestone and B. Harrison, *The Deindustrialization of America* (New York: Basic Books, 1982).

28. Marshall Kaplan and Franklin James (eds.), *The Future of National Urban Policy* (Durham, N.C.: Duke University Press, 1990); Paul E. Peterson (ed.), *The New Urban Reality* (Washington, D.C.: The Brookings Institution, 1985) 14.

29. Paul Blumberg, *Inequality in an Age of Decline* (New York: Oxford University Press, 1980).

30. Mark Naison, *Communists in Harlem During the Depression Years* (New York: Grove Press, 1983); John Ehrenreich, *The Altruistic Imagination*.

31. Bart Landry, *The New Black Middle Class* (Berkeley, Calif.: University of California Press, 1987).

32. Green and Wilson, *The Struggle for Black Empowerment in New York City*; Osofsky, *Harlem, The Making of a Ghetto*; Andrew Billingsley, *Black Families in White America* (Englewood Cliffs, N.J.: Prentice-Hall, 1968).

33. Peterson, *The New Urban Reality*, 14.

34. Catherine A. Sunshine, *The Caribbean: Survival, Struggle and Sovereignty* (Washington, D.C.: EPICA, 1985); also, Department of City Planning, New York, "The Newest New Yorkers: An Analysis of Immigration into New York City During the 1980s," 1992.

35. Judith H. Dobreznski, "The New Jobs: A Growing Number Are Good Ones," in *The New York Times* (Sunday, July 21,1996, Section 3).

36. William Julius Wilson, "Work," in *The New York Times Magazine* (August 18, 1996), 29.

37. Bureau of Labor Statistics (New York State Regional Office); see also: Meredith Bagby, "Annual Reports of the United States of America" (1997, Section 4 2/1).

38. These figures were gathered from the Bureau of Labor Statistics (New York State Regional Office, June, 2000).

39. Dobreznski, "The New Jobs."

40. The Multi-City Study and Harry Holzer's investigation are reported by the Russell Sage Foundation (RSF NEWS, Issue No. 2, 1997, 1–4).

41. W. J. Wilson in "Work," 30.

42. Avery Gordon, "Globalism and the Prison Industrial Complex: An Interview with Angela Davis," in *Race & Class* (Vol. 40, No. 2/3, 1998/9) 145.

43. Andrew Hacker, *Two Nations: Black and White, Separate, Hostile, Unequal* (New York: Ballantine Books, 1992) (chapter 11 on Crime and Race).

44. Gordon, "Globalism and the Prison Industrial Complex," 148.

45. Hacker, in *Two Nations,* cites U.S. Census Bureau Current Population Survey data, pages 230–231.

46. The Organization for Economic Cooperation and Development (OECD) bloc comprises the 26 richest countries in the world: Australia, Austria, Belgium, Canada, Czech Republic, Denmark, Finland, France, Germany, Greece, Ireland, Iceland, Italy, Japan, Luxembourg, Netherlands, New Zealand, Norway, Portugal, Spain, Sweden, Switzerland, United Kingdom, United States, Turkey, and Mexico. These countries contain roughly 16 percent of the world's population but control two-thirds of its merchandise (or tradable goods).

47. Steven A. Holmes, "U.S. Reports Drop in Rate of Births to Unwed Women," in *The New York Times* (October 5, 1996), A1; World Bank Atlas for 1997 (Section on People), 17; also, Sklar, *Chaos or Community?* (especially chapter 1, "Wealth and Poverty").

48. Green and Wilson, *The Struggle for Black Empowerment in New York City* (chapter 2, 46).

49. Carl Ginzberg describes this growing trend and the negative effect for communities, health care professionals, and patient care. One conglomerate, Columbia Healthcare Corp., headquartered in Nashville, Tennessee, is singled out. This $20 billion corporation aims to own 10 percent of America's hospitals. Already, it has acquired more than 348 hospitals across the country. See Carl Ginzberg, "The Patient as Profit Center: Hospital Inc. Comes to Town," in *The Nation* (Nov. 18, 1996),18–22.

50. According to Jonathan Kozol, there is state, and to a lesser degree, federal funding, but property tax is the decisive force in shaping inequality between poor urban school districts and their suburban counterparts. This method was first introduced during the 1920s. See Kozol, *Savage Inequalities: Children in America's Schools* (New York: Harper Collins, 1991) (especially pages 54–57 and 207–210).

51. Dobreznski, "The New Jobs."

52. In Joseph G. Conti and Brad Stetson (eds.), *Challenging the Civil Rights Establishment: Profiles of a New Black Vanguard.* (Westport, Conn.: Praeger, 1993). See essays by Thomas Sowell, "The Four Targets of a Maverick Thinker"; Shelby Steele, "Beyond Comic Strip Racism"; and Glen C. Loury, "Black Dignity and Self-Help."

53. Charles W. Mills, "Rethinking Race, Rethinking Class," in *Third World Viewpoints* (Vol. 1, No. 4, Summer 1995), 12.

54. See Frances F. Piven and Richard A. Cloward, *Regulating the Poor*; William J. Wilson, *The Truly Disadvantaged* (Chicago: University of Chicago Press, 1987).

55. W. J. Wilson, *When Work Disappears: The World of the New Urban Poor* (New York: Alfred A. Knopf, 1996), 165–170.

56. See Francis X. Clines, "Clinton Signs Bill Cutting Welfare; States in New Role," in *The New York Times,* (1996) A1, A22.

57. Nathan Glazer, *Affirmative Discrimination: Ethnic Inequality and Public Policy* (New York: Basic Books, 1975).

58. Glazer, *Affirmative Discrimination.*

59. Jervis Anderson, "Black and Blue" in *The New Yorker* (Special Issue on Blacks In America, April/May 1996), 62–64.

60. See also Melvin L. Oliver and Thomas M. Shapiro, *Black Wealth/White Wealth: A New Perspective on Racial Inequality* (New York: Routledge, 1997); also, Hacker, *Two Nations* (chapter on Employment and Race).

61. Bagby, "Annual Reports," 1997 (Section 3/6).

62. Gary Webb, "Dark Alliance: The Story Behind the Crack Explosion," in *San Jose Mercury News*, (August 18, 1996), 1–5.

63. Nelson Blackstock, *Cointelpro: The FBI's Secret War on Political Freedom* (New York: Pathfinder, 1988); See David J. Garrow's discussion of Cointelpro in connection with SNCC, Black Nationalists, and others in *The FBI and Martin Luther King, Jr.* (New York: Penguin, 1981) (chapter 5); Green, "Genocide, Victimization, and America's Inner-Cities"; Clarence Lusane, *Race in the Global Era* (Boston, Mass.: South End Press, 1997), 124–134; Clayborne Carson, *In Struggle: SNCC and the Black Awakening of the 1960s* (Cambridge, Mass.: Harvard University Press, 1981).

64. Journalists discuss Rep. Maxine Waters' untiring search for the truth in this case. See Andrea Ford and Michael K. Frisby, "Maximum Effect," in *Emerge* (April 1997), 40–46.

65. Gerald Horne, "The Political Economy of the Black Urban Future: A History," in Charles Green (ed.), *Globalization and Survival in the Black Diaspora: The New Urban Challenge* (Albany, N.Y.: State University of New York Press, 1997); also by Horne, *The Fire This Time: The Watts Uprising and the 1960s* (Charlottesville, Va.: University Press of Virginia, 1995).

66. A committee of the U.S. House of Representatives headed by John Conyers Jr. (D-Detroit, Mich.) reports that racism is a major factor in police misconduct in the city. See also: Green and Wilson, *The Struggle for Black Empowerment in New York City*, 132–133; Selwyn Raab, "City's Police Brutality Report Card: Complaints Down, Needs Improving," in *The New York Times* (August 17, 1997), Metro Section, 41. Rep. John Conyers returned to New York City on Nov. 18, 1997 to reconvene open hearings on police misconduct at Brooklyn's Medgar Evers College.

67. "The Militia Threat," a *New York Times* editorial (June 14, 1997), 20.

68. Kenneth B. Clark, *Dark Ghetto*; Cornel West, *Race Matters* (Boston, Mass.: Beacon Press, 1993); Elijah Anderson, *Streetwise: Race, Class and Change in an Urban Community* (Chicago: University of Chicago Press, 1990).

69. Jervis Anderson, "Black and Blue."

70. George Moschis, *Consumer Socialization: A Life Cycle Perspective* (Lexington, Mass.: Lexington Books, 1987).

71. Mary Pattillo-McCoy, "Consumer Culture Among Cuban and Black American Youth" in *Souls* (Vol. 1, No. 2, Spring 1999).

72. The Yankelovich Partners Inc. Survey of Black America surveyed 1,200 African Americans nationally. See also: Jervis Anderson, "Black and Blue," 63–64.

73. Findings from Jennifer Hochschild's 1995 work, *Facing Up to the American Dream*, are cited extensively in Jervis Anderson's article, "Black and Blue," on page 64.

74. Cornel West, *Race Matters*; Douglas Glasgow, *The Black Underclass* (New York: Vintage, 1981); Kotolowitz, *There Are No Children Here*; Green in *Genocide, War, and Human Survival*; also, Robert J. Lifton, "Beyond Psychic Numbing: A Call to Awareness," in *American Journal of Orthopsychiatry*, 1983, 52: 619–629.

75. Katherine S. Newman, *No Shame in My Game: The Working Poor in the Inner City* (New York: Alfred A. Knopf and Russell Sage Foundation, 1999).

76. Terry Williams and Willian Kornblum, *The Uptown Kids: Struggle and Hope in the Projects* (New York: Putnam, 1994).

77. Patterson, O., "Toward a Future That Has No Past, " in *Public Interest,* 1972.

78. Obika Gray, "Power and Identity Among the Urban Poor of Jamaica," in Charles Green (ed.), *Globalization and Survival in the Black Diaspora* (Albany, N.Y.: SUNY Press, 1997), 199–227.

3

The Urban Nemesis and the Contemporary Caribbean

Identifying the roots of a problem is never a simple task, particularly when our energy is directed to a region comprising disparate island states and sociocultural, linguistic, and political differences must be taken into account. In this chapter our objective is to examine the roots of the urban crisis in the anglophone Caribbean[1] that pose a serious threat to the future of Caribbean civil society and the relationship of this crisis to that in America's urban black belt. The leading argument is that the Caribbean crisis, which evolved sometime after the U.S. crisis and proceeded at a much slower pace, is accelerating in the present global economic climate.

Furthermore, it will be argued that the urban crisis is an effect of the frail economies of the small island states that comprise the region, their dependency on the advanced metropoles, and the political and sociocultural ramifications that stem from their geographical proximity to the United States. Another important effect is the legacy of European colonialism that was replete with uncertainty and competition. We learn that the immediate post-Spanish colonial period was characterized by competition as the Caribbean became an important arena for muscle flexing and squaring off between imperialist powers. In the latter part of the eighteenth century, many of the islands flip-flopped between French, British, and Dutch control. Tiny Dominica, for example, changed hands a total of 12 times.[2]

A disturbing observation is that when it comes to discussing the Caribbean region, or for that matter, the African continent, journalists and scholars often address it in monolithic terms. Of course, the opposite is true when these same writers and scholars address countries on the European continent. This view can be overheard at the airport terminal where island-bound tourists, bubbling with excitement, await their flights. Much of their chatter concerns which islands they enjoy most, which hotels to avoid, and so on. A remark that is almost assured is, "The islands are lovely, but they are essentially the same; if you've seen one, you've seen them all." This view of the Caribbean, which is supported by travel agencies' colorful brochures depicting the region as a stream of islands surrounded by white sandy beaches lined with palm trees and luxurious hotels, is inaccurate. The Caribbean, home to more than 35 million people, is made up of 16 independent countries including Belize, Guyana, and Suriname. It comprises many ethnic groups and five dominant language groups, namely Anglo, Franco, Creole, Spanish, and Dutch and Papimento (a Creolized form of the Dutch language spoken mainly in the territories of Aruba and Curaçao).[3] Most of the island territories are independent but some remain colonies or dependencies of Britain, France, Holland, and the United States.

In the preceding chapter we unraveled some of the factors deemed responsible for the rise of the American urban black belt and the condition of hyperghettoization. In an attempt to determine the relationship between the urban situation in the United States and the Caribbean, many of these same conditions are considered.

URBANIZATION AND THE CARIBBEAN

As living conditions continue to deteriorate for Caribbean folk who live in the countryside, their gravitation to the towns and central cities will continue so long as they see hope for work, usually in the informal sector[4] and satisfying their other basic needs such as health care and education, as located strictly in the urban centers. Newcomers to the towns come face to face with the massive social and spatial inequalities that prevail in the city and are soon confronted with their own powerlessness to change their living conditions.[5]

The trend toward urbanization in the Caribbean is fairly recent and coincides with the period of global recession that began in the 1980s. A point that should be clarified when speaking about urbanization in the small island states of the Caribbean is that there is a shallow dividing line between rural and urban in most cases. Literally speaking, one can shift from the country into the town or central city within minutes. For certain, in the context of globalization, the proximity between rural and urban areas is having a significant impact on the changing social and cultural patterns in the countryside. In 1985, roughly 52.2 percent of the region's population was living in urban areas, having increased from a level of 38.2 percent in 1960.[6] Current UNDP Population Division data indicate that this trend continues, although unevenly so, with some countries experiencing higher levels of urbanization than others. In Trinidad and Tobago and Jamaica for example, it was reported that 71.7 percent and 53.7 percent of their populations, respectively, resided in areas defined as urban, whereas for St. Vincent and the Grenadines and Barbados, it was 40.1 percent and 47.3 percent, respectively.[7] Table 3.1 below shows this current trend for select Caribbean countries between 1950 and 1990.

Table 3.1 Urban Trends in Selected Caribbean Countries, 1950–1990 (as a percent of the overall population)

	1950	*1960*	*1970*	*1980*	*1990*
T'dad & Tobago	63.9	64.5	63.0	63.1	69.1
U.S. V.I.	44.5	44.5	44.5	44.5	44.5
St.Vincent & Gren.	12.5	13.7	15.2	27.2	40.6
Dominica	48.3	47.4	46.9	63.4	67.7

Source: World Urbanization Prospects: The 1996 Revision, May 1, 1997. United Nations Population Division.

POPULATION DIVISION

Urban researchers have found a strong positive correlation between levels of urbanization, a country's Gross Domestic Product (GDP) and, too, the tendency toward urban primacy. Urban primacy, sometimes referred to as "urban bias," is a common feature of developing societies whereby a town or specific towns become the center of gravity. It is a consequence of colonialism in which the towns were customarily administrative ports and retail centers.[8] An interesting footnote is that while urban primacy has been the preferred terminology to describe this phenomenon for developing societies, it is either substituted or carefully eschewed in the literature when describing the same condition in the developed metropoles. New York City and Los Angeles are two examples of American cities that continue to draw internal and international migrants in search of work and other amenities. Unlike much of the developing world, they may not be the capital cities per se but are nonetheless considered major. Simply stated, these data can be interpreted to mean that for the more developed Third World countries, the pull factor to the urban centers would be far greater than for poorer countries. In the cases of Trinidad and Tobago and Barbados, with higher per capita GDPs than their closest neighbors, it was found that in the past, urbanization and urban primacy levels exceeded that of other islands such as Dominica, St. Vincent and the Grenadines, Grenada, and Haiti.[9] But the current situation is different, due in large measure to the region's high poverty rates. According to the World Bank's report on poverty in the region, poverty averages roughly 38 percent of the total population, ranging from a high of 65 percent in Haiti to a low of 5 percent in the Bahamas. Excluding Haiti, approximately 25 percent of the total population is poor.[10] These estimates place the Caribbean close to a world aggregate average of poverty in the developing countries. As a consequence, feelings of desperation have surmounted and triggered rapid urbanization with primacy given to the central cities and their surrounding districts. This dilemma is not the monopoly of any one island state; it is regional. From Port of Spain, Kingston, Kingstown, and

St. George's, to Bridgetown, Roseau, and Charlotte Amalie, these and other cities have become the receptacles for this onrushing sea of human desperation.

Jones (1980) found that urban immigrants act not upon objective characteristics but upon their perceptions of them. It matters little that unemployment is chronic or that there are raging social dislocations in the capital cities of Kingston and Caracas—the desperate will migrate there anyway.[11] This fact alone should confirm that urbanward migration in Third World societies is occurring not merely for the lure of bright city lights but for structural reasons that are central to the political economies of the various countries themselves.

Overall, urbanization, with an emphasis on urban primacy, has been devastating to the small island states of the Caribbean. This emphasis has created greater isolation and inequality in the nonindustrialized areas, which have as a result become even more underdeveloped. Importantly, it has impeded the emergence of secondary city areas that would share some of the economic growth (or whatever measure of economic growth is taking place) and help to slow down the population growth and overurbanization that engulf the capital cities.[12] Some analysts have come to view the current urbanization not merely as contradicting the development objective but as pathological. Such views draw upon the work carried out by American sociologist Louis Wirth in the 1930s, which envisaged social problems as inextricably tied to urbanism.[13]

Urbanism is believed to have brought about a distinct personality type based on secondary relationships, anonymity, greater social and spatial mobility, and weakened bonds of kinship and neighborhood. As was demonstrated in our discussion of the United States, rural-to-urban migration of African Americans is a consequence of capital's need to satisfy its industrial interests. It is also the result of unflinching white racism, particularly in the rural South, with the objective of instilling fear in the black community and keeping blacks permanently subjugated. While race cannot be overlooked in the context of the Caribbean, it has, however, functioned differently than in America. Africans were enslaved throughout the Americas, which included the Caribbean and the 13 settlements of colonial America. Of the 10 million or more slaves brought to the Americas, the Caribbean received 47 percent.[14] The abolitionist movement that took root in England preceded that movement's development in America. As a result, slaves were emancipated in the British territories in 1835, whereas those brought to America would have to wait nearly 30 years to achieve their freedom. Thus, the predominance of African slaves over white plantation owners and settlers in the Caribbean, and their head start as freed men and women, are essential for understanding the role that race would come to play in those societies versus the United States.[15]

Patterson (1972) compared and contrasted the role that race has played in the United States, the Caribbean, and Latin America. Whereas in the United States a classificatory system of race prevails—that is to say, racial shading among the minority black population is not recognized—in the anglophone Caribbean and in

Latin America race is a much more complicated matter. There we find a system of racial shading does exist. However, it is class or one's social background, education, and economic position that determines one's mobility in the social structure. The Caribbean system is described as continuous denotative, in which a majority of blacks and a minority of whites compete and are included alongside each other. In such a system, blacks are able to achieve various roles such as prime minister, judge, police commissioner, and teacher and serve as models for the next generation. The system in Latin America resembles the United States in that although racial shading exists, the white descendants of Europeans are ascribed a status of privilege above and beyond the other racial categories. Patterson defines this system as a discontinuous denotative system.[16]

In summary, while race may be articulated or constructed differently in the Caribbean and the United States, in both cases the fact of black powerlessness remains. Most critical to understanding urbanization in the Caribbean, and the bridge between it and the African American experience, is the adverse effect that social and economic dislocation in the urban districts has had on one of its most vulnerable cohorts: the youth on whom the future rests. Data for the Caribbean Community and Common Market (CARICOM) member states define youth as the 15 to 25 year olds and furthermore indicates that this cohort represents 25 to 30 percent of their general populations.[17] Such a high proportion in this subpopulation is particularly worrisome: At the threshold of adulthood they are without the support and resources needed to develop to their fullest potentials. Needless to say, this places a serious burden on these already frail and small economies.

THE ROOTS OF CRISIS AND POWERLESSNESS

In the case of the Caribbean it is not sufficient to advance the view that the present urban dislocation is strictly an effect of the international recession that was introduced in the 1980s or, as some would have it, an act of fate. Geopolitics, the dependency syndrome, and the debt burden must be factored in. Let us briefly examine each of these.

Geopolitics and Proximity to the United States

While the U.S. role in the Caribbean in the wake of the Spanish–American War was deferred to Britain and the competing European powers, the United States stayed involved in trade and kept a watchful eye on the activities taking place within the hemisphere. From the Monroe Doctrine in 1823, followed by Teddy Roosevelt's "Big Stick" diplomacy, to the Truman Doctrine and beyond, the view that anything that moves in its immediate hemisphere is its business sums up the history and course of U.S. foreign policy in the Caribbean. For that very reason, official recognition of Haiti as the first sovereign black state in the hemisphere following the Haitian Revolution in 1804 was resisted, and it is this same ambivalence that has steered the politics of intervention and destabilization in Haitian affairs throughout the twentieth century. Moreover, it explains the U.S. 30-year trade embargo against the Cuban socialist state while normalization has been pursued with certain of its former nemeses like Vietnam and North Korea. Probably the most conspicuous of these normalization efforts is recognized in the case of China, which despite U.S. charges of human rights violations, continues to enjoy uninterrupted "most favorite nation trade status."

Choice words such as "basin" and "backyard" occupy a special place in the American political lexicon when referring to the Caribbean. Former U.S. President Ronald Reagan was particularly fond of this phraseology when referring to the region. Its usage is probably best recalled during the period leading up to the U.S. invasion of the tiny island state of Grenada in 1983, when Reagan took to the national airwaves armed with maps to show the Cuban intrusion in the "basin" under the pretext of constructing an international airport.[18] It was only natural that the term would be featured in framing the Caribbean "Basin" Initiative (CBI). On January 1, 1984, the United States implemented the CBI to encourage the people of the region to participate in the political and economic growth of their countries. It represents a combination of long-term trade, aid, and investment incentives designed to encourage new business while providing political and social stability. CBI was based on the premise that the government sector would provide an educated, healthy workforce; transportation and communication networks; and infrastructures essential to sustained economic growth and, importantly, that the private sector would provide entrepreneurs who were willing to assume risks, foster business development, and lead the way to growth and development. Once again we see foreign interests who are privileged with knowing what is best and offering a standardized model of development for all.

The people of the Caribbean enjoyed relative prosperity during the 1960s and early 1970s. This was the result of expanded (although brief) production and the high price paid for raw materials such as bauxite, petroleum, and sugar, and the favorable export of certain produce goods to North America. Tourism began to flourish following the Cuban Revolution, and the United States imposed the embargo shortly thereafter. With the acceleration of immigration, initially to Britain but later to the United States and Canada, the region's population burden was somewhat relieved.[19] Some writers have credited this acceleration for their decision to pull out of the budding Federation of the West Indies in the 1960s, a vision well ahead of its time. But this early experiment in formal regional integration between 1958 and 1962 was guaranteed to fail. Jamaica, the Federation's largest member, was preoccupied with its success in the bauxite and tourism industries. Trinidad and Tobago, with its healthy deposits of petroleum and natural gas and assured economic success, soon followed suit. Consequently, both states opted for independence and decided to pull out of the agreement altogether. It is speculated that had it succeeded, the Federation might have resulted in a

Caribbean region significantly different, politically and economically, from that which we see today.[20]

Chronic Dependency

But adversity was just around the corner, so to speak, by the time the 1980s rolled around. For many observers, this represented a watershed for the present regional urban crisis. A series of events propelled the international economic recession of the early 1980s. Coinciding with the United States' decision to go off the gold standard in 1974 was a sharp decline in worldwide production and trade growth rates. Trade, which had grown at an average 8.7 percent a year from 1965 to 1973, declined to 4.6 percent between 1973 and 1980, and to 2.4 percent between 1980 and 1985.[21] The oil crisis triggered by OPEC's price hike per barrel of crude between 1972 and 1973 and again in 1979 was devastating for the non-oil-producing countries whether developed or developing. But it was the unprecedented impact it had on the major capitalist countries that precipitated the international recession that followed. The leading industrial nations responded with belt-tightening measures, not to mention long-overdue energy conservation strategies. The oil debacle and the capitalist world's response to it signaled ominous consequences for the Caribbean and for the Third World as a whole. With the decline in foreign investments in the region and the major players shifting to substitute markets for traditional Caribbean exports of bauxite, sugar, and even tourism, macroeconomic imbalances unlike any observed in the recent past began to take root.[22] We have come to know these all too well as balance of payments problems and the debt crisis. The dependency trap is an easy one to fall victim to if we are discussing small and historically fragile open economies that typify the Caribbean. As Deere and colleagues note, "The consequence of this degree of openness is that any change in international demand for the region's exports, for example, a change in import prices or the availability of external finance, will have a disproportionate effect on the level of Caribbean income."[23]

A chief objective behind colonialism was to impose an economic structure on the colonies that would be profitable to the colonial empire. Dependency was a natural and intended effect of the colonial relationship that guaranteed the marginalization of the subjects. For this reason, George Beckford (1988) argues, the history of enslavement and the plantation system cannot be left out of the analysis, as they provide the basis for stagnated poverty in the region in the late twentieth century and for the social, political, and economic powerlessness that is strangling the masses.[24]

By colonial design, the single-crop economy flourished in the territories, which meant that sugar, bananas, spices, coffee, and later, oil and bauxite, were anointed as the cash earners for specific islands. That they inherited this model after gaining their independence was not the only problem for the newly formed governments: Another serious problem was that they did not vigorously seek to diversify their economies. The following passage captures the region-wide problem of non-diversification that is one of its most serious economic pitfalls.

> In 1985, petroleum products accounted for 82 percent of Trinidad and Tobago's merchandise exports while bauxite and alumina accounted for 68 percent of Jamaica's, 76 percent of Suriname's, and 43 percent of Guyana's export earnings. Sugar constituted 74 percent of total exports in Cuba, 46 percent in Belize, 35 percent in Guyana, and 21 percent in the Dominican Republic. Bananas accounted for 50 percent of export earnings in St. Lucia, 44 percent in Dominica, and 21 percent in St. Vincent and the Grenadines.[25]

The seriousness of the situation becomes even clearer if one adds to this the fact that the structuring of commodity prices for goods produced as well as exchange rates and special trade incentives do not originate with the Third World countries themselves but is the business of external bodies such as the World Trade Organization (WTO). A people with limited control or no control at all over the flow and direction of their economic existence are unmistakably a powerless people.

Most countries in the immediate post-independence period witnessed an intensification of Caribbean dependency on the United States for trade, investment, tourism, and security via military support. Dependency, of course, carries certain limitations and consequences. Once the central player in that relationship has decided to sever its commitment to dependents, crisis usually follows. Finding a way out of what is commonly referred to as the cycle of dependency or the dependency syndrome is the ultimate challenge facing the sovereign states in the region.

The Debt Crisis

Referring to the Third World's debt burden, Susan George probes the question of whether there is a fate worse than debt itself.[26] Between 1980 and 1986 the external debt owed by CARICOM countries rose from $3.1 billion to $6.5 billion, with Jamaica and Trinidad and Tobago leading the pack. Presently, the Caribbean debt that soars at approximately $636.6 billion[27] is owed chiefly to commercial banks and international lending institutions such as the International Monetary Fund and the World Bank. An increased supply of loans from commercial banks was presented to the Third World with the first oil-price hike in 1973 and more so after the second price hike in 1979, when an abundance of OPEC profits found their way into American banks as investments and deposits. Stunned by the crisis and needing money to purchase oil, the governments of these poor non-oil-producing countries eagerly reached out for the easy loans. As this pattern continued, they eventually lost track of the soaring interest burden attached to the loans and lost sight of their ability to service their debts. It should be noted that interest is usually offered at variable rates, meaning that they can fluctuate upward or downward according to economic trends. Before long, a debt crisis was born.[28]

Structural adjustment policies (SAPs) and the IMF are very familiar to the people of the Caribbean and other developing regions. SAPs are reforms initiated in order to properly manage balance of payments, reduce fiscal deficits, increase efficiency, and encourage private sector investments and export-oriented production. SAPs employ such measures as devaluation of the local currency, reduction of public borrowing, and government expenditure, particularly in the social sectors. Other measures include trade liberalism, tariff reductions, abolition of price controls, privatization of public controlled companies sometimes referred to as parastatals and, of course, the reduction of the public workforce.[29] Both the IMF and its sister institution, the World Bank, which were adopted at the summit of world powers at Bretton Woods, New Hampshire in 1944, are headquartered in Washington, D.C., and are dominated by the United States. The fervor these institutions have created around the world is not simply a fact of the harsh conditions imposed on borrowers for loan repayment; it is the unreasonable interest payments that virtually ensure that debtors remain debtors. For most, an alarming reality, if not a clear contradiction, is the fact that the world's greatest debtor nation, the United States, with an external debt that now exceeds $5 trillion, is not yet a client of the IMF.

A unique site stands in the heart of New York City's business district at 42nd Street and Avenue of the Americas. There, a digital clock sponsored by a major corporation records the constantly changing national debt for all to see. Displayed alongside the debt are the interest burden and the per capita share of the burden for every American family. A startling observation is the unperturbed manner with which New Yorkers stroll by this monument without giving it as much as a glance. This example underscores the acute insensitivity on the part of a major superpower and its citizens to the debt problem of less fortunate states, even though the problem has found its way to their doorstep. Protests that have erupted in various parts of the developing world are kindled not by the elites whose decisions inspired the loans in the first place but by the angst of the masses who must bear the brunt of their decisions each and every day. Following is an account of one such anti-IMF protest in Caracas, Venezuela, in 1989 that is indicative of the frustration and indignation felt by poor and working-class people who experience firsthand the stranglehold of the international lending institutions' policies. Antidebt protests of this dimension have not erupted in the Caribbean as such.

On February 16, 1989, President Carlos Andrés Pérez announced that the government had signed an agreement with the IMF. The agreement, known by Venezuelans as *el paquete*, increased hardship and sacrifices for the Venezuelan people, including the rise in gasoline prices, the devaluation of the bolivar, the suspension of subsidies for basic consumer products and necessities, the elimination of price controls, and increased taxes. It led to the privatization of many state-owned companies such as VIASA, the major Venezuelan airline, and CANTV, the telephone company. And the agreement also included using one-third of the national budget to satisfy debt payments. On February 26, the president increased the price of gasoline and that was the straw that broke the camel's back. In the early hours of February 27, the popular protest erupted, and thousands of people including students, urban workers, housewives, and poor people from the barrios flooded the streets of Caracas and other cities for over 24 hours. They took over commercial establishments, especially supermarkets, grocery stores, and appliance stores. On February 28, the city was virtually paralyzed. To control the movement, the government sent out the national guard, the police, and eventually, the army to repress the situation. While the official toll was estimated between 200 to 350 deaths, human rights organizations placed it between 1,000 and 1,300.[30]

That this protest occurred in a country so close to the Caribbean has aroused the anxiety among regional leaders about the threat to their own stability and the fear that it could also happen on their soil.

It is commonly understood that the effects of SAPs have been hardest felt by those most vulnerable, that is, the poor, the powerless, women (heads of households), children, and youth in the urban areas. The urban poor tend to be more vulnerable than the rural poor to changes in the economic environment because they are more fully integrated into the monetized economy and often have fewer safety nets than the rural poor (such as the extended family and the benefit of home gardens to grow their own food). Their misery is translated into rising food and housing prices, the slashing of the welfare safety nets, privatization of basic institutions, and unemployment and underemployment. Due to these conditions, many have been forced to migrate out of the region entirely or to the urban areas where they believe their chances of finding work and surviving is greater.

Out migration has proven to be a crucial survival strategy for a fortunate few but it also has implications for family dislocation. One estimation is that the Caribbean as a whole sends out a greater percentage of its population than does any other world region, with the United States and Canada being the prime targets.[31] While the recent migration has absorbed those from the professional ranks who have not been able to realize their fullest potential, in the wake of economic austerity it is the less fortunate who have been left behind and forced to turn to the urban areas as the last resort. This migration is important in the context of finding work and improving one's standard of living, but paramount are the remittances that flow to family members back home when one member migrates. These remittances help bolster the region's weak economies and have become an important source of foreign exchange.[32] Recognizing this and the sheer volume of immigrants, money wire services like Western Union are enjoying a bonanza and in cities such as New York, have increased their operations to meet the demand.

Added to the problems of the urban poor is the breakdown of traditional family life characterized by a high proportion of absentee parents and single-parent households. It should be noted here that absentee parents are fathers who have abandoned households and, increasingly, mothers who have migrated to the United States and Canada, leaving their children in the care of relatives and friends while they work mainly as domestics, child care givers, and hospital workers.[33] For certain, a dependency has developed around their monetary remittances but of equal importance are the barrels (tall sturdy cardboard drums) they send home that contain many of the items that bombard locals across the television airwaves: designer sneakers, jeans, the latest CDs and videos, foods, and certain essentials either not available to them or available at exorbitant prices.[34]

As the United States and Canada weather their immediate economic storms and tighten immigration policies, the likelihood that migration to those countries will remain a prime survival option for Caribbean people is extremely tenuous. The shift in U.S. immigration policy has been propelled by an inordinate rise in xenophobic sentiments. So strong is the anti-immigration sentiment in the United States that a referendum was put before voters in California, one of the nation's largest immigrant states. The controversial Proposition 187 seeks to limit services and other entitlements to undocumented immigrants and their children. In the aftermath of heated national controversy and the growth of the economy, the governor of California rescinded his opposition to Proposition 187 in July 1999. Shifts and turns in the immigration policies by the United States and other leading receiving countries impact the less fortunate sending countries of the world. In Trinidad and Tobago, for example, would-be migrants, including youth and other prime members of the working age population, have been forced to remain at home. That has in part explained the increase in this segment of Trinidad and Tobago's population over the recent decade.[35] Overall, the formal safety net in many countries has proved inadequate in terms of coverage and benefit levels. The real value of social insurance programs that have aided mainly the elderly has declined over time and individuals employed in the informal sector are rarely covered. With the exception of Barbados, no real provision is made for unemployment insurance nor are the unemployed eligible for social assistance.[36]

We have already noted that in the case of the U.S. urban black belt, severe economic conditions have increased family breakups and separations and have contributed to the rise of female-headed, mostly poor households and ultimately to the breakdown in the supervision of the children. In the Caribbean, more women are being forced into the labor force as the men's prospects for work have dimmed, making it that much more difficult for them to carry out their traditional role as household provider.[37] Men and women are both visible as vendors and operators in the thriving informal sector; wages in that sector tend to be low, however.[38] These breakdowns and the undersupervision of children, particularly as they occur in the urban areas, are associated with a higher incidence of street crime, gang violence, and drug abuse.[39] Unskilled youth, but also school dropouts, who are afflicted with high unemployment rates throughout the region, have little hope of ever entering the formal labor sector. The result is frustration

that too often leads to their involvement in crime and other forms of antisocial behavior. Most perpetrators of urban crime throughout the region tend to be young
males between the ages of 16 and 34, are from large, low-income families, have
left school, and are involved in the drug subculture either as users or smugglers.
They are, increasingly, repeat offenders.[40] Interestingly, crime and the fear of
crime in the central cities has eroded the population's sense of trust while at the
same time raised anxiety levels and broken down communities. The state of
health in general has also declined in the urban areas. An arguable indicator of a
nation's health status is its infant mortality rate.[41] Infant mortality rates—which
had begun to show signs of improvement in the 1980s as the result of internal efforts and the work of international health organizations—were lower in the 1990s
but remain in double-digit figures. This is demonstrated by 1990 UNESCO figures showing rates of infant deaths per 1,000 live births during the first year for
selected countries: St. Vincent and the Grenadines (21), Trinidad and Tobago
(20), Dominica (18), and Jamaica (16).[42]

To better understand the implication of these developments for the youth, one
would have to return to the matter of out migration and absentee parents who are
based abroad. Frequently, distant mothers promise to send for a child left behind
once sufficient resources have been saved up. Unfortunately, promises have been
known to remain unfulfilled and what was a month becomes a year, frustration
sets in, and problems erupt at school. According to University of the West Indies
sociologist Rhoda Reddock, many of the youth seen hanging out on street corners
and getting into trouble in the urban district of Port of Spain could very well be
migration related. The dearth of social workers and counselors in the country to
work with these young people exacerbates the problem.[43]

The World Bank and the IMF are quick to point out that the imposition of
structural adjustment policies is not the culprit or even the critical link to understanding protracted poverty in the region. While the effects of adversity and dis-
comfort are admitted, it is their position that these conditionalities must be imposed for the simple reason that these countries were unable to help themselves
and that alternative policy choices would produce even harsher consequences for
the poor. In its recent report on poverty in the region, the World Bank defends the
use of exchange rate devaluation and the reduction of public sector employment
while arguing that much of the debate about SAPs is based on deficient assump-
tions and methods. Insofar as solutions are concerned, the Bank's position is un-
wavering in its support for a macroeconomic environment that favors more foreign investment, privatization, the establishment of growth enterprises, and an
international environment of free trade and the free flow of investment under conditions of fair competition.[44]

From this overview of the urban condition in the contemporary Caribbean we
can begin to see certain parallels with that of the United States. To examine this
relationship more closely, we now shift our attention to specific territories in the
region. Providing the setting for this section are the capital districts of four

Caribbean countries: Port of Spain, Trinidad and Tobago; Kingstown, St. Vincent and the Grenadines; Roseau, Dominica; and Charlotte Amalie, St. Thomas, U.S. Virgin Islands. These territories were selected because of the presence of urban unrest but also, generally speaking, they are overlooked in the media and the scholarly literature compared with the more popular tourist destinations like Jamaica, Barbados, Puerto Rico, and the Dominican Republic (see appendix A).

Trinidad and Tobago

The small twin island Republic of Trinidad and Tobago, the southernmost of the West Indian archipelago situated at the northeast tip of Venezuela, won its independence from Britain on August 31, 1962. It is a fair statement that Trinidad and Tobago is a stranger to most Americans. Some Trinbagonians have commented that Hansley Crawford's upset victory at the 1976 Summer Olympic Games in Montreal to become "the world's fastest human" was equally important because it helped to put Trinidad and Tobago squarely on the map. Trinidad and Tobago's obscurity has much to do with the fact that oil, petrochemicals, and natural gas rather than tourism are among its chief revenue earners. These natural resources have permitted Trinidad and Tobago to enjoy a relatively high per capita income compared with most other states in the immediate area. To poor struggling folk from smaller islands who have never stepped foot outside the region, or their island for that matter, a city like Port of Spain is on par with New York City. This is how Sharon, a 21-year-old woman who worked as a domestic in training at a guest house near the Cane Field Airport in Dominica, described her first experience outside of Dominica: "Compared to downtown Roseau, downtown Port of Spain was exciting and big. There were plenty of shops along Frederick Street with so many things to buy. By night, there was a lot of action."[45]

In 1995 approximately 69.1 percent of the nation's 1.2 million population resided in towns and cities. The capital city, Port of Spain, located on the larger island of Trinidad, is the most populous city, followed by San Fernando to the south and Arima to the east. Residential data belie the actual numbers of people who live just outside on the periphery and are drawn to these centers each day as formal workers but also as members of the informal economy and even as squatters. Trinidad and Tobago's urban crisis can be traced to the early 1980s and the end of the short-lived oil boom period. OPEC's price hike in the 1970s boosted the nation's economy while expanding its appetite for luxury imports. While the nation enjoyed prosperity and some government officials succumbed to corruption, little effort was directed toward diversifying the oil-centered economy and planning for the inevitable post-boom period. When the bottom finally fell out in 1981,[46] the imports and spending continued and in 1988 the newly elected National Alliance for Reconstruction (NAR) government was forced to enter into an agreement with the IMF.

Trinidad and Tobago has staged a massive economic restructuring. Currently Trinidad and Tobago is the largest exporter in the CARICOM community. Approximately 120,000 to 130,000 barrels of crude oil are produced daily. The nation leads the world in its production of natural gas, methane, and ammonia. Trinidad and Tobago is steadily increasing its production of steel and there is an aluminum smelter under construction. What is important to note is that all of this capital funding is foreign. Trinidad and Tobago is the second largest recipient of U.S. long-term investment in the hemisphere. According to David Abdullah of the Trade Union OWTU (the region's largest trade union founded in Trinidad in 1937), Trinidad and Tobago is perceived as "a good boy"—a cooperative partner that will positively influence the other CARICOM members."[47] The social costs associated with restructuring the nation's economy are most visible in urban districts like Port of Spain. Unemployment, which continues to rage in double-digit figures, has disrupted families and escalated the phenomenon of female-run households that are barely able to make ends meet. Hovering around 45 percent,[48] unemployment is demoralizing for youth who have completed school as well as for those who have dropped out due to failing grades and their belief that school is a waste of one's time. The inability of the state to control the influx of hard drugs that enter the country and the use of the nation's waterways by the South American drug cartels as a transshipment point for drugs destined for the United States and Europe has increased crime and violence to levels unprecedented in the nation's history.[49]

Aiding and abetting the drug menace is the problem of police corruption. Police, like other workers, have been forced to tighten their belts and exist on meager salaries. The thriving drug enterprise provides an easy way for them to supplement their incomes. A major social cost of this has been the growing mistrust of the police by youth and allegations of police misconduct.[50] My interviews with Port of Spain and other urban residents reflect their fear of street crime and violence and the belief that their problems are the byproducts of an encroaching American mass culture. Doris, a middle-aged woman from Port of Spain, remarked: "Down here getting real dread [bad], just like [dat Yankee place] de States. Trinidad ain't no different from Brooklyn an' [or] Harlem. Is deh TV and deh drugs from up deh [there] dat making dis place so bad."[51]

Statements such as this are not uncommon. Fueling them is the firm grip of the United States on the nation's economy but also the rapid displacement of indigenous culture by the globalized fast food chains such as Pizza Hut, Kentucky Fried Chicken, and McDonald's, and fashions and communications technology from abroad. As far as the urban youth are concerned, their preferred dress styles and material cultural adaptation are unmistakably African American.[52]

Trinidad and Tobago youth respondents to our survey indicated that while 47.3 percent live in intact families, 32.4 percent live in households headed by a single mother. In listing problems that concern them, unemployment, the drug menace, AIDS, the lack of adult guidance, and street crime were underscored. Mistrust of law enforcement personnel, namely the police, was evident, with 73.7 percent of the sample disagreeing that police treat all equally and fairly and 85 percent feeling that the police should protect and serve. Another interesting finding was that while these youth are marginally connected to formal activities in their communities, 40 percent informed that they spent at least two to four hours in front of the television every day (see appendix B).

Complicating the urban situation in Trinidad and Tobago is its history of ethnic relations. The Afro-Trinbagonian population at 39.9 percent, once the largest, trails the East Indian population which is now 40.3 percent.[53] When African slaves were manumitted in 1835, the indentureship of Asian Indians (East Indians)[54] was begun. They were introduced essentially to assume work in the fields vacated by recently freed blacks. Years of economic sacrifice added to the values of the Hindu religion enabled the Indian population to rise to their present status as the leading economic force in the country. The rise of Indian nationalism, heightened with the election of the nation's first prime minister of Indian descent, has led to feelings of uneasiness on the part of the African population and has given rise to a new torrent of black nationalism. We see, for example, a growing enthusiasm by blacks to participate at annual Emancipation Week activities and other forms of cultural awareness projects. Because this neonationalism has developed mainly in response to Indian nationalism and empowerment there is reason to question its sustainability.

Politically, Trinidad and Tobago is proud of its democratic tradition as a multiparty state. Following the death of the nation's first leader, Eric Williams, on March 29, 1981, the People's National Movement (PNM) began its decline amid allegations of fiscal mismanagement, corruption, and the end of the oil boom. Because the PNM had run the nation uninterrupted since independence, the timing was ripe for the opposition: In 1986, the PNM was defeated by the NAR. In part because it inherited a near fiscally broken government and its inability to fully win the confidence of the masses, NAR, under the leadership of Prime Minister A. N. R. Robinson, was forced to settle for one term, only to be succeeded by another PNM administration headed by Patrick Manning. During this period of political musical chairs, the crisis of the state worsened. For the first time in its history, the nation that once enjoyed economic surplus was forced in 1988 to enter into an agreement with the IMF.

On July 27, 1990, there was an attempted coup to overthrow the NAR government by an urban-based group of youthful black Muslims, the Jumaat al Muslimeen. This action by the Jumaat was determined to be a form of resistance to an impotent government that was perceived as either unable or unwilling to address the needs of common folk. The last elections, held in 1995, saw yet another shift, this time in favor of the East Indians. The victor was Basedo Panday, a former union leader and head of the United National Congress (UNC). UNC narrowly won the election when it received the swing and decisive vote from NAR party head A. N. R. Robinson.

Changing the guards may convey healthy messages of political dynamism and good governance,[55] but for all of the shifting, the leadership of the nation is void of any new vision and serious insight about how to stem the tide of social and economic decline and build the nation. Some believe that the last glitter of light beamed earlier during Eric Williams' administration and has not shone since. Prime Minister Panday's immediate mission for the nation seems to be tied to winning the confidence of Washington. He has surrounded himself with a cabinet that is essentially East Indian and has not been successful in convincing Afro-Trinbagonians that their interests are just as important as the East Indian community's. In the meantime, we find that the social cost of economic readjustment and debt repayment has been severe and that, disproportionately, the African community and its youth are at the center of the urban crisis.

St. Thomas, U.S. Virgin Islands

On March 31, 1917, the United States purchased from Denmark three minor isles east of Puerto Rico: St. Croix, St. Thomas, and St. John, together called the Virgin Islands. For most Americans, this news was nothing more than an obscurity. Today, beyond recognizing the isles as a favorite vacation stop, Americans don't know much more about this territory than they did then. Together, the three U.S. territories have a population of 101,809, predominantly persons of African descent. St. Thomas, with a population of 48,000, is the second largest of the three isles and is the site of the capital and central city, Charlotte Amalie (population about 12,331). Absence of the Virgin Islands from the international spotlight and evidence of urban social dislocation in and around the capital city were key but not the only criteria for inclusion in this study. Another important consideration was the rare opportunity to observe the impact of U.S. colonialism in the anglophone Caribbean and the qualitative differences between this territory and the sovereign island states in the region.

Politically, the United States affixed its relationship to the territories in a policy of "nonincorporation," meaning that its Congress and not the process of self-determination by the locals would determine vital political and economic policy for the islands. Within that framework, tax and trade concessions, unavailable to U.S. states or independent Caribbean countries, were made available to the territory. In 1924, citizenship was granted to Virgin Islanders with all the rights accorded that status except the vote in presidential elections, the same status granted to Puerto Ricans.[56] As citizens, they would be free to travel between the islands and the mainland. This latter privilege raises an empirical question of whether feelings of hopelessness about the future—identified as an issue among black urban dwellers, especially the youth—in other territories would be minimized in the case of the Virgin Islanders. During the "Development Decade" of the 1960s, a flow of jobs was created as the United States extended its investment in the tourist industry (which is now estimated at 60 percent of GDP) to make it competitive with other islands. One of the world's largest oil refineries (Amerada Hess Oil) was installed on the island of St. Croix while St. Thomas was maintained as the hub of tourism and the central port city. The Virgin Islands have also received about $200 million a year in federal aid for housing subsidies, education grants, welfare, and food stamps. Even though the income of one-third of the Virgin Islands population falls below the official (U.S.) poverty line and per capita income is only half that of the United States, at approximately $12,000, it is among the highest in the Caribbean. Other economically prosperous islands, some of which are known as off-shore banking centers, are the Grand Cayman Islands, the Bahamas, Bermuda, and the Netherlands Antilles.[57]

Recognizing its dependency on the mainland economy is essential to understanding the present urban crisis in the Virgin Islands. Predictably, when the economy of the parent experiences a downturn, the stability of its dependents is jeopardized. The recessionary environment of the 1970s and early 1980s led to sharp downturns in the Virgin Islands' economy as visitors, exports, and employment stagnated. However, one must consider the vulnerability of the islands to recession, owing to their heavy reliance on imported goods from the U.S. mainland and Puerto Rico. This is due to the limited agricultural potential of the territories. The Virgin Islands terrain is mostly hilly to rugged and mountainous with only 15 percent arable land. An effect of this has been the persistence of higher local prices and inflation rates than on the mainland.

As social safety-net programs—food stamps, public assistance, and Medicaid—on the mainland come under assault by conservative legislative initiatives, living standards for the islands' working-class and poor residents also have worsened. Compared to other island economies where unemployment coasts in double digit figures, the current estimated 6 percent unemployment for the Virgin Islands would offer little cause for alarm. But relative to the history of the territory, where unemployment rallied at 8.2 percent in 1983 after leveling off to about 3 percent, the present figure is viewed as substantial.[58] What should be factored in is the transmigratory nature of Virgin Islands society whereby nationals travel back and forth between the mainland and, through that process, help contain unemployment. Including this transmigratory cohort with the regular labor force would undoubtedly increase unemployment levels.

Racial construction and subjugation, an imposition of the American colonial structure, is another distinguishing characteristic of Virgin Islands society in the anglophone Caribbean that further explains the frustration and hostility that presently overshadows the society. Nationalist groups associate the violence and crime that have exploded in the urban areas with the issue of race. The fact that Virgin Islands transmigrants come in direct contact with mainland blacks in New York City, where nationalist trends are fervently rooted, gives an important boost and support to these island-based activities. The population of mainland whites on the islands has increased since the development decade of the 1960s; in St. Thomas, whites now account for 15 percent of the population.

The race factor has intensified with increased labor segmentation. Whites disproportionately occupy managerial, professional, and administrative positions at private firms, and blacks are distributed along the lower wage spectrum. Understandably, nationalist stirrings have begun to create feelings of unease among the island's white minority population. In an interview in 1994, a middle-aged white American resident described an incident that took place in a St. Thomas supermarket where she was verbally abused by a group of blacks simply because she was white. She mentioned that a number of her white friends were also coming forward with similar experiences. As the incidence of interracial hostility between native Virgin Islanders and foreigners increases, intraracial conflict between the native blacks and the influx of foreign blacks (mainly from the Eastern Caribbean islands who have migrated for the lucrative job opportunities) has also climbed. Presently, the foreign black population is about 40 percent of the island's black population.

The U.S. economy, as we noted in the preceding chapter, is experiencing an upswing. However, with each downturn, tremors can be expected in the territories. Moreover, the residual effects of the lackluster American economy are still being felt. At least 27 percent of all black families from 1989 to 1990 were reported to be functioning at or below the poverty level; families with children under 18 were functioning at 36.6 percent below the poverty level. Households headed by single women, who are at the lowest income ranges, are proliferating.[59] This has been accompanied by a breakdown in discipline in the schools and an increase in the high school dropout rate as well as the crime rate.

Journalist Melvin Claxton reported that homicide was the leading cause of death among the Virgin Islands' male population between the ages of 15 and 30 with the average of one homicide committed every 11 days. In fact crime by youth has increased 45 percent since 1989. Claxton informs that: "Each year the killers get younger, the weapons deadlier, and the crimes more brutal. The escalating violence has put the community on edge and threatens the territory's billion dollar tourism industry."[60] More than 21,000 guns (two-thirds of which are unregistered handguns) are reported to be in the territories and are used in the acts of robberies, rapes and other assaults, and drug warfare. A recidivism rate of 40 percent is a reality in the absence of rehabilitation and educational programs for prison inmates. As is the case throughout the region, drugs are inordinately linked to the crimes as the Virgin Islands have become yet another major transshipment site for drugs headed to the mainland. Exacerbating the problem is the implication of the police in criminal activity and the subsequent breakdown in respect for law by the youth. A sociologist at the University of the Virgin Islands assessed that crime in the territory is not monopolized by impoverished desperate youth; it also involves youth who are caught up in the culture of material possessions and have come to see little merit in applying approved means to achieve those ends.[61]

Without a doubt the privileges granted under the U.S. colonial structure have enabled many Virgin Islanders to enjoy a standard of living that is the envy of others in the region. But privilege has its limits, and not all of the islands' residents have prospered as is popularly believed. A limiting effect of prolonged U.S. colonialism is the problem of "identity crisis." On the one hand is a majority of blacks who identify with American cultural values and on the other is a growing movement by nationalists seeking to reclaim their heritage and culture as West Indians. As colonial subjects, the powerlessness that Virgin Islanders endure denies them a full voice in the decisions that affect their political and economic destinies. Quite similar to Puerto Ricans living under American colonial rule, Virgin Islanders elect one representative to the U.S. House of Representatives, a governor, and a lieutenant governor. But the power of these officials is limited. As well, the judicial system is under the strict direction of the United States. Albeit U.S. citizens since 1917, Virgin Islanders are unable to vote in the presidential elections. The result is frustration that has given rise to nationalist sentiments and movements for sovereignty. The frustration has also led to social dislocation that is most conspicuous in the urban centers like Charlotte Amalie, where housing projects for the poor and the bulk of marginalized working-class folk are concentrated.

On a variety of items, responses to our youth survey by the St. Thomas sample seemed to overlap with the U.S. and Trinidad and Tobago samples: 53.3 percent informed that they live with their mother only and 37.8 percent with both parents. Problems such as unemployment, street crime, drugs, and the lack of guidance from adults are front-runners. That unemployment would receive such high priority is understandable in light of the large numbers of school dropouts who do not have jobs awaiting them. They are marginally attached to social clubs and other organized activities. Interestingly, 44.7 percent reported that they spend at least 2 to 4 hours per day in front of the television. Dissatisfaction with the government for its inability to respond to their needs and problems was registered by 95.6 percent of the youth. Their resounding agreement that the police have an important role to play in the community as protectors of residents was contradicted by their overwhelming disagreement with the statement (81 percent) that the police treat all people equally and fairly.

The Eastern Caribbean

Another overlooked territory is the Eastern Caribbean. It encompasses a group of small islands including Antigua and Barbuda, Dominica, Grenada, Montserrat, St. Christopher and Nevis, St. Lucia, and St. Vincent and the Grenadines. For the most part, these economies are both agriculturally based (accounting for 20 percent of the GDP in some cases) and tourist driven. Because some islands are unable to produce sufficiently to meet their needs, they must rely on food imports. The island of Dominica, for example, is very hilly and not suitable for growing varieties of crops. Whereas Trinidad and Tobago and the tourist-driven island of St. Thomas might be considered cosmopolitan, this is contrasted by the more traditional and slower pace of several other Caribbean states. The inclusion of this subregion adds an important dimension to the analysis by providing us the opportunity to observe the impact of globalization and urban transformation on small, traditionally agrarian-based island states compared to larger, more developed ones.

Two eastern states were selected for this study: Dominica and St. Vincent and the Grenadines. Dominica received independence from Britain on November 3, 1978 and St. Vincent and the Grenadines on October 27, 1979. Linking them are their small population size (Dominica, 82,926 and St. Vincent, 118,344), economies, and various social and cultural patterns.[62] Their economies correspond to those of most other island states in that they lack diversification, and consequently are highly dependent on a single crop, in this case bananas, as their most important revenue earner. The other revenue earner is tourism, followed by small produce such as coconuts, mangoes, and avocados. As we saw in the case of Trinidad and Tobago's oil industry, when all of the cards are falling neatly into place, a successful single crop can facilitate an economic "boom." But the case of Trinidad and Tobago also reminds us of the ephemeral nature of economic booms.

There have been profitable periods for the Dominican and Vincentian banana industry, but these governments do not exercise power in the larger export and trade markets. They are currently enduring stringent competition from the Central America-grown crop and the powerful multinationals like Chiquita Brands and Dole, whose crops are cheaper to buy on the international market and considered to be of a finer quality. Moreover, the future of preferential treatment afforded their produce in the single European market is uncertain.[63] Adverse weather conditions is yet another devastating force with which they must contend, as witnessed when hurricanes David and Hugo struck in 1989 and Marilyn and Luis in 1995, destroying much of Dominica's and St. Vincent's crop.

It is believed that these small island states never fully recovered from the international recession of the 1970s and 1980s. Vulnerable, they fell immediately into the debt trap. Presently, the external debts of Dominica and St. Vincent are $89.5 million and $118.2 million respectively.[64] With the imposition of structural adjustment policies, unemployment for all labor sectors combined has reached dismal proportions of over 20 percent in both countries. In St. Vincent and the Grenadines, following the gradual pullout of the low-grade manufacturing industry by multinationals in the mid-1980s, unemployment has skyrocketed. The unemployment rate in Dominica hovers around 15 percent; for youth it has been roughly 21 percent.[65] One effect is that more people are flocking to the central cities of Roseau, Dominica and Kingstown, St. Vincent to stake their chances in the informal labor economy.

All of this is taking place at a very different period in the history of Dominica and St. Vincent and the Grenadines. It is a period marked by an increased penetration of foreign mass culture in the form of communications technology, the satellite dish, consumerism, and the restructuring of indigenous cultural values. This is significant within the context of these small societies. In the not-so-distant past, traditional values and indigenous institutions helped shape personal outlooks and provided support to people during difficult times. Now they are being replaced by modern practices.

The relationship between television and violence, consumer patterns, and the shaping of young people's values is well documented. Thus the availability and integration of television and other communications technologies throughout the societies would explain the differing pace of the crisis in certain territories compared with others. About 6 percent of the population in Dominica own television sets and about 18 percent own telephones. In St. Vincent and the Grenadines, about 18 percent of the population own televisions. Also noted are the fewer number of cinema houses on these two islands compared with Trinidad and Tobago and St. Thomas. In Trinidad and Tobago there are several television broadcast stations with cable channels. In 1992, well over one-half the population owned television sets and 15 percent had telephones. In the Virgin Islands, 65 percent of the population owned television sets with a similar percentage having telephone service.[66] It is quite clear that youth are putting their television sets to use. Based on responses to our surveys conducted in St. Vincent and the Grenadines and Dominica, 18 percent and 11 percent respectively of the youth reported that they spend more than 4 hours per day watching television.

The pace of this transformation and the response to it by the masses may be slower than observed elsewhere in the region, as the cases of Trinidad and Tobago and St. Thomas reveal. Nevertheless, a casual glance at the daily newsprint from both countries indicates that momentum is building. Since 1994, editorials and daily columns in two of St. Vincent's newspapers, *The Vincentia* and *Searchlight,* have consistently carried reports about domestic violence, drugs, and weapon possession by teens. Letters to the editor criticizing the inundation by foreign cable services and television programs and the impact on local culture are commonplace.

The effect of this cultural transformation on the youth subculture became apparent to me in 1993 when I visited Leyou, St. Vincent, a small village located just a few kilometers outside the capital city of Kingstown. Without incident one evening, my companion, a retired Vincentian man, and I came face to face with five teenage males whose demeanor was menacing. Their dress style, large gold necklaces, hair styles, expensive sneakers, and body language led me to doubt for that brief moment that I was actually on that small Caribbean island and not in one of New York City's urban districts. In another instance, riding in a taxi from Cane Field International Airport in Dominica, the driver revealed to me his dismay that a tiny island like Dominica was being wired to receive additional cable channels. In his own words, "this cable business is destroying our little country."

One gathers that people from these islands are spellbound and still adjusting to the thunderous intrusion by foreign mass culture. Mingling among the population one gets a better feel for the differences in outlook between the so-called "small island" and big island folk and how small island folk come to define the sweeping changes taking place before their very eyes. Chatting with common folk from these two islands one senses that they feel more bound to the land and more laid back than those from the more cosmopolitan islands. This was borne out during my informal chats with recently returned Vincentian nationals who had lived abroad in the United States and England for a number of years. They managed to achieve middle-class income status, yet their dream was to return home, build a modest house, and cultivate small crops and simple livestock. This was in contrast to their counterparts from Trinidad and Tobago. For the latter group of returnees, a spacious suburban home without too much horticultural distraction came closest to their idea of the retired life back home.

Alongside crime and domestic violence,[67] households headed by single women[68] in Dominica and St. Vincent and the Grenadines are on the rise. The majority of these households in St. Vincent and the Grenadines, for example, are headed by poor and working-class women and comprise roughly 39 percent of the families in the nation. Feeling trapped and despondent, many such women came to regard migration to the United States and Canada as their only option. Children were left with grandmothers and other surrogates, and mothers would send remittances to maintain them. In a number of cases, these children, distraught over the family disruption, are expressing their rage out on the streets, manifested by an escalation of crime and drug-related violence. The entire eastern coastal corridor has become a key transshipment site for drugs that eventually find their way to North America and Europe. More and more we find that these drugs are entering the societies and that youth in Dominica and St. Vincent and the Grenadines are participants either as sellers or users.

This stultifying outcome is the combined effect of declining economic conditions and youths' uncertainty about the future, the loosening of traditional norms and customs, and the growing importance assigned to material possessions that are bombarding them across the television airwaves. With school dropouts unable to find work, levels of unemployment unprecedented in the territories' history now prevail. In Dominica, for example, youth unemployment for the age group 15 through 24 in 1970 was 38.8 percent. By 1981 it was 79.5 percent. By 1990 it had leveled off but was still high at 39 percent. Unemployment among female heads of household in Dominica in 1970 was 2.6 percent compared to 1.6 percent for male-headed households. By 1981 that figure had risen to 9.2 percent.[69] Behind these problems lurks the real issue of globalization which has affected the terms and extent of foreign investment and has contributed to structural adjustment programs, government downsizings, and generally the poor quality of life for all residents.

On the issue of crime, the capital city of Roseau led other Dominican urban districts between 1990 and 1993. For each year there was only one reported homicide, but thefts, burglaries, robberies, and drug offences remained constant. This underscored the feeling of desperation that was amassing and the impact that developments in the wider international sphere were having on the economy of this small island nation. Table 3.2 below compares crime data for Dominica and Trinidad between 1991 and 1993. It is intended to dramatize the proportional difference in the dimension and pace of urban dislocation between a small island state and a more cosmopolitan state. Thus, it shows the highest crime rates for the year 1992 in the areas of theft, burglaries, and drug arrests and that the pace of crime has escalated in both island states but that Trinidad and Tobago is well ahead.

Table 3.2 Comparison of Crime in Dominica and Trinidad & Tobago, 1991–1993

| | *Theft* | | *Burglary* | | *Robbery* | | *Drugs* | |
	Dom.	*T&T*	*Dom.*	*T&T*	*Dom.*	*T&T*	*Dom.*	*T&T*
1991	1	97	357	7,313	5	3,099	75	1,078
1992	1	109	588	7,941	8	3,783	76	967
1993	1	108	278	8,419	13	4,723	46	1,079

Source: Commissioner of Police National Documentation Centre on Dominica. Trinidad & Tobago Police Survey of Crime Statistics Division adapted from C. Griffin, p.190.[70]

Our survey data of youth from Dominica and St. Vincent and the Grenadines showed that youth from both countries are experiencing similar levels of dislocation. For example, 38.5 percent of those from Dominica and 33.3 percent from St. Vincent indicated that they live with their mother alone, while 33.2 percent and 32.1 percent, respectively, live with both parents. Their attachment to organized social clubs and activities seems to be less tenuous than their Trinidad and Tobago and Virgin Island counterparts. Unemployment was listed as the number one problem facing young people alongside the drug problem, AIDS, and the lack of adult guidance. In their opinion, government could do much more than it is presently doing to address their concerns. Most seemed to mistrust the police as indicated by their disagreement with the survey statement that the police treat all people equally and fairly (see appendix B).

Unlike Trinidad and Tobago, ethnic and racial conflict is not such a useful factor for explaining the urban crisis in St.Vincent and the Grenadines and Dominica considering that Africans are the predominant racial group in these territories. But we must be reminded that just because blacks represent the majority in one territory is no guarantee that they will be empowered compared to black minorities elsewhere. Their effective leadership and organization are key. Without these, the majority versus minority dialectic has little significance.

The party that led the country into independence in St. Vincent was the St. Vincent Labour Party (LP) headed by the first prime minister and lawyer, Milton Cato. Essentially it was a middle-class-backed government. In 1984 the Labour Party was defeated by the New Democratic Party (NDP) headed by professional politician James "Son" Mitchell. Ideologically, few if any differences are detected between the two parties with neither ever having possessed a clear vision about how to develop the country and move it forward. The Vincentian left enjoyed a brief moment of attention with the rise of the New Jewel Movement in Grenada in 1979; however, with the collapse of the Grenadian Revolution in 1983, the left has receded into obscurity.

From Patrick John to Eugenia Charles, the picture in neighboring Dominica is not much different. Patrick John, the first prime minister at the time of independence, was crippled by allegations of corruption and certain undemocratic practices. In 1980, John's Democratic Labour Party (DLP) was replaced by the Democratic Freedom Party (DFP) headed by a successful lawyer, Eugenia Charles, who would become the region's first woman prime minister. Her right-of-center posture made her one of the most favorite Caribbean leaders in the eyes of Washington and assisted her in procuring loans and aid packages from international organizations, which she used to repair the country's ailing infrastructure. Charles' unpopular support of the Reagan administration's invasion of Grenada in 1983 won her the title "Iron Lady." In 1995 Dominicans voted into power the United Workers Party (UWP) headed by Edison James. There does not appear to be a dearth of parties and leaders in St. Vincent and Dominica. Nevertheless, the social and economic conditions continue to deteriorate and there appears to be little evidence that the parties, the leaders, and their politics of nothingness will be able to support the policies required to challenge those external forces that are the source of the problem.

CONCLUSION

This chapter set out to explore the roots of the urban nemesis in the contemporary Caribbean and to consider what, if any, differences exist between the crisis in that region and that which is taking place in the United States. The discussion pointed to commonalities but also to structural, environmental, and sociocultural distinctions between the two settings. A key distinction was the difference in the pace of the urban crisis. Moreover, not only were differences found to exist between the United States and the Caribbean, but also within the Caribbean sample as well.

A few people today continue to cling to the belief that there are societies in the world (non-Western to be exact) that have managed to escape the tentacles of postmodern mass culture and are still heavily guided by their indigenous ways of life. In light of the fierce economic and cultural globalization penetration of societies worldwide, such a belief, though judged to be desirable and necessary by the standards of some, does not appear realistic.[71] A hypothesis that was unraveled in this chapter and which warrants further consideration concerns the matter of pace. That is to say, while all the world's cultures are experiencing the effects of external cultural penetration as a direct result of globalization, for some non-Western societies, that effect is markedly reduced. This, needless to say, would be an important basis for comparison. The logical setting to explore this and related questions for non-Western blacks is the African continent. With that in mind, we now shift our attention to the continent's East African subregion.

NOTES

1. The Caribbean, unless otherwise specified, refers to the anglophone island states of Greater and Lesser Antilles including Guyana.

2. Catherine A. Sunshine, *The Caribbean: Survival, Struggle and Sovereignty* (Washington, D.C.: EPICA, 1985), 12.

3. Sunshine, *The Caribbean*, 2; Carmen Deere, Peggy Antrobus, Lynn Boles, Edwin Melendez, Peter Phillips, Marcia Rivera, Helen Safa, *In the Shadows of the Sun: Caribbean Development Alternatives and U.S. Policy* (Boulder, Colo.: Westview, 1990), 12.

4. Keith Hart coined the term "informal sector" as a result of his groundbreaking field research conducted between 1965–1968 with a Northern Ghananian group, the Frafras. It was later popularized by the International Labour Organization's (ILO) study of Kenya in 1972. See Keith Hart, "Informal Income Opportunities and Urban Employment in Ghana" in *Journal of Modern African Studies* (Vol. 11, 1973), 61–89.

5. Robert B. Potter, *Urbanization and Planning in the Third World* (New York: St. Martin's Press, 1985), 7–8; also, Potter, *Urbanization and Planning in the Caribbean* (London: Mansell Pub., 1989), chapter 1.

6. Potter, *Urbanization and Planning in the Third World*, 66.

7. UNDP, Human Development Report, 1995; also demographics update from UNDP Population Division, June, 2000.

8. Urban primacy, otherwise referred to as "urban bias," is a feature of developing societies. It is a major consequence of colonialism, in which the towns were customarily ports and administrative and retail centers. See C.G. Clark, "Urbanization in the Caribbean," in *Geography* (59, 1974), 223–232; Andrew Webster, *Introduction to the Sociology of Development* (London: Macmillan,1984); A. Portes, J. Itzigsohn, C. Cabral-Dore, "Urbanization in the Caribbean Basin: Social Change During the Years of Crisis" in *Latin American Research Review* (Spring 1994); also, Potter, *Urbanization and Planning in the Third World*, 67.

9. Potter, *Urbanization and Planning in the Third World*, 67–70.

10. According to the World Bank's 1997 report, poverty in the region averages roughly 38 percent of the total population, ranging from a high of 65 percent in Haiti to a low of 5 percent in the Bahamas. Excluding Haiti, approximately 25 percent of the total population is poor. These estimates place the Caribbean close to a world aggregate average of poverty in the developing countries (see page 1).

11. See R.C. Jones, "The Role of Perception in Urban In-Migration: A Path Analytic Model" in *Geographical Analysis* (Vol. 12, 1980), 98–108.

12. R. Hope Kempe, *Urbanization in the Commonwealth Caribbean* (Boulder, Colo.: Westview, 1986), 102–103.

13. Malcolm Cross, *Urbanization and Urban Growth in the Caribbean: An Essay on Social Change in Dependent Societies* (Cambridge: Cambridge University Press, 1979), 15–16.

14. Franklin Knight and Colin Palmer (eds.), *The Modern Caribbean* (Chapel Hill, N.C.: University of North Carolina Press, 1989, Introduction), 7.

15. Howard Zinn, *A People's History of the United States* (New York: Harper Perennial, 1990). It should be pointed out that other ethnic groups are present (Chinese, East Indians) who arrived as indentured servants mainly in Trinidad and Tobago and Guyana after the African Emancipation in 1834. In Trinidad and Tobago and Guyana, the East Indian population is roughly 50 percent of the entire population. See Sunshine, *The Caribbean: Survival, Struggle and Sovereignty* (chapter 1); Deere, et al., *In the Shadows of the Sun: Caribbean Development Alternatives and U.S. Policy*, 8.

16. Orlando Patterson, "Toward a Future That Has No Past—Reflections on the Fate of Blacks in the Americas" in *Public Interest* (27, 1972); also, Charles Green and Basil Wilson, *The Struggle for Black Empowerment in New York City: Beyond the Politics of Pigmentation* (New York: McGraw-Hill, 1992) (chapter 5, "Afro-Carib Dialectic").

17. Godfrey St. Bernard, "Labour Market Challenges and Contemporary Youth in Caribbean Societies" (University of West Indies, St. Augustine, Trinidad, unpublished paper presented at the 23rd Conference of the Caribbean Studies Association, St. John's, Antigua, 1998).

18. See Maurice Bishop, *Forward Ever: The Years of the Grenadian Revolution, Speeches of Maurice Bishop* (Sydney, Australia: Pathfinder Press, 1982); Clive Y. Thomas, *The Poor and the Powerless: Economic Policy and Change in the Caribbean* (New York: Monthly Review Press, 1988) (see chapter 1, "The Caribbean Dilemma"); Michael Manley, *Jamaica: Struggle in the Periphery* (London: Third World Media Ltd., 1982).

19. Carmen Deere, et al., *In the Shadows of the Sun*, 5.

20. Eric Williams, *Forged from the Love of Liberty: Selected Speeches of Dr. Eric Williams* (compiled by Paul K. Sutton) 1981. Sunshine, *The Caribbean*; Gordon Lewis, *The Growth of the Modern West Indies* (New York: Monthly Review, 1968); Franklin W. Knight, *The Caribbean: The Genesis of a Fragmented Nationalism* (New York: Oxford University Press, 1968); "Caribbean Policy: From Subregional Federation to Regional Association," (excerpted from chapter 14 by Professor Alan K. Henrikson, The Fletcher School of Law and Diplomacy, Tufts University, *A Continent of Islands: Searching for the Caribbean Destiny* [Reading, Mass.: Addison-Wesley, 1990]).

21. Carmen Deere, et al., *In the Shadows of the Sun*, 17.

22. Deere, et al., *In the Shadows of the Sun*, 21–24.

23. Deere, et al., *In the Shadows of the Sun*, 22.

24. George L. Beckford, *Persistent Poverty: Underdevelopment in Plantation Economies of the Third World* (Morant Bay, Jamaica: Maroon Pub., 1988).

25. Carmen Deere, et al., *In the Shadows of the Sun*, 23.

26. Susan George, *A Fate Worse than Debt: The World Financial Crisis and the Poor* (New York: Grove, 1988).

27. *Global Development Finance* (Vol. 1, A World Bank Book [Caribbean and Latin America Debt, 1997]), 196–197.

28. Susan George, *A Fate Worse than Debt* (chapter 2, "Money Mongers").

29. Cheryl Payer, *The Debt Trap* (New York: Monthly Review Press, 1974); Susan George, *A Fate Worse than Debt*; Deere, et al., *In the Shadows of the Sun*, 44.

30. Esther Madriz, "Neoliberalism in Venezuela: From Urban Riots to Presidential Impeachment," in Charles Green (ed.), *Globalization and Survival in the Black Diaspora: The New Urban Challenge* (Albany, New York: SUNY Press, 1997), 129–149.

31. Elas Chaney, *Migration from the Caribbean Region: Determinants and Effects of Current Movements* (Washington, D.C.: Center for Immigration and Refugee Assistance, 1986), 15; also, New York City Planning Dept., *The Newest New Yorkers*; World Bank Report on Poverty, xi, 43–45.

32. Alejandro Portes and Ruben G. Rumbaut, *Immigrant America*, (Berkeley, California: University of California Press, 1990).

33. Aubrey A. Bonnett, "The New Female West Indian Immigrant: Dilemmas of Coping in the Host Society" in R. W. Palmer (ed.), *In Search of a Better Life* (New York: Praeger); Susan Michael, "Children of the New Wave Immigration: An Exploration" in A. W. Bonnett and L. Watson (eds.), *Emerging Perspectives on the Black Diaspora* (Maryland: University Press of America, 1990); Joyce Toney, "The Perpetuation of a Culture of Migration: West Indian Ties With Home, 1900–1979" (an unpublished paper delivered at Annual CSA Meeting, St. George's Grenada, 1992).

34. B. Larmer, "The Barrel Children" in *Newsweek* (February 19, 1996), 45–48.

35. Joan C. Neil, "Social Programmes for Poverty Alleviation in the Republic of Trinidad and Tobago" (a working paper) (Port of Spain: Economic Commission for Latin America and the Caribbean, 1992).

36. *Poverty Reduction and Human Resource Development in the Caribbean.* (World Bank Report No. 15342 LAC, 1996), x.

37. Deere, et al., *In the Shadows of the Sun*, 62; Bonacich, et al., explain that women are preferred in most of the assembly factory and textile work settings over men as they are perceived as being more submissive and less likely to succumb to the calls of union organizers.

38. World Bank Report (No. 15342 LAC, 1996), ix.

39. World Bank Report, 9.

40. World Bank Report, 6, 10.

41. Andrew Webster, in *Introduction to the Sociology of Development,* considers the infant mortality rate a poor indicator of development. Infant mortality rates—which had begun to show positive signs of improvement in the 1980s as the result of internal efforts and the work by international health organizations—have lowered in the 1990s but remain in double-digit figures.

42. According to figures provided by UNESCO for 1992, rates of infant deaths per 1,000 live births during the first year demonstrate this for selected countries: St. Vincent and the Grenadines (21), Trinidad and Tobago (20), Dominica (18), Jamaica (16).

43. Excerpt from a radio interview with Prof. Rhoda Reddock on WBAI aired August, 1997; Margaret Chatoor, *Mothers Don't Come in Barrels* (a documentary film, book, and song prepared by the St. Joseph's Convent Port of Spain Young Leaders), Port of Spain, Trinidad and Tobago, 1999.

44. World Bank Report, ix, 15.

45. Interview with Dominican young woman, August 1993.

46. David Abdulah, "The IMF/World Bank and Trinidad and Tobago" (A statement by OWTU presented to The People's Tribunal, Berlin, 1988), page 2.

47. David Abdullah radio interview on Pacifica Radio WBAI, New York, April 7, 1998.

48. See St. Bernard, "Labour Market Challenges and Contemporary Youth in Caribbean Societies."

49. See discussion on drugs and crime: World Bank Report on Poverty, No. 15342 LAC; *Trinidad and Tobago Poverty and Unemployment in an Oil Based Economy* (World Bank Report No. 14382–TR, 1995); Cathy Booth, "Caribbean Blizzard," Feb. 26, 1996.

50. Clifford E. Griffin, *Democracy and Neoliberalism in the Developing World: Lessons from the Anglophone Caribbean* (Brookfield, Vt.: Ashgate, 1997) (see chapter 9, "Neoliberalism in Trinidad and Tobago").

51. Interview with woman from Port of Spain, Trinidad, August 1993.

52. Charles Green, "Urbanism, Transnationalism, and the Caribbean: The Case of Trinidad and Tobago," in Green (ed.), *Globalization and Survival in the Black Diaspora*, 171–199.

53. Based on 1990 Census of the Population, *CSO of Trinidad and Tobago*; also, see Peter Lewis, M.D., "Drug Abuse: The Trinidad and Tobago Experience" (Port of Spain, Trinidad: CEWG Publication, December, 1994).

54. East Indian is a locally used term to describe the mostly Hindu Indo population; also, see Gordon Lewis, *The Growth of the Modern West Indies*; Selwyn R. Cudjoe, *Basedo Panday and the Politics of Race* (Wellesley, Mass.: Calaloux Publications, 1997).

55. Selwyn Ryan gives an excellent discussion of this in "The Decline of Good Governance in the Anglophone Caribbean," a paper delivered at XXTH CSA Conference, Willemstad, Curaçao, May 1995.

56. Janet Domingo, "Security and Self-Development in the U.S. Virgin Islands," in Ivelaw Griffith (ed.), *Strategy and Security in the Caribbean* (New York: Praeger, 1991), 179; also, Domingo, "Employment, Income, and Economic Identity in the U.S. Virgin Islands," (Summer 1989, Vol. 18, No. 1), 37–56.

57. Domingo, *Strategy and Security in the Caribbean*, 176–180.

58. Domingo, *Strategy and Security in the Caribbean*.

59. In the V.I., female-headed households represented 27.1 percent and those with children under 18 years of age was 18.6 percent. See Domingo, "Employment, Income, and Economic Identity in the U.S. Virgin Islands"; also, *Social and Economic Characteristics for Virgin Islands of the United States for 1980 and 1990* (U.S. Department of Commerce); also, see Domingo, *Strategy and Security in the Caribbean*.

60. Between March and December of 1994, journalist Melvin Claxton authored a six-part series on drugs, violence, and crime in the V.I. and the Caribbean. See his "V.I. Drugs Linked to Antigua" (March 3, 1994), 2 of 5.

61. Telephone interview with Dr. Dione Phillips, February 1996.

62. Population statistics for St. Vincent and the Grenadines and Dominica provided by *World Urbanization Prospects: The 1996 Revision* (United Nations Population Division, May 1997).

63. Renwick Rose, "Undermining Our Own Interests" in *Searchlight* (October 11, 1996), 10; *The EUROPA World Yearbook 1996; World Development Report 1992*. The World Bank.

64. External debts data for St. Vincent and the Grenadines and Dominica. *World Debt Tables* (October 1994–December 1995, and 1996, Vol. 2). The World Bank.

65. See St. Bernard, "Labour Market Challenges and Contemporary Youth in Caribbean Societies."

66. U.S. Government Fact Sheets on St. Vincent and the Grenadines and Dominica, 1996.

67. *Digest of Crime Statistics for the Years 1989–1991* (Statistical Unit of Central Planning Division, St. Vincent and the Grenadines).

68. Joyce Toney, "The New Urbanism and the Impact Upon Women and Family Rela-

tions: The Case of St. Vincent." C. Green (ed.), *Globalization and Survival in the Black Diaspora*, 227–247.

69. *Report of the 1970 Census for Dominica* (Vol. 4, Table 2); *Report of the 1981 Census for Dominica* (Vol. 1, Table 2.2); *Dominica Labour Force Survey* (Sept. 1989).

70. Clifford Griffin, *Democracy and Neoliberalism in the Developing World,* 190.

71. Wade Davis, "Vanishing Cultures," in *National Geographic* (Vol. 196, No. 2, August 7, 1999), 62–90.

4

An Urban Storm Brews in East Africa

For many Westerners, the thought of journeying into Africa's urban corridor might seem a bit peculiar. One explanation for Westerners' unfamiliarity with urban Africa could be their preconception of Africa as an agrarian space. Perhaps a more plausible explanation for their unfamiliarity with urban Africa is related to the images of Africa that are projected via cable television or satellite dish into their living rooms. These images are not recent and date back to television's earliest programming including the weekly "Tarzan" series and consistent portrayals of Africa as the "Dark Continent," a view that was popularized with the publication of Henry Morton Stanley's work, *Through the Dark Continent* in 1878. Africa's contemporary portrayal is that of a vast wildlife preserve encompassing the continent's immense Rift Valley where daring European scientists intrigue their audiences nightly with their latest discoveries and action-packed video from the wild. Other images depict misery-prone people constantly fleeing the ravages of drought or internecine warfare. It is seldom if ever conveyed that people residing on the continent and its urban spaces today are educated, fun loving, and hard working, and that they have many of the same aspirations for themselves, their children, and the future of their homeland as do people on other continents. I found Andrew Hacker's chapter, "Being Black in America," from his work, *Two Nations,* not only accurate but timely when he wrote, "Much of the rest of the world regards Africa as the primal continent: the most backward, the least developed, by almost every modern measure. The message persists that it [Africa] must receive outside help because there is little likelihood that it will set things right by itself."[1]

Africans, like other peoples around the world, are increasingly becoming urbanized with nearly 35 percent of the continent's population reportedly living in urban areas. Urbanization under normal circumstances can pose social and environmental consequences for the newcomers. Rapid urban growth is another matter altogether. The pace of urban growth in Africa is presently the highest in the world. Whereas in 1970 only about 16 percent of Africa's people lived in urban areas, the United Nations estimates that this figure will grow exponentially and will reach 51 percent by the year 2025.[2] A central concern that White (1989) and Stren and White (1989)[3] address is the management of rapid urban growth in African cities, particularly during the present period of strained human and institutional resources. As we have noted elsewhere, a catalyst for this recent trend is economic globalization and the inability of the state to mount an effective response. African cities to the west and south such as Lagos, Dakar, Abidjan, Harare, and Lusaka have already begun to demonstrate the effects of rapid urbanization and globalization.[4] The winds now appear to be gathering in the east, affecting such major cities as Dar es Salaam, Kampala, and Nairobi. This chapter draws attention to the problems associated with urbanization and globalization that are engulfing Africa's eastern subregion. It explores the uniqueness of that experience vis à vis the United States and, too, the Caribbean regions.

What the peoples of the world are coming to realize is that geographical distance from the West offers little if any protection against the penetration of Western-based mass culture.[5] We argue that compared to the U.S. black belt and the Caribbean, the socioeconomic and cultural crisis that is unraveling in Africa's eastern subregion is taking place at a moderate pace for which several factors can be identified. Distance from the West is an obvious contributing factor, but as the case of Tanzania illustrates, a competing factor is the nature of political relations between a given African state and the West at a given point in time. Proximity to the West and political relations notwithstanding, East Africa's reliance on subsistence farming and the degree to which traditional lifestyles continue to influence the body culture cannot be overlooked in explaining the moderate pace of that subregion's urban crisis. Also to be factored in is the level of communications technology development in the society. Our examination of the urban crisis in this subregion will be guided by a critical look at two key territories, Tanzania and Kenya. At the outset it is necessary to offer some background information on the subregion as well as recent developments in the political economies of both countries that have triggered the crisis in their urban districts.

Of the plethora of problems that challenge Africa's sub-Saharan region, debt is believed to be salient. According to the World Bank, the total short- and long-term liabilities of these countries increased dramatically, from $6 billion in 1970 to $58 billion by 1988 and to $174.2 billion in 1995.[6] It rose from $38.5 billion in 1978 to $80 billion in 1984, which amounted to 30 percent and 50 percent respectively of the region's total GNP. Currently sub-Sahara Africa's debt burden exceeds $300 billion. The headache, of course, is the cost of servicing the African debt which has reached unsustainable levels. For example, the total debt service increased from $6.4 billion in 1983 to $7.9 billion in 1984. The debt service ratio of 21.6 percent in 1984 rose to 33.2 percent in 1985 for the continent as a whole.[7] Needless to say, the matter of arrears for the region is startling. Like other debtor regions in the developing world, more capital flows from Africa than to it. In 1986 it was found that the continent was paying back more to the IMF than it was receiving from the Fund in new loans. Havnevik found that the greatest burden of the debt crisis and the hardship of adjustment so far in the world has been borne by the African countries and the majority of poor people who reside there.[8]

The United States has come forward with a plan that it feels can once and for all address sub-Sahara Africa's social and economic growth problems and bring it into the twenty-first century. Concern for Africa should not be construed as a spontaneous stroke of goodwill by the Americans to begin to take Africa and the plight of its people seriously. Prompting the Americans was the stark realization that the Asians (most specifically Japan and China) and certain NATO allies have been much more visible on the continent. In the light of the current preoccupation with economic globalization and heightened international competition, such initiatives by the major economic players are more suspect today of being driven by the prospects of new investment profits and geopolitics than with the urgency for human development. As far as the Americans are concerned, future relations with the continent will be guided by the steady arm of trade, not aid. To pave the way, the Clinton Administration sent Secretary of State Madeline K. Albright on a seven-nation African tour in December 1997. Albright limited her visit to Central and Southern Africa with the countries of the Congo, Zimbabwe, and South Africa heading the list. Albright's visit culminated with the administration's launching of the Africa Growth and Opportunity Act in 1998. The bill was passed in the U.S. House of Representatives but lost in the Senate. In February 1999 it was relaunched under a new title, The Africa Trade and Development Act and finally passed by Congress in May 2000. Two main objectives of this bill was for the United States to lead the task of integrating Africa more fully into the global economy and to build a more valuable partnership between Africa and the United States that would benefit citizens of both lands. More specifically though, the bill would require that African countries adopt the standard structural adjustment policies of deregulation, liberalization, and privatization in order to trade with America. The bill provides no additional aid money and forces African governments to adhere to the intellectual property rights regime of the World Trade Organization.[9]

THE EAST AFRICA SUBREGION

Most analysts seem to agree that East Africa consists of three contiguous states: Tanzania, Kenya, and Uganda. On occasion, however, there is room for discussion. Malawi, Somalia, and Ethiopia, for example, have also been added to that trio, as have other states.[10] Kiswahili is the spoken language, mainly in Tanzania and Kenya, and to a lesser degree in Uganda, alongside English and multiple indigenous languages. Bridging these territories are their colonial histories, their impoverished status, and unmistakably, their wealth in minerals and other natural resources prevalent throughout the continent. Complementing East Africa's importance as a source of natural wealth (according to some historians) is its direct link to the origin of mankind. It has been noted that:

> Ancient civilizations of Egypt, Southern India, and Arabia maintained trade connections with East Africa as early as 3,000 years ago [and] were greatest along the East African Coast giving rise to the Waswahili people and the Kiswahili language. Indigenous people of East Africa included the Bantu, who expanded into the area at least five centuries ago and Hilotic and Hamitic people from the West and North.[11]

Perhaps Kilbride and Kilbride (1990) are clearest in their assessment of the causes of the growing powerlessness among men and women, the erosion of the village society, and the changing family life in East Africa. They cast their net on modernization and the process of European cultural and economic penetration that began in the fifteenth century mainly with the exploits of Portugal and Spain. They maintain that normative and positive interrelated patterns of child care have been preserved to some degree in East Africa today, as have the reliance on the extended family for support, a subsistence economy with women and men as agriculturalists, and a moral system with elders as moral leaders. However, the process of "delocalization" globalization is charged with the systematic breakdown of this social arrangement.[12] Villagers of various ages have been forced into the cities and towns in search of work and survival. Kayere (1980) reports that in Kenya, 50 percent of the jobs in the modern economy sector are in the cities of Nairobi and Mombasa, and that the migrants are mainly young adult males with some form of education. Noted among the consequences is the shifting responsibilities on the part of some men to their families, a problem that has been extremely stressful for women and children. The incidence of child abuse and neglect is also believed to be more prevalent throughout Kenya, occurring primarily in Nairobi, but also in Uganda's urban areas.[13]

Tanzania and Kenya were selected for this investigation because of their overlapping sociocultural and political histories but also because of their peculiarities.[14] A key divide was their different development of capitalism, which is directly related to their colonial experiences. Kenya was a British settlement colony whereas Tanzania became a British mandate after World War I. Prior to that it was a colony of Germany. Following the German defeat in WWI, it was decided by the League of Nations that Germany's African territories would be divided among Britain, France, and South Africa. Thus, Tanganyika (or German East Africa) went to Britain, Namibia (or German Southern Africa) was assigned to South Africa, and Togo and Cameroon (or German West Africa) went to the French.

The British interpreted their responsibility to Tanzania purely as a nation complying with the mandate issued by the League of Nations. There was little personal investment or interest in the country; in fact, much of what one sees infrastructurally in the city of Dar es Salaam today can be dated back to the pre-British period. Throughout that time, Britain's preoccupation rested with its main colony, Kenya, and the capital city of Nairobi. Tanzania would remain, in Western terminology, economically "backward," but Kenya would be allowed to "take off."[15] This brief mention is instructive as we proceed with our discussion of the two countries. Analyzed in this politicoeconomic and historical context, we are better able to appreciate Tanzania's slower development pace along Western lines in relation to its regional neighbors.

Both countries won independence from Britain in the early 1960s; Tanzania in 1961 and Kenya in 1963. In 1962 Julius K. Nyerere, a former schoolteacher, became the first president of Tanzania and was reelected for four consecutive terms. In 1985, Ali Hassan Mwinyi replaced Nyerere as president. His succession to the presidency coincided with the nation's shift in economic policy in which acceptance of the IMF's prescriptions for the removal of government subsidies, monetary devaluation, and budgeting restraint was by far an easier undertaking than it might have been under Nyerere.[16] In 1947 Jomo Kenyatta, a Kikuyu, Kenya's largest ethnic group, became president of Kenyan African Union (KAU). In 1953 he was detained after it was alleged that he was involved in the Mau Mau offensive against the British government; he was released in 1961. Kenya was granted self-government in June 1963 and independence on December 12, 1963. KAU became KANU, Kenyan African National Union, and Kenyatta became the nation's first prime minister in 1963, and president in 1964.

While both leaders perceived some form of socialism as necessary for their respective countries, Nyerere threaded that path with greater zeal and commitment than his Kenyan counterpart. Nyerere's policy, known as "ujamaa," a form of nationalistic socialism, was formalized in 1967 with his Arusha Declaration.[17] That declaration was highly suspicious of Western cultural penetration and its demonstrative insensitivity toward indigenous cultures. It offers partial explanation why Tanzania's communications technology in the form of television and cable television development was not prioritized. Television would not arrive to mainland Tanzania until 1994. Coincidentally, this occurred at the zenith of radical economic restructuring and liberalization in the country, which forced the opening up of the Tanzanian economy to foreign markets and investors. On the other hand, in neighboring Kenya, the state-owned television system was developed shortly after independence. At that point, the single network featured foreign (mainly Western) programming. The existence of this medium and its subsequent expansion throughout the nation since independence has contributed significantly to the shaping of the Kenyan social and political mindset. Combined, Nyerere's mission, Kenya's embrace of the West in that state's development process, and the deleterious impact of the international recessions of the 1970s and early 1980s, heighten our awareness about the urban condition in these two territories and the subregion as a whole.

THE TERRITORIES

Kenya and Tanzania are essentially rural societies with over 90 percent of their populations engaged in some form of agriculture such as growing food for domestic consumption or exporting crops, the most important of which are coffee, tea, and sisal. Crude tools such as the hand hoe are the norm. The composition of the population by age has important consequences for the allocation of resources insofar as health, education, and welfare are concerned. Sub-Saharan Africa, like other parts of the developing world, could be classified as youthful; however, this condition poses immediate and long-term implications. According to Bennars (1985:8)[18] the youth population (15–24) in Africa will grow from 39 million in 1950 to 292 million by the year 2025, an increase of nearly 650 percent.

By contrast, the youth population in the more developed nations has increased by only a fraction of that amount. For poorer, developing countries, a youthful population can be burdensome. The World Population Projections reported that the East African subregion—which is consistent with the finding for the continent as a whole—is disproportionately youthful with over 35 percent of the overall population of Tanzania, Kenya, and Uganda between the ages of 10 and 24.[19] Fifty-two percent of the population are children through age 17, and 10.9 percent are above 50 years of age. Translated, that means that roughly 37 percent of the population are the most active economically and have to support 63 percent of the population who comprise the young and the old in the society. For thriving, advanced economies, meeting this obligation should be negligible. However, in the case of poor, destitute states, meeting that obligation is virtually impossible. It is to be expected, therefore, that in the absence of these monetary resources, Africa's youth would experience an uneven share of poverty, unemployment, malnutrition, ill health, and poor housing.[20]

GDP figures show that Kenya has grown more rapidly than Tanzania in both the agricultural and nonagricultural sectors. Both countries experienced a rise in coffee export between 1976 and 1978 when the world price for coffee quadrupled. But in the aftermath of this boom, Tanzania especially experienced a severe foreign exchange crisis. In 1981 and 1982 both countries received food aid, although Tanzania had been receiving such aid since the mid-1970s. Aid dependence had become so great that a considerable component of recurrent government expenditure was financed by it.[21] At this writing, Tanzania is still the recipient of the largest amount of aid of any country in sub-Sahara Africa with bilateral aid emanating from such countries as Japan, Scandinavian states, Germany, Italy, the UK, and Canada.[22] According to critics, this has only served to increase Tanzania's dependency and powerlessness.

Let us begin by taking a closer look at Tanzania followed by Kenya. Before doing so, it should be mentioned that there is only a handful of urban sociologists from the East African subregion whose scholarly work has centered on East Africa's urban crisis and has earned recognition in the West. For that reason, Joe Lugalla's work on Dar es Salaam, Tanzania and Kinuthia Macharia's on Nairobi, Kenya are cited extensively in the discussion that follows.

TANZANIA AND THE ORIGINS OF THE URBAN CRISIS

O'Neill and Mustafa (1990) and Lugalla (1996) link the current development crisis in Tanzania to the world recession concomitant with the effects of the oil price hikes, the increased costs of fertilizer and capital goods, drought, a deterioration in the terms of trade, and the cumulative costs involved in carrying the burden of war in 1979 to liberate Uganda from Idi Amin's dictatorship.[23] Among the internal factors are state borrowing from the national bank at levels that fueled inflation, strategic errors in the allocation of foreign exchange, insufficient attention to export potential, and bureaucratic mismanagement.[24] The agricultural sector policies Tanzania adopted since independence have suppressed agricultural sector produce prices. They also have destabilized the rural settlements and social institutions through the introduction of preplanned and ad hoc ujamma villages, sometimes expressed as the process of villagization policies. Moreover, these policies set in motion the preconditions for the start of the agrarian crisis that Tanzania is currently experiencing.

The pre-colonial period is of enduring significance in shaping the modern history of Tanzania as is the case with many other African countries. Tanganyika won its independence from Britain on December 9, 1961 following 75 years of colonialism that included 30 years under Germany and 45 years under the British. Independent Tanganyika became Tanzania in 1964 when it was united with the island sultanate of Zanzibar. Presently, the population of Tanzania is 26 million, of which 76 percent is rural and 24 percent is urban based. This figure represents an increase of 17 percent since 1970, the decade that marked the migratory sprint toward the urban areas.

With a population of 2,474,260 (or 35 percent of the nation's urban population) Dar es Salaam is the largest and most populous urban area. Dar es Salaam remains central notwithstanding the 1973 decision of the ruling Chama Cha Mapinduzi Party (CCM)[25] to shift the capital from Dar es Salaam to the more centrally located Dodoma. Between 1948 and 1978 Tanzania's urban population on the mainland increased 18.5 times while its share of the country's total population increased fivefold over the same period. Tanzania, which had been experiencing urbanization since colonialism, has witnessed an increase of 9 percent annually and has doubled every 10 years between 1948 and 1993. By 1988 the urban population was 17.9 percent of the country's population of 22.5 million. Alarmingly, the urban population growth is faster than the rate of growth of the total population. It is expected that Tanzania's population will increase more than fivefold and one in every three people will live in urban areas.[26] But why is Dar es Salaam so important and heavily urbanized? Well, for starters, it is the region's largest seaport and the industrial, commercial, and communications center. All of the major transportation routes by air, sea, rail, and road that connect various parts of the country as well as those that link Tanzania to the rest of the world, originate in Dar es Salaam. Of the 220 industries that were carried over from colonialism and that employed more than 10 people, 52.89 percent were situated in Dar es Salaam.[27] Infrastructurally, the city benefited little from the years of British rule following Germany's defeat in World War I. That fact provides an interesting dimension when we compare the city of Dar es Salaam to other former British urban centers such as Nairobi, Kampala, and Harare.

Based on Lugalla's survey of 280 of Dar es Salaam's residents from low-, medium-, and high-income areas, it is learned that 87 percent of the population supplement their incomes through the informal sector or through petty trading activities. As a visiting lecturer at the University of Dar es Salaam between 1989 and 1990, this investigator can recall seeing a transport vehicle, or "dalla-dalla,"[28] overflowing with passengers; it was later identified as owned by a respected university professor. In present day Tanzania, members of the middle class and professionals must subsidize their meager salaries by engaging in the informal economy. For some this may mean purchasing a vehicle to be used for transportation and employing a driver or perhaps cultivating citrus crops on a plot of rented or owned land commonly referred to in Kiswahili as a "shamba." Poor boys (shamba boys) are employed to help with the harvest and its sale at the local marketplace.

The bottom-most class in the social structure is comprised of the unemployed, domestic servants, hawkers, street vendors and those whose survival depends on luck and the vagaries of the urban system. Their fates rest solely with the informal sector. Wealth continues to be concentrated in the hands of a few at the expense of the many. A conservative estimate is that 1 percent of the Tanzanian population controls 80 percent of the wealth.[29] As Lugalla points out, the very wealthy in the country—such as contractors, industrialists, merchants, and other members of the bourgeoisie—are mostly Asians, Arabs, and semi-Arabs with business contracts abroad. Just beneath them are the senior officials, government officials, heads of parastatals, diplomats, university professors, and so on. They can be easily identified by the license tags on the vehicles they drive or are driven about in. They are the direct beneficiaries of globalization and the new liberalization policies that have been introduced in the nation. Their appetite for Western culture is enormous, evidenced by their flair for luxurious motor cars, satellite dishes, and new television sets since television's recent introduction.

Unlike their Caribbean and U.S. counterparts, poor urban youth generally do not sport the latest fashions and other material imports from abroad. In other words, the probability of seeing scores of youth sporting National Basketball Association teams' paraphernalia or expensive Nike sneakers through the streets of Nairobi is limited, with the odds even greater in Dar es Salaam. This form of material aggrandizement appears to be the preserve of youth from better-off classes who are able to enjoy the largesse of their parents. Still, it is slowly beginning to seep through on the backs of hawkers who may sport them as they try to peddle them. For urban and rural poor school dropouts, hope is tied to migration to any one of the main cities. Hope is also tied to pot luck. In Dar es Salaam, boys have formed street gangs for their survival with names like the Posta Group, Ja la Kuu, and the Kariakoo group. They engage in small crimes (stealing, purse-snatching, and hustling). Girls and young women turn to prostitution for the very same reason we find in other parts of the developing and developed world. To meet their basic clothing, food, and shelter needs, they have come to feel that there is no other way. Lugalla states that anywhere from 60 to 100 children can be seen daily in the cafeteria of the University of Dar es Salaam scavenging food remains during lunch and supper time. It is essentially these youth, then, who are the ones involved in illegal activities, cheating, trickstering, theft, and mugging and who smoke bhang, the Swahili term for marijuana. Some are even known to smoke glue to escape their misery.[30]

Also contributing to the migration problem is the influx of mainly teenage boys from the southern areas of the country. Historically, this region has provided much of the reserve labor force. During the colonial period, the southern region exported labor to other parts of the country and beyond. Consequently, able-bodied people (usually males) were always away from home and in transit. The southern regions played a vital role during the struggle for liberation, which was waged by the African National Congress (ANC) in South Africa and used as a training ground for the liberation fighters. For some, this factor contributed to their decision to migrate from an inhospitable south to the cities northward.[31]

In the current atmosphere of neoliberalism, whereby the government has ceased being the principal employer, finding work has become more difficult. The majority of the youthful southern migrants or "machingas" (marching boys in the Kiswahili language) are engaged in informal activities. Roughly 25,000 machingas are believed to be in the city of Dar es Salaam alone.[32] They can be found along the roadsides, but especially along Congo Street in the Kariakoo district, peddling their wares—mostly clothing, shoes, and household products. Like other vendors, they procure the merchandise from wholesalers for whom they work. Most of the wholesalers hail from the Asian and Arab communities.

It is estimated that urban unemployment has increased 140 percent over the last 10 years. In 1994, there were about 1.5 million unemployed people in Tanzania. Every year more than 400,000 youths complete school but without any prospect for formal employment due to the fact that there are only about 20,000 new jobs open each year. The industrial sector is not growing fast enough to keep pace with the ever-growing labor output and the private sector in Tanzania, which is in its infancy and incapable of absorbing the demand.[33]

Other causes have been cited for the problem of youth unemployment in Tanzania. Among them are distortions in the labor markets, which have overvalued exchange rates and distorted prices—particularly the large income differentials between the educated and the less educated. Political social pressures are credited with an overexpansion of education relative to job opportunities, and the overemphasis of educational credentials in job selection has led to unrealistic aspirations.[34] We should not overlook the legacy of colonialism, when education was restricted to the privileged few. That system was abolished in the immediate post-independence period.

At the time of independence in 1961, Tanzania faced an acute shortage of both middle- and highly skilled manpower. Thus, when drawing up the nation's first 5 Year Plan to meet these needs, the new government called for the expansion of primary school enrollment and placed heavy emphasis on the expansion of secondary and tertiary education preparation. There were also the elements of power and prestige associated with education and the belief that attaining it would lead to high-salaried white collar jobs. Unfortunately, this belief system served to undermine the larger development needs of the nation. After completing school, educated rural youth became fascinated by the fabricated opportunities in the urban centers, where they could enjoy life and connect with educated colleagues already residing there. It has also been found that parents, feeling the need for economic assistance, persuaded their educated children to become wage earners in the city. With the importance of agriculture declining, when the choice of agriculture versus the classroom was posed, it is not surprising which emerged the victor.

According to a World Bank report, 10 percent of Tanzanian households are headed by females; in the rural areas it is 5.8 percent. In Dar es Salaam alone, the rate is 13.1 percent. Abandonment and out-of-wedlock births help explain these data for the urban areas. Our youth survey found that more than one-half of the respondents (54.9 percent) indicated that they live with both parents and that only 14 percent indicated that they live with a single parent (see Appendix C). Overall, these may not be startling figures when compared to Western societies such as the United States and the Caribbean but they do point to the fact that change is taking place within traditional African civil society. With regard to poverty, the Bank estimated that 50 percent of all Tanzanians are living in households classified as poor, while 36 percent live in households classified as chronically poor. About 59 percent of the people living in rural villages are poor, while 39 percent of those in the urban areas other than Dar es Salaam are poor.[35]

With the introduction of the Human Resources Deployment Act (1983), the state attempted to curb the rural—urban migratory flow. It sought to tackle the problem of unemployment in the urban centers by redirecting the hard-to-place job seekers to the rural areas where they would become more productive. At the time of its passage, 1.4 million people were living in Dar es Salaam City with only 166,000 employed. Of that figure, 830,000 were dependent (roughly

320,000 of them schoolchildren), and 470,000 people, including youth, engaged in some kind of business in the informal sector. Rather than being seen as a sensitive policy measure, the Act by its very language had the outward appearance of blaming the victims, with the poor and unemployed seen as parasites draining the productivity of able-bodied residents. It was eventually repealed.

In the monograph, "Freedom and Rural Development," Julius Nyerere outlined a strategy to help ease the problem of urban growth and urban primacy in the city of Dar es Salaam. However, this measure was seriously contradicted by its "anti-urban" overtone and perception of urban as "parasitic." Furthermore, it did not carefully define what was unacceptable and undesirable about the urban areas.[36] The "New Growth Pole Centre" was announced as part of the second 5 Year Plan. It stated that any further industrial development was to be located in Morogoro, Dodoma, Mbeyea, Mwanza, Mtwara, Tabora, Tanga, Moshi, and Arusha. But while small-scale industrial development began to take off in these other districts, primacy nonetheless did not recede in Dar es Salaam as industries and other investments continued to relocate there. Of the 265 new industrial establishments between 1969 and 1979, 129, or 46.8, percent were located in Dar es Salaam. The result, according to Lugalla, is that the process of overurbanization in Dar has continued unabated. Approximately 33.6 percent of the nation's people engaged in manufacturing in 1988 resided in Dar es Salaam and by 1990, the greatest portion of the nation's electricity consumption was accommodated by the city.[37]

Preceding these measures was "ujamaa," a controversial policy that was highly criticized in Tanzania because of its failure to develop the nation. Between the period 1967 to 1973, President Nyerere's chief aim and concern for the development of Tanzania was the promotion of the ujamaa village policy. The initial policy stressed voluntary movement into the villages utilizing persuasive socialist techniques. Later, during the period 1974 to 1976, coercion was used to encourage villagization, the objective of which was to create ujamaa villages and to use the villages as instruments for accomplishing the broader goals and objectives of socialism.

During the second phase, 1969 to 1973, heavy emphasis was placed on expropriating a consciousness raising about the ujamaa philosophy and policy by the government throughout the country.[38] Some of the problems with the policy included the government's need to use coercion and the difficulty in measuring villagers' use of true collective work patterns. Other problems concerned the mixed and often confused messages that were conveyed to the Tanzanian people. There was strong resistance from the more prosperous farmers in the Kilimanjaro area to the north who were growers of cotton, tea, and coffee. Because the sympathies of these rich farmers rested with the city dwellers and not necessarily with the poor peasants, they were reluctant to form ujamaas in their areas and their subsequent reduction in output resulted in frequent food shortages and even famine in the mid-1970s. This in turn increased the need to import food with the accompanying effect of spiraling the nation's foreign debt obligation.[39]

By the mid-1970s, Tanzania was well on the road to economic downturn. The precipitating factors were the world prices for sisal exports and the union of Tanganyika and Zanzibar in 1964. While the union strengthened the new government's relationship with East Germany, it traumatized relations with the West and led to the termination of economic support from the West Germans. Later on, the break in relations with Britain over Rhodesia (now Zimbabwe)[40] further devastated the economy and there was the matter of rising wage rates that reduced the profitability of investments in new or expanded production. While all of this was taking place, the demand for more services and a greater redistribution of wealth was on the rise. The Arusha Declaration of 1967 could be viewed as a final effort to salvage the failing policy of ujamaa. It sought the nationalization of major economic institutions. It imposed restrictions on conspicuous consumption, progressive taxation, and the decolonization of the school curriculum. It appealed to the need for economic diversification. Most important of all, it sought to marshal the commitment to self-reliance.[41]

URBAN CRISIS AND THE GLOBAL SETTING

During the 1970s, several events jolted the international economy, carrying severe consequences for the developing countries. With the abandonment of the gold standard, the major industrial countries adopted the floating exchange rate system. On the heels of that were two major oil crises.[42] This in turn disturbed the balance of payments, inflation rates, and economic growth rates of many developing countries, and to a lesser extent, certain non-oil-producing developed countries. By the late 1970s, the economic crisis became manifested in the form of uncontrollable inflation, increased balance-of-payments difficulties, declining real per capita income, and substantial fiscal difficulties. The importation of raw materials climbed, leading to a dramatic deterioration of capital stock, spare parts, and other commodities. In 1970 the Tanzanian long-term foreign debt was $188 million. By 1994 that amount rose to $6.2 billion. All of this eventuated in economic recovery negotiations with the International Monetary Fund and the World Bank.

Scholarly observers of the Tanzanian crisis have not succeeded in convincing the leading international financial institutions that the root cause of the crisis is the legacy of colonialism and neo-colonialism in the form economic globalization. The Bretton Woods twins, or the IMF and the World Bank's, explanation for Tanzania's economic crisis centers around internal matters such as insufficient production incentive and poor marketing facilities, inadequate resources directed toward agriculture versus industry, and the excessive growth of the public sector leading to increased government spending and related inflationary pressure. As a result the financial institutions insist on their usual conditionalities, including the devaluation of the Tanzanian shilling, the imposition of fees for secondary schooling, and an end to subsidies for fertilizers.[43] Tanzania's recovery efforts have primarily concerned shifting income protection and other resources away from urban earners to the rural population. Structural reforms have meant adjusting the economy to efficiently manage balance of payments, reduce the fiscal deficits, increase economic efficiency, and encourage private-sector investments and export-oriented production. Major measures have included control of money supply, devaluation of local currency, reduction of the public's borrowing, and government expenditure, especially in the social sector. These were supplemented by other externally imposed measures, namely trade liberalization, privatization, and the deregulation of laws protecting job security.[44]

In the area of health care, because of unlivable wages and unbearable work conditions, demoralized health workers are now reacting bitterly against the state. Doctors' strikes and nurse go-slows, events uncharacteristic in Tanzania's health sector, became common in the 1990s. The state acted swiftly in 1991, using the well-trained Field Force Police Unit to end the doctors' strike at Muhimbili Medical Centre in Dar es Salaam, the country's largest facility. The police unit beat them and their families and removed them by force from hospital-owned housing. Growing hostility between the state and health personnel has worsened the delivery of health services even further.[45] Throughout sub-Saharan Africa, the policy debate in health care has shifted from demand-oriented questions on what the population needs and what is feasible and effective to meet them, toward supply-oriented questions of what is affordable and cost effective.

Extending the discussion on the impact of SAPs, Lugalla explains that some children are dropping out of school to assist in the household economy through involvement in petty trading activities.[46] Some less fortunate are subject to abandonment, which has led to Tanzania's street children problem. It would be inaccurate to say that SAPs have been instrumental in causing all of these problems, as some of these problems are long standing. SAPs have only intensified them and highlighted the government's inability to effect the policies necessary to address the problems.

Omari (1991) does not fail to consider the role of the political economy to understand the rise of prostitution, school dropouts, and other social problems that plague the urban areas. He quickly points to the declining importance of traditional institutions in the body culture that included the elaborate age-grade system among the Maasai, youth communities among Nyakyusan Obusoka, and initiation rites and institutions like Mshitu-ngasu among the Pare. Historically, these institutions were vital for imparting the societally determined values to the young. In the advent and maturing of Western religions and institutions, there has been an appreciable decline of indigenous culture, not to mention traditional family lifestyles. Omari bemoans that "most of the people under the age of forty years who have gone through modern education do not know much of this cultural background."[47]

Colonialism, race, and urbanization have played out interestingly in Tanzania. In fact, throughout the black diaspora where there was colonialism—despite the

remaining black majorities—the legacy of race is inseparable. Upon examining residential infrastructure, one will discover that the design of the colonial towns was
planned by and for Europeans. Lugalla notes that "the towns were nonindustrial
adding that their relationship with rural Tanzania was exploitative and parasitic
rather than generative. Hence, they enhanced rural underdevelopment and poverty
instead of prosperity and good standards of living."[48] In the countryside, this blue-
print has served as an impetus for rural–urban migration. Racial class segregation
became evident by the landscape: the physical layout reflected the social distances
of hierarchic colonial social organization. Europeans lived in low-density suburbs in
large, well-built houses with expensive gardens and full recreational amenities. They
occupied such areas as Oyster Bay in Dar es Salaam, Gangilonga in Iringa, and Ki-
jongi in Arusha. Locals called these areas "uzunguni," or white European areas.
Asian Indians lived in Upanga, also known by the Kiswahili name, "uhindini,"
meaning an area of moderate density. Poor Africans were left to reside in high-den-
sity, impoverished, unplanned settlements like Ilala and Magomeni.[49] This residential structuring remains intact today except that the wealthiest Tanzanians have replaced many of the European foreigners in the affluent areas.

     The disruptive force of colonialism cannot be glossed over when analyzing Tan-
zania's current urban condition. That structure is credited with the introduction of
other destabilizing forces such as rural and urban capitalism and an economic system based on commodity production. It inspired rural-to-urban migration and imposed a system of racial and ethnic stratification that was unknown to indigenous
Africans. Independence, and the leadership of the nationalist–socialist Julius
Nyerere, helped infuse Tanzanians with a sense of self-reliance, cultural pride, and
moral commitment that strengthened them in the wake of abject poverty. As we
have discussed, in the face of international pressure and insurmountable hardship,
great philosophies and nationalist ideals are often forced to succumb. With the onset
of world recession and the expansion of economic globalization, rural-to-urban migration in Tanzania, which had begun as a flurry, was developing into a storm.

     From 1989 to the present, not quite a decade, the changes to Tanzania's urban
districts have been rapid. With the introduction of television in 1994 and other technologies, widespread changes are inevitable. A 1996 survey of urban Tanzanian
households showed that 6 percent owned a television set—an increase of 5 percent
since the 1991 survey. This reflects the introduction of three television stations in
the interim of the two surveys.[50] Unofficial surveys have found that television is
concentrated in the urban areas and that social class is the determining factor as to
ownership. Seventy percent of Tanzanians live in squatter settlements and of the
remaining 30 percent, one-half live in better housing. It is that other half who tend
to own televisions. A number of pubs in the squatter settlements have television sets
and that is where many of the poor and working-class residents go to watch. Three
television networks are privately owned: one (Independent Television Network) by
a black Tanzanian; the other two (Coastal Television Network and Dar es Salaam
Television Network) are Asian-owned. As expected, these new networks are heav-

ily influenced by the West. CNN and MTV are featured alongside other programs, for which commercials are unedited. Shifting to Tanzania's next-door neighbor, Kenya, "the gem of the West" will provide us the opportunity to compare and better appreciate the extent of Tanzania's urban upheaval.

Despite the small sample size, our survey of Tanzanian youth enlightened us about the struggles of young people in that changing society and the extent of their feelings of powerlessness and frustration in their quest for a better life. In that regard, 92.2 percent felt that their government could do more to assist them. For the greatest part, youth believe that the role of the police is to protect and serve the community; however, 31.3 percent disagreed that the police treat all equally and fairly. Recent conflicts in the city of Dar es Salaam between the police and the machingas, their harassment of vagrants, and their treatment of striking medical personnel and university students have contributed to the youths' growing mistrust of the police. Most of the youth (82.7 percent) believed that, in general, they have little control over their environment. On the question of their ability to change things that are happening around them, there appeared to be some uncertainty, or at least mixed emotions (see Appendix C). One is better able to appreciate their sentiments by examining youths' ranking of selected social problems. AIDS, alongside unemployment and poverty, were atop their list. While the majority indicated not having experienced arrest, at least 25.7 percent admitted having friends who were arrested.

KENYA

To debate Kenya's status as the shining star of East Africa, given the attention afforded it during the colonial and post-colonial period compared with its immediate neighbors, would be a meaningless exercise. Kenya's "favorite nation" status in the eyes of the West can be attributed not only to President Jomo Kenyatta's political posturing, but unequivocally to his successor, Daniel arap Moi's unmistaken embrace of overzealous Western investors. This elite has occupied the presidency since 1978, following the death of Kenyatta. Solidifying Moi's rule has been his strong-arm tactics, which are codified by a constitution that embraces colonial-era laws that give the president sweeping powers to jail dissidents, ban political parties, and break up political demonstrations. He has not hesitated to use brute force to subdue popular protest by students and workers against the government. President Moi's uninhibited disdain for the democratic process of open and fair elections finally gave way to internal and international pressure, and in 1992, Kenya's multi-party system was voted into law. The country's first multi-party elections took place on December 29, 1992. Because Moi was accused of using undemocratic tactics in the past, prominent foreign observers were called in for the 1992 elections. Despite allegations that he had provoked ethnic violence to ensure his victory, Moi was reelected for a fourth term. More significant than Moi's victory was the fact that the political status quo was finally turned upside down. It signaled the loosening but not the end to Daniel arap Moi's grip on the country and future elections. Since the 1992 election, the nation's politics have become more entrenched in tribal loyalties and conflict and competition for patronage. In this environment, the struggle for empowerment by Kenya's powerless has become that much more formidable. Macharia (1997) argues that close ties to the West have accelerated class formation in the last 30 years. Kenya's growth fell from 7 percent in the 1970s to about 3 percent in the 1980s as a result of the structural adjustment policies imposed by IMF and the World Bank.[51] Unemployment and squatter settlements in the urban areas proliferated.

Quite similar to other African cities, Nairobi experienced rapid increase in rural-to-urban migration after independence. Accompanying this was the proliferation of small-scale trade and urban petty-commodity production, including nonserviced and unauthorized housing.[52] The situation inherited at the time of independence was that of a city designed for capitalist expansion and highly segregated by race and income with extreme inequalities in the level of services provided in different areas.[53] Rapid rural-to-urban migration that followed averaged 5.4 percent per annum in the first decade and 7.9 percent per annum in the second decade after independence. Although Kenya has productive agricultural regions, more than half of the country is arid or semi-arid. Currently, the total population is 24 million. During the 1970s, Kenya's 4 percent annual population growth rate was considered the highest in the world. Fortunately, the response by international health and family-planning nongovernmental organizations helped bring down the growth rate to below 4 percent, where it presently stands. However, work must continue in order to sustain a tolerable population growth rate. What is important, though, is that rapid population growth together with the shortage of cultivable land hastened the migration to Nairobi and, to a lesser degree, to the city of Mombasa. While the overall population growth rate in Kenya was increasing since 1962, it was taking place concomitant with an even faster urban growth rate. The annual urban growth rate increased from 671,000 in 1962 to 1.082 million in 1969, growing at the rate of 7.1 percent per annum. In 1969 this represented 9.9 percent of the total population. Nairobi continues to have the largest share of urban residents and presently between 9 million and 10 million (over one-fourth) of the nation's population live in urban centers.[54] During the colonial era, migration was restricted, but with the relaxation of these laws in 1963 following independence, the great urban leap forward was under way.

THE CITY OF NAIROBI AND THE URBAN CRISIS

The city of Nairobi, with an estimated population of 2.5 million, was started as a colonial railway workshop in the late 1890s. The British, who liked Nairobi's cool climate, moved the capital from Mombasa, located along the coast, to Nairobi in

1920. Marked by skyscrapers and Western-designed motorways, the city's prosperous appearance is contradicted by massive squatter settlements and an informal economy. Nairobi's roadways and general infrastructure, once the envy of others in the region, are rapidly deteriorating due to a combination of government corruption and poor maintenance. The more affluent suburbs, concentrated in the west and south of the city, are a legacy of colonial town planning; the deprived neighborhoods occupy most of the eastern and northeastern parts of the city. Clusters of the urban poor can be found in the squatter settlements of Mathare Valley, Korogocho, Mukuru, Kayaba, Fuala, and Kibera.[55] The infrastructure in the squatter settlements is appalling. Roads, sewerage, waste disposal, lighting, and drainage are dilapidated or nonexistent. Dwellings comprise old stone buildings or semipermanent ones made of mud or cardboard boxes. Mathare Valley, the most densely populated area in the country, has become an international symbol of misery and impoverishment. In 1998, nearly two-thirds of the city's population were poor with only a handful of them educated. The young and those older than 45 are the most vulnerable, and women and single mothers tend to be poorer than their male counterparts. Within a short time, rapid urbanization has devastated the city's and the state's ability to meet rising demands. Consequently, at least 50 percent of Nairobi's population is struggling to make ends meet and even to survive in the informal sector commonly referred to as jua kali, or "hot sun." According to Macharia, the term comes from the Kiswahili language and refers to the open (roofless) locations where various self-employed business activities like metal art-working, welding, and the hawking of various commercial goods take place.

Colonial Nairobi, like the city of Dar es Salaam in Tanzania, began as a city with distinct racial ethnic categories. There were European whites, followed by Asians, Arabs, and Africans. Urban space was allocated along racial lines. This colonial structure was not altered when the independent government came into power. Instead, black elites picked up where the Europeans left off. In fact, when one considers the issues of class configuration, ethnic mix, and the racial divide, Nairobi closely resembles its neighbor, Dar es Salaam. Insofar as the interethnic mix is concerned, Asian Indians represent the largest foreign group, followed by Arabs and a small, white, mostly British elite. While they constitute only 1 percent of the overall population, Asians dominate the economy. Nearly 80 percent of retail businesses are owned by Asians, and more than 25 percent of the garment firms are Asian-owned.[56] Accounting for this is their tradition as an urban people—versus the indigenous Africans—and their successful accumulation of capital and strong familial, political, and professional networks.

Another explanation for the rapid urban migration is the unbearable rural living conditions that began in the 1980s. Throughout the 1980s, the country's environment was plagued with soil erosion, a depletion of water resources, drought, and food shortages. Poor land management, a constant problem, did not help. With the collapse of the primary export commodities on the international market—including coffee, tea, cotton, and tobacco—a drastic decline in rural incomes and open joblessness set in as fewer laborers were needed in the exportation of agriculture. According to Mary Kinyanjui (1994), the process of deagrarianization deprived large numbers of men and women of their social, cultural, and economic autonomy. These displaced persons began to trek to the urban centers, which in their estimation was the logical place to search for an alternative livelihood. It is important to add that as education spread to the rural areas during the post-independence period, rural school dropouts were unable to locate jobs. They too joined the urban trek.[57] Rapid migration to Kenya's central cities was triggered by the same structural forces that gripped Tanzania, namely international recession, excessive borrowing, a severe decline in trade, and consequently, balance of payments deficits. Kenya's long-term debt went from US $409 million in 1970 to $6.1 billion in 1994.[58]

YOUTH, CRISIS, AND THE URBAN FUTURE

A major frustration for the deagrarianized migrants is the unavailability of work once they arrive in the cities. Unemployment is a perennial problem in Kenya that is exacerbated by population trends of high fertility rates. That is where the jua kali steps in. It would be a mistake to assume that entry into the informal sector is automatic. Life is hard for newcomers to the city, and it is important for them to maintain their rural ties and connections (at least for food supplies), as getting situated in the informal economy is not automatic.[59] Frustration on the part of the general population is one thing; the germination of frustration by youth who constitute a significant portion of the population is yet another. Our survey of youth from the city of Nairobi found that 79.2 percent were unemployed. While many of the respondents to our survey were not actively looking for work, on the question that asked them to rank social problems, unemployment ranked the highest (see Appendix C).

A United Nations Population Division prediction at the start of the 1980s was that Kenya's youth population would increase from 2.9 million to 7.8 million between 1980 and 2000, representing an increase of 149.1 percent.[60] That prediction was on the mark, as the UNDP Population Division updates for 2000 show that 44 percent of Kenya's population are youth. This has serious implications for unemployment nationally, but as we will see, especially so for the central cities. In 1986 the government released a Sessional Paper No. 2 on "Unemployment" that presented what it perceived to be the central causes behind the problem:

Rapid growth of the population and the consequent growth of the labor force; the inability of the economy to grow at a rate that would stimulate enough employment creation to absorb all job seekers; job selectivity among school leavers; seasonality of jobs; skills imbalance which has resulted in vacancies co-existing with surplus labor; inappropriate technological applications and failure of development programmes to focus more sharply on areas with greater employment creation potential.[61]

A major setback in the government's ability to provide needed employment is the discrepancy between the amount of monetary resources expected to be invested in the modernization sector versus the amount allocated to replace ageing capital. In that respect, only 1.4 million jobs were anticipated between 1984 and 2000, which would leave 6 million workers—40 percent of the labor force—without jobs by the year 2000. Evidently the situation is more severe than predicted. Updated statistics from the UNDP Population Division and the International Labour Organization indicate that nearly 50 percent of the nation's population are unemployed or fall outside the formal labor sector. The state's concentration on modernization and capital-intensive investment has been at the expense of the rural area development. The other major problem facing Kenya is the fact that most of its individual output is owned and controlled by foreign transnational corporations that utilize capital-intensive modes of production. This functions contrary to the country's surplus labor problem, ergo little if any new employment has been achieved. The net effect of these conditions is the spiraling youth unemployment problem. Each year, more than 260,000 youthful school dropouts join the labor force; however, only a disappointing 23 percent, or 60,000, are actually placed.[62] The only alternative for them is the informal sector where job creation is relatively cheaper and where wages are low and flexible. Paradoxically, the Kenyan government, not unlike most other states, recognizes the important role of the informal sector, yet it seeks to deny its existence and limit it through the constant harassment of its participants.[63]

It is necessary to reiterate that 85 percent of Kenyans still live and work in the rural areas, with 75 percent of that population engaged in farming and pastoralism. However, the attitudes of youth, as we saw in the case of Tanzania, are rapidly shifting away from this lifestyle and they are outrightly coming to despise agrarian work. They and their families have fixed their aspirations around white collar jobs that are available only in the urban areas. The state's concentration on modernization capabilities has not helped stem the migration crisis; in fact it continues to reinforce the idea of urban prominence. Rapid urbanization and related social problems of prostitution and crime erupt as these rural-to-urban migrants fail to procure the expected employment and other rewards in the cities. As rural migrants rush to the big city it only contributes to higher rates of unemployment. Reality soon sets in that economic globalization is steadily eroding the relevance of school certificates and diplomas as steppingstones to formal employment in the private and public sectors. Making matters worse, Nzoma (1984) and Pinheiro (1993) discuss the fact that newcomers feel frustrated when confronted with the reality of the high costs of living in the city and the absence of work. They reported that the Kenyan government was wholeheartedly involved in the import of expatriates (so-called experts) to do jobs that might otherwise go to nationals.[64]

In Kenya, concern for survival has placed enormous pressure on traditional family life and values in the rural areas and particularly in the cities. Although the majority of youth from our survey (67.9 percent) responded that they live with both parents, this traditional model is currently being challenged. Women and children constitute the majority of the poor—a sector that was once predominantly male—and, as such, they must engage in various informal activities for survival. Due to the breakdown of key social control mechanisms, including traditional values and the family structure, alongside the impersonality of urban life and life in the squatter settlements, many youth are forced into street gangs, violence, and crime.

Obudho and Owuor (1994) found that the major thrust of crimes committed fall into the category of bodily assaults, robbery, break-ins, and auto thefts. Offenses such as manslaughter and dangerous drug offenses are, however, less common.[65] Two items from our youth survey probed the youths' criminal activity. While the majority indicated that they had never been arrested, that same majority (65.3 percent) indicated that they had friends who experienced arrest. Whether or not these respondents were honest when answering the first question, the fact that so many had friends who were arrested corroborates Obudho and Owuor's findings about the rising urban crime problem.

Nairobi's streets are indeed "mean streets," a picture that has characterized Nairobi for quite some time. Visitors and nationals alike must be constantly on alert for hustlers and petty thieves. Compared to Dar es Salaam, Tanzania's central city, Nairobi is correctly described as patterned along the lines of a major Western city in terms of its physical layout, the hustle and bustle, and the added distraction of crime and violence However, the pace of criminal activity, though greater than Dar es Salaam, is still appreciably less than that typically found in many Western inner cities when homicide rates, the drug subculture, and youth gang violence are taken into account. Because Nairobi is the more cosmopolitan and tourist-oriented city with a developed communications technology, the appurtenances of Western society are far more visible there than in Dar es Salaam.

CONCLUSION

Ironically, the urban crisis now brewing in East Africa is beginning to resemble the Caribbean and possibly the United States. However, compared to the Caribbean, the pace of Western influence in East Africa is much slower but steady. Unlike their counterparts in the Caribbean, East Africa's poor and working class do not have relatives abroad in the United States and Canada who can send barrels filled with material symbols of the Western good life. Thus, they have not become fully immersed into the Western-based consumer subculture.

Despite the political differences that separated them earlier in their independence histories, parallels can now be drawn between Tanzania and Kenya insofar as their internal problems are concerned and specifically, their urban condition. The followers of ujamaa and scientific socialism appear to be in the race to catch up. By any reasonable account, the city of Dar es Salaam appears to be well on its way to a convergence with Nairobi. An immediate internal threat they share is the fact that their youth populations are in the throes of crisis and that they are rapidly being drawn into the ranks of the powerless. As we have posited, such a situation casts an ominous cloud over the future of these regions and their people. Unlike the United States, yet similar to the Caribbean, the black masses from these East African regions constitute the majority. Majority status, as we have already noted, is a meaningless indicator of group status if the group in question is not permitted to share power or is without access to those vital institutional links to power within the society. In Kenya and Tanzania, a minority of Asian Indians control major sectors of the economy. Recently in Tanzania, inter-ethnic tension has flared between Asian Indians and Africans. This experience alone links Tanzanians to their African American and Caribbean counterparts.

Tajudeen Abdul Raheem is General Secretary of the Global Pan African Movement, which was formed in 1992 and is headquartered in Kampala, Uganda. At a talk he gave in New York City in November 1997, Dr. Raheem pointed out that the problem for Africa is not poverty. Africa is wealthy—it is the Africans who are poor. It is poverty not strictly in economic terms but of outlook, identity, and vision that continues to pull its youngest and brightest sons and daughters into the ranks of the powerless. East Africa is just one region on the continent where this prevails. How to get Africa and the Africans moving *again* should be center stage in the international debate. Emphasis is placed on *again* in recognition of Africa's culturally rich history that predates the development of European civilization.

Up to this point we have examined the urban situation for the United States, the Caribbean, and East Africa. In the chapter that follows, the three regions are compared.

NOTES

1. Andrew Hacker, *Two Nations: Black and White, Separate, Hostile, Unequal* (New York: Ballantine Books, 1992), 33; These views permeate the feature article by Jeffery Goldberg, "Their Africa Problem and Ours," *The New York Times Magazine* (March 2, 1997).

2. Kenneth Watts, *The Courier* (No. 131, Jan.–Feb., 1992), 62; also, Saitiel Kulaba, "Local Government and the Management of Urban Services in Tanzania," in Richard E. Stren and Rodney R. White (eds.), *African Cities in Crisis* (Boulder Colorado: Westview Press, 1989), 206–245.

3. Rodney R. White, "The Influence of Environmental and Economic Factors on the Urban Crisis," in Stren and White, *African Cities in Crisis*; also, Saitiel Kulaba, "Local Government and the Management of Urban Services in Tanzania," pages 206–245.

4. Carolyn Somerville, "Reaction and Resistance: Confronting Economic Crisis, Structural Adjustment, and Devaluation in Dakar, Senegal," in Charles Green, *Globalization and Survival in the Black Diaspora: The New Urban Challenge* (Albany, N.Y.: SUNY Press, 1997).

5. A special issue of *National Geographic* is devoted to this subject. See "Global Culture," *National Geographic* (Vol. 196, No. 2 (August, 1999).

6. External debts data for sub-Saharan Africa. World Debt Tables, October 1994–December 1995, and 1996, Vol. 2. The World Bank.

7. Kjell J. Havnevik (ed.), *The IMF and The World Bank In Africa* (Sweden, Ekblad Co.: 1987) (see Introduction by Havnevik, 13).

8. Havnevik (ed.), *The IMF and The World Bank In Africa*, 14.

9. Horace Campbell, "U.S. Partnership or Domination of Africa: Reflections on the Discussions over the Africa Growth and Opportunity Bill" (International Committee of the Black Radical Congress, February 10, 1999).

10. Philip L. Kilbride and Janet C. Kilbride, *Changing Family Life in East Africa* (Nairobi, Kenya: Gideon and Were Press, 1990). To this foursome has been added the states of Rwanda and Burundi (see: J. P. L. Lugalla; Omari and Shaidi include Zambia and Botswana) (see C. K. Omari and L. P. Shaidi [eds.], Social Problems in Eastern Africa. Dar es Salaam: University of Dar es Salaam Press, 1991).

11. Omari and Shaidi, *Social Problems in Eastern Africa*, 152.

12. Kilbride and Kilbride, *Changing Family Life in East Africa*, 50.

13. J. Kayere, "Rural Female Roles: Some Reflections" (1980) cited in Kilbride and Kilbride, *Changing Family Life in East Africa*, 16–17.

14. To compare the political economies of Kenya and Tanzania, see O'Neill and Mustafa (eds.), *Capitalism, Socialism and the Development Crisis in Tanzania*. (Aldershot, England: Averbury, 1990, xi, 15); Omari and Shaidi, *Social Problems in Eastern Africa;* Kilbride and Kilbride, *Changing Family Life in East Africa*; David Bevan, Arne Bigsten, Paul Collier, and Jan W. Gunning, *East African Lessons on Economic Liberalization* (London: Trade Policy Research Centre, 1987 (chapter 1, "Kenyan and Tanzanian Economies Compared," 2–15).

15. For a comprehensive treatment of this, see John Iliffe's discussion in "A Modern History of Tanganyika" (Cambridge: Cambridge University Press, 1979); also Joe L. P. Lugalla, *Crisis, Urbanization, and Urban Poverty in Tanzania: A Study of Urban Poverty and Survival Politics* (Lanham, Md.: University Press of America, 1995); also, R. H. Sabot, *Economic Development and Urban Migration in Tanzania, 1900–1971* (Oxford, U.K.: Oxford University Press, 1979).

16. O'Neill and Mustafa, *Capitalism, Socialism and the Development Crisis in Tanzania* (Introduction by O'Neill and Mustafa, p. 16).

17. O'Neill and Mustafa, *Capitalism, Socialism and the Development Crisis in Tanzania*, 13–14.

18. G. A. Bennars, "African Youth in the 1980s Documentation," in *Basic Education Resource Centre Bulletin* (Vol. 12, 1985), 8.

19. Eduard Bos, et al., World Population Projections, 1994–1995 (Washington, D.C.: A World Bank Book); also, Population for Sub-Saharan Africa. World Urbanization Prospects: The 1996 Revision. United Nations Population Division (May 1997).

20. David Bevan, et al., *East African Lessons*, 1–3, 18.

21. O'Neill and Mustafa, *Capitalism*, 1–3.

22. David Bevan, et al., *East African Lessons*, p. 18.

23. O'Neill and Mustafa, *Capitalism*, xi–xii; and Lugalla, *Crisis*.

24. O'Neill and Mustafa, *Capitalism*, xii.

25. In 1977, TANU (Tanganyika African National Union) and the Afro–Shirazi Party (the Zanzibaran central party) amalgamated to form Chama Cha Mapinduzi, or CCM.

26. Lugalla, *Crisis*, 21; Lugalla, "Where Do the Majority Live in Tanzania: Why and How?" in Charles Green (ed.), *Globalization and Survival in the Black Diaspora*, 61.

27. Lugalla, "Where Do the Majority Live in Tanzania?"

28. "Dalla-dalla" is a nickname for the buses that since 1983 have operated informally and transport people in Dar es Salaam. They have eased the burden on the official city transportation company, Usafiri Dar es Salaam (UDA). The nickname came from a Tanzanian five shilling coin, which resembles the American silver dollar. The buses got this name because they used to charge five Tanzanian shillings for fare. See Lugalla, *Crisis*, 1995, 114.

29. The Bank's report recognized Tanzania as one of the poorest countries in the world and discusses wealth inequality. See World Bank, 1993, Tanzania: A Poverty Profile (Draft Report No. 12298), Washington, D.C.; Lugalla, *Crisis*, 127–129; M. S. Bagachwa (ed.), *Poverty Alleviation in Dar es Salaam* (Dar es Salaam: University of Dar es Salaam Press, 1994).

30. Lugalla, *Crisis*, 132, 138, 142, 152.

31. Dorothy A. Mbilinyi and Cuthbert K. Omari, *Rural–Urban Migration and Poverty Alleviation in Tanzania* (Dar es Salaam: University of Dar es Salaam Press, 1996), 6.

32. C. K. Omari and L. P. Shaidi (eds.), *Social Problems in Eastern Africa* (Dar es Salaam: University of Dar es Salaam Press, 1991) (see chapter 2 by Omari, "Some Youth Social Problems in Tanzania," 12–25).

33. Omari and Shaidi, *Social Problems*, 20.

34. George A. Malekela, "Educated Youth Unemployment in Tanzania," in Omari and Shaidi, *Social Problems*, 47.

35. World Bank, "Tanzania: A Poverty Profile" (Draft Report No. 12298, 1993), Washington, D.C.

36. Julius K. Nyerere, "Freedom and Development" (originally a policy booklet presented October 1968) in *Man And Development* (London: Oxford University Press, 1974), 25–39.

37. Lugalla, *Crisis*, 30.

38. Rukhsana A. Siddiqui, "Socialism and the Ujamaa Ideology," in O'Neill and Mustafa, *Capitalism*, 27, 38.

39. Siddiqui in *Capitalism*, 44.

40. Independent Tanzania has always taken an active and supportive stance on behalf of liberation struggles by victims around the world.

41. Cited in Rukhsana A. Siddiqui's article in *Capitalism*, 49.

42. J. Wagao, "Beyond the International Monetary Fund Package in Tanzania," in Omari and Shaidi, *Social Problems*, 224.

43. Salvator Rugumisa, *A Review of the Tanzanian Economic Recovery Programme*. (Research Report No. 1, 1989, Tanzanian Development Research Group); also, *Daily News*, "Salient Tips on Dar's ERP II, March 9, 1990); also, see Lugalla, "The Impact of Structural Adjustment Policies on Women and Children's Health in Tanzania," in *Review of African Political Economy*, No. 63:43–53, 1995), 44.

44. Lugalla, *Crisis*, 45.

45. Lugalla, *Crisis*, 47, 51–52.

46. Lugalla, *Crisis*.

47. Omari and Shaidi, *Social Problems*.

48. Lugalla, *Crisis*, 62.

49. Lugalla, *Crisis,* 63.

50. Tanzania Demographic & Health Survey, 1996. Bureau of Statistics, Planning Commission, Dar es Salaam and Macro International Inc., Calverton, Maryland, USA, August 1997.

51. Kinuthia Macharia, in Green, *Globalization and Survival,* 143.

52. Diana Lee-Smith, "Urban Management in Nairobi: A Case Study of the Matatu Mode of Public Transportation," in Stren and White, *African Cities in Crisis,* 276.

53. Mary Kinyanjui, "Entrepreneurs in the Diaspora: Cultural Foundations of Poverty Alleviation" (unpublished version, 1994) University of Nairobi. Page 13 cites works by Manuel Castells, *The Urban Question* (1977) and David Harvey, *Social Justice and the City* (1973), which discuss how Third World countries are a product of the expansionary nature of the world capitalist system.

54. These figures were estimated by Lee-Smith, "Urban Management in Nairobi," 281; see also, Kinthia Macharia, *Social and Political Dynamics of the Informal Economy in African Cities* (Lanham, Maryland: University Press of America, 1997), 26. The UNDP confirmed these figures for 2000.

55. Mary Kinyanjui, "Entrepreneurs in the Diaspora," 1.

56. Dorothy McCormick, et al., "Networks, Markets and Growth in Nairobi's Garment Industry: Barriers to Growth" (ICEG Final Report, Nairobi, 1994).

57. Mary Kinyanjui, "Entrepreneurs in the Diaspora," 3, 4.

58. World Debt Tables, October 1994–1995. The World Bank.

59. Macharia discusses the size of Nairobi's jua kali in Green, *Globalization and Survival.*

60. Charles B. K. Nzioka, "The Youth Unemployment Problem in Kenya" in Omari and Shaidi, *Social Problems,* 58.

61. Republic of Kenya, "Sessional Paper No. 2 on Unemployment" (Nairobi Government Press, 1985). 7; ILO Report, "Employment, Incomes and Inequality: A Strategy for Increasing Productive Employment in Kenya" (Geneva, 1972), 2.

62. R. A. Obudho and S. O. Owuor, "Urbanization and Crime in Kenya," in Isaac O. Albert, J. Adisa, T. Agbola, and G. Herault (eds.) *Urban Management and Urban Violence in Africa,* Vol. 2. (Ibadan, Nigeria: IFRA Press, 1994), 41–51.

63. Obudho and Owuor, "Urbanization and Crime in Kenya."

64. N. D. Nzoma, "The Socio-economic Consequence of Kenya's Changed Formal Education" (1984), 9 (cited in Charles B. K. Nzioka, "The Youth Unemployment Problem in Kenya," pages 61–65).

65. Obudho and Owuor, "Urbanization and Crime in Kenya," 41–45.

5

The Urban Problem: A Comparative View

To alert world public opinion about the aspirations of young people and to ensure that they participate more actively in economic and social development and in the construction of peace. UNESCO[1]

Youth, or the future generation, are major players in the urban crisis in the black diaspora. Their empowerment is conditioned on a clear understanding and inter-pretation of their perception of the problems in their environment as well as their aspirations for the future. This would underscore the need for comparative data of youth cross culturally.

In this chapter, data from the surveys administered to youth are presented and compared, with special attention directed to the similarities, the differences, and the pace of the crisis. We compare the Caribbean and the United States and East Africa and the United States. Comparative data for the Caribbean and East Africa are also analyzed and presented. The survey items covered a number of areas (see appendix A). Selected for this analysis were items related to the issues of power-lessness, social integration, and social dislocation.

Modern democracies promote the idea that the primary concern of law en-forcement personnel should be to protect all citizens equally regardless of race, ethnicity, class, or religious orientation. But in many democracies throughout the modern world (developed and developing nations alike), this precept is starkly contradicted. Police in many free societies are considered to be the eyes and ears of the state and the protectors of the rights and privileges of the elite. Some law enforcement personnel succumb to corruption and rationalize their misdeeds on account of their meager wages. Several survey items pertaining to the role of the police were included for that reason. Because of their high visibility in the urban ghettos, the police are a potential source of support and encouragement for young people. But they can also serve as the inhibitors of positive personal development and responsible citizenship. For these reasons, it was important to explore youths'

111

perception of the police in their communities and determine the effect on youth empowerment.

Table 5.1 presents frequency distributions for the United States and the Caribbean for several survey items related to the powerlessness factor. Among these are two items that pertain to the police role in the community and their treatment of residents. Of the Caribbean respondents, 87.6 percent—compared to 71.3 percent of the U.S. sample—agreed that the police are necessary for the security and protection of residents. Differences, while small, might be explained by the longer history of exploitation and abuse by white police officers in the African American community. As a result, African Americans appear to be more suspicious and cynical about the role of the police in their neighborhoods. When asked whether the police treat everybody equally, 75.8 percent Caribbean and 67.6 percent United States disagreed. On the other hand, Table 5.2 shows that only 38.5 percent of the East Africans disagreed with the question.

Table 5.1. Comparing Powerlessness between United States and Caribbean Respondents

	United States				Caribbean			
	Agree[a]	Disagree[b]	No opinion	Total N	Agree	Disagree	No opinion	Total N
Adult care	243	14	43	300	148	32	43	223
	(81.0)	(4.7)	(14.3)	(100.0)	(66.4)	(14.3)	(19.3)	(100.0)
Government help	261	10	30	301	213	7	15	235
	(86.7)	(3.3)	(10.0)	(100.0)	(90.6)	(3.0)	(6.4)	(100.0)
Police protection	214	39	47	300	197	12	16	225
	(71.3)	(13.0)	(15.7)	(100.0)	(87.6)	(5.3)	(7.1)	(100.0)
Police treatment	15	100	33	148	15	91	14	120
	(10.1)	(67.6)	(22.3)	(100.0)	(12.5)	(75.8)	(11.7)	(100.0)
Fair trial	79	92	77	248	58	36	52	146
	(31.9)	(37.1)	(31.0)	(100.0)	(39.7)	(24.7)	(35.6)	(100.0)
No youth control	67	202	35	304	36	168	22	226
	(22.0)	(66.4)	(11.5)	(100.0)	(15.9)	(74.3)	(9.7)	(100.0)
Your ability to change	212	33	60	305	184	13	28	225
	(69.5)	(10.8)	(19.7)	(100.0)	(81.8)	(5.8)	(12.4)	(100.0)

NOTE: Numbers in parentheses are percentages.
a) Agree denotes two response categories: strongly agree and agree.
b) Disagree denotes two response categories: strongly disagree and disagree.

Table 5.2. Comparing Powerlessness between United States and Eastern African Respondents

	United States				Africa			
	Agree[a]	Disagree[b]	No opinion	Total N	Agree	Disagree	No opinion	Total N
Adult care	243 (81.0)	14 (4.7)	43 (14.3)	300 (100.0)	93 (82.3)	8 (7.1)	12 (10.6)	113 (100.0)
Government help	261 (86.7)	10 (3.3)	30 (10.0)	301 (100.0)	104 (91.2)	7 (6.1)	3 (2.6)	114 (100.0)
Police protection	214 (71.3)	39 (13.0)	47 (15.7)	300 (100.0)	111 (93.3)	6 (5.0)	2 (1.7)	119 (100.0)
Police treatment	15 (10.1)	100 (67.6)	33 (22.3)	148 (100.0)	52 (57.1)	35 (38.5)	4 (4.4)	91 (100.0)
Fair trial	79 (31.9)	92 (37.1)	77 (31.0)	248 (100.0)	56 (49.6)	28 (24.8)	29 (25.7)	113 (100.0)
No youth control	67 (22.0)	202 (66.4)	35 (11.5)	304 (100.0)	56 (45.9)	41 (33.6)	25 (20.5)	122 (100.0)
Your ability to change	212 (69.5)	33 (10.8)	60 (19.7)	305 (100.0)	59 (62.8)	25 (26.6)	10 (10.6)	94 (100.0)

NOTE: Numbers in parentheses are percentages.
a) Agree denotes two response categories: strongly agree and agree.
b) Disagree denotes two response categories: strongly disagree and disagree.

Institutionalized racism in the United States cannot be overlooked in explaining these differences. As socioeconomic conditions continue to deteriorate in the Caribbean, and more and more people from the lower strata are forced to resort to socially unacceptable means of survival, the expectation is that relations between them and the police will continue to deteriorate. To understand the discrepancy between East African respondents on this question, it will be necessary to explore the *internal* territorial data (see appendix C). Contributing to this discrepancy in the East African sample is Tanzania, where 67.2 percent were in agreement that they received fair treatment from police versus 29.2 percent of the Kenyans. Political and historical factors that were raised in chapter 4 provide some explanation for this finding. Whereas the pernicious regime of President Daniel arap Moi since 1978 has guaranteed a system of preferential treatment for the Kenyan elite and disdain for the poor and working classes, this does not reflect the experience of independent Tanzania. However, intolerance on the part of the Tanzanian state is steadily increasing

as people from the lower strata struggle to adapt to economic hardship resulting from liberalization and privatization policies imposed since the mid-1980s.
The Caribbean and U.S. respondents appear to be similarly ambivalent on the
question, "If you get arrested do you think you will get a fair trial?" Once again,
the discrepancy with the East African sample informs us about the regional differences. In this case, 60.6 percent of the Tanzanians, compared to 31.7 percent of the
Kenyans, have faith in the system and believe that they would receive a fair trial.

Frustration and feelings of hopelessness are said to be prevalent among inner-
city youth in the diaspora, and a substantial portion of the discussion in earlier
chapters was devoted to that issue. Two survey items included in Table 5.1 dealt
specifically with this concern: "People your age can change things that happen in
your country"; and "You have no control over the events taking place in your
life." Of the Caribbean sample, 81.8 percent—compared to 69.5 percent of the
U.S. sample—agreed that they possess the ability to correct things that are happening in their environment. In part, the higher Caribbean score might be explained by the effect that being a racial majority lends to the identity question and
also to feelings (real or imagined) associated with being in charge. It is interesting to see how this compares with the East African respondents. Examining Table
5.2, we find similar levels of agreement between East Africans and U.S. youth
concerning their perceived ability to change things. On the other hand, there was
a marked discrepancy on the statement concerning youths' ability to control
things, with more East Africans (45.9 percent) agreeing that youth are unable to
control things in their environment. By exploring within the East African sample,
we are better able to understand this. Looking at appendix C, we find that the Tanzanian sample lags behind the Kenyan sample on this question. For example, only
53.5 percent of these youth compared to 70.6 percent of the Kenyans believe in
their ability to change things. Also, there is greater agreement (82.7 percent)
among Tanzanian youth versus Kenyan youth (37.1 percent) that they are unable
to take control of their lives. Despite the economic and social transformation that
is currently taking place in Tanzania, it is likely that the legacy of that state's role
under ujamaa and state socialism of the recent past explains their ambivalence toward the idea that people can or should take charge of their surrounding problems
independent of the government. Because the Kenyan state since independence
became structured along an opposite set of political values, it is understandable
that their responses would support a more independent viewpoint concerning
their role in relation to the state.

Two items probed youths' impression of adults (see Table 5.1 and Table 5.2).
When asked, "Are adults concerned about young people?" the result was relatively high agreement among the U.S. and Caribbean youth. But when the question was posed, "Could government do more to help improve the conditions of
young people?" respondents expressed reservations. Reservations were similarly
expressed across the regions about their governments' responsiveness. One interpretation of these findings is that young people for the most part have not given

up on adults and desire guidance and support from them. The problem is that they are not in receipt of these. Adults who are charged with running the government are not viewed as effective or capable of creating the conditions necessary for a brighter future. This was clearly articulated at a focus group session that this investigator conducted with a group of young people in Port of Spain, Trinidad and Tobago. The youth indicated that persistent double-digit unemployment contributes to youth frustration and low self-esteem. Despite receiving the required "O" level passes,[2] there is no guarantee of employment for youth. One young woman in the group said, "Those who run the government are paid to lead but they do not seem to have a single clue about what to do."[3] Following this statement, all of the youth, including the young woman who made the statement, burst out in laughter that spoke to the entire group's cynicism and lack of confidence in their government. Furthermore, this seems to suggest the extent to which young people in the diaspora are generally confused and powerless.

Related to youths' perception of the police is their experience with arrests. Table 5.3 shows Caribbean and U.S. youth responses to the question about their involvement with the criminal justice system.

The majority responded that they had never experienced arrest. For the U.S. youth, that figure was nearly 80 percent and for the Caribbean youth it was 94 percent. But when asked the question, "Have any of your friends ever been arrested?" the responses changed dramatically with the majority of both groups responding affirmatively. Table 5.4 shows that the East African youth responded at similar levels to the question but there was some variation from the U.S. sample on the question of friends' arrests.

Examining the internal Caribbean data (see appendix B) reveals marginal differences between and among the territories. The higher figure concerning arrest of friends for Trinidad and Tobago (76.9 percent) could be explained by its more advanced condition of urban dislocation vis a vis the others. It is also possible that a discrepancy in youth responses between personal experiences with arrests and that of their friends might have to do with voluntary misreporting. Such a universal error, however, seems a bit unlikely. As well, there is room for the coincidence that the youth in this study just happen to be those urban youth who are struggling to stay out of trouble. In any event, the fact that so many would indicate that they know people who have been arrested confirms that a vast number of young people today throughout the diaspora are no strangers to the legal system. Furthermore, it might also help explain youths' ambivalence toward the police. Likewise, when we shift to the internal region data (see appendix C), differences between the Kenyan and Tanzanian samples appear. Most Kenyan youth (65.3 percent) indicated that they had friends who experienced arrest compared to only 25.7 percent for the Tanzania sample. Unquestionably, once again this finding points to the matter of the pace of social change between the two territories, as crime and social dislocation in the towns and cities of Kenya have been under way for some time.

Table 5.3. A Comparison of Social Issues between United States and Caribbean Youth

	United States			Caribbean		
	Yes	No	Total N	Yes	No	Total N
SOCIAL ISSUES						
Youth arrest	66 (20.4)	257 (79.6)	323 (100.0)	15 (6.2)	227 (93.8)	242 (100.0)
Arrest of friends	226 (72.4)	86 (27.6)	312 (100.0)	116 (56.3)	90 (43.7)	206 (100.0)
Drug use	85 (27.2)	228 (72.8)	313 (100.0)	38 (15.9)	201 (84.1)	239 (100.0)
Employment	108 (34.1)	209 (65.9)	317 (100.0)	53 (22.2)	186 (77.8)	239 (100.0)

	N	Percent	Rank	N	Percent	Rank
MEDIA EXPOSURE						
Watch TV						
1–2 hrs	69	(22.0)		73	(32.2)	
2–4 hrs	134	(42.7)		94	(41.4)	
over 4 hrs	111	(35.3)		60	(26.4)	
(total)	314	(100.0)		227	(100.0)	
TV program						
Comedy	123	(51.5)	1	65	(34.9)	1
Drama	10	(4.2)	6	31	(16.7)	2
News	5	(2.1)	8	7	(3.8)	8
Nature education	6	(2.5)	7	12	(6.5)	6
Police education	11	(4.6)	5	26	(14.0)	3
Soap operas	29	(12.1)	3	18	(9.7)	5
Sports	33	(13.8)	2	19	(10.2)	4
Talk shows	22	(9.2)	4	8	(4.3)	7
(total)	239	(100.0)		186	(100.0)	
YOUTH PROBLEMS						
AIDS	65	(26.0)	1	18	(9.0)	6

Continued

Table 5.3. (Continued)

	United States			Caribbean		
	N	Percent	Rank	N	Percent	Rank
Street crime	32	(12.6)	5	20	(10.0)	4
Drugs	50	(19.6)	3	47	(23.4)	2
Lack of education	35	(13.8)	4	19	(9.5)	5
Poverty	5	(2.0)	6	2	(1.0)	8
Suicide	1	(0.4)	9	2	(1.0)	8
Unemployment	4	(1.6)	8	59	(29.4)	1
Poor government services	5	(2.0)	6	8	(4.0)	7
Lack of guidance	56	(22.0)	2	26	(12.9)	3
(total)	254	(100.0)		201	(100.0)	
FAMILY LIFE						
Live with						
Both parents	112	(36.0)	2	92	(38.3)	1
Mother	136	(43.7)	1	90	(37.5)	2
Father	10	(3.2)	5	5	(2.1)	6
Grandparents	19	(6.1)	3	13	(5.4)	4
Other relatives	14	(4.5)	4	26	(10.8)	3
Alone	6	(1.9)	6	3	(1.3)	7
Friends	6	(1.9)	6	1	(0.4)	9
Partner	5	(1.6)	8	7	(2.9)	5
Spouse	3	(1.0)	9	3	(1.3)	7
(total)	311	(100.0)		240	(100.0)	
FUTURE PROJECTIONS						
Life in 2 yrs						
Working	53	(19.6)	2	76	(35.0)	1
Secondary school	26	(9.6)	4	13	(6.0)	4
University	120	(44.3)	1	52	(24.0)	3
Married	4	(1.5)	6	5	(1.8)	7
Having children	3	(1.1)	7	—[c]	—	
Pursue career	44	(16.2)	3	60	(27.6)	2
Unemployed	—	—		5	(2.3)	6
Others	21	(7.7)	5	7	(3.2)	5
(total)	271	(100.0)		217	(100.0)	
Life in 5 yrs						
Working	75	(28.3)	1	63	(31.3)	1
Secondary school	4	(1.5)	7	—	—	
University	68	(25.7)	2	32	(15.9)	4

Continued

Table 5.3. (Continued)

	United States			Caribbean		
	N	Percent	Rank	N	Percent	Rank
Married	28	(10.6)	**4**	49	(24.4)	**2**
Having children	10	(3.8)	**6**	6	(3.0)	**6**
Pursue career	61	(23.0)	**3**	40	(19.9)	**3**
Others	19	(7.2)	**5**	10	(5.0)	**5**
(total)	265	(100.0)		201	(100.0)	

NOTE: Numbers in parentheses are percentages.
c) — denotes no response to that category.

Table 5.4. A Comparison of Social Issues between United States and Eastern African Youth

	United States			Africa		
	Yes	No	Total N	Yes	No	Total N
SOCIAL ISSUES						
Youth arrest	66	257	323	17	105	122
	(20.4)	(79.6)	(100.0)	(13.9)	(86.1)	(100.0)
Arrest of friends	226	86	312	51	69	120
	(72.4)	(27.6)	(100.0)	(42.5)	(57.5)	(100.0)
Drug use	85	228	313	27	95	122
	(27.2)	(72.8)	(100.0)	(22.1)	(77.9)	(100.0)
Employment	108	209	317	16	108	124
	(34.1)	(65.9)	(100.0)	(12.9)	(87.1)	(100.0)
MEDIA EXPOSURE						
Watch TV						
1-2 hrs	69	(22.0)		24	(44.4)	
2-4hrs	134	(42.7)		15	(27.8)	
over 4 hrs	111	(35.3)		15	(27.8)	
(total)	314	(100.0)		54	(100.0)	
TV program						
Comedy	123	(51.5)	**1**	15	(28.8)	**1**
Drama	10	(4.2)	**6**	5	(9.6)	**5**
News	5	(2.1)	**8**	2	(3.8)	**6**
Nature education	6	(2.5)	**7**	1	(1.9)	**7**
Police education	11	(4.6)	**5**	10	(19.2)	**3**

Continued

Table 5.4. (Continued)

	United States			Africa		
	N	Percent	Rank	N	Percent	Rank
Soap operas	29	(12.1)	3	8	(15.4)	4
Sports	33	(13.8)	2	11	(21.2)	2
Talk shows	22	(9.2)	4	—c)	—	
(total)	239	(100.0)		52	(100.0)	
YOUTH PROBLEMS						
AIDS	65	(26.0)	1	24	(20.2)	2
Street crime	32	(12.6)	5	6	(5.0)	6
Drugs	50	(19.6)	3	24	(20.2)	2
Lack of education	35	(13.8)	4	8	(6.7)	5
Poverty	5	(2.0)	6	15	(12.6)	4
Suicide	1	(0.4)	9	3	(2.5)	8
Unemployment	4	(1.6)	8	30	(25.2)	1
Poor government services	5	(2.0)	6	3	(2.5)	8
Lack of guidance	56	(22.0)	2	6	(5.0)	6
(total)	254	(100.0)		119	(100.0)	
FAMILY LIFE						
Live with						
Both parents	112	(36.0)	2	75	(60.5)	1
Mother	136	(43.7)	1	12	(9.7)	2
Father	10	(3.2)	5	6	(4.8)	6
Grandparents	19	(6.1)	3	2	(1.6)	7
Other relatives	14	(4.5)	4	11	(8.9)	3
Alone	6	(1.9)	6	7	(5.6)	4
Friends	6	(1.9)	6	2	(1.6)	7
Partner	5	(1.6)	8	7	(5.6)	4
Spouse	3	(1.0)	9	2	(1.6)	7
(total)	311	(100.0)		124	(100.0)	
FUTURE PROJECTIONS						
Life in 2 yrs						
Working	53	(19.6)	2	35	(28.9)	1
Secondary school	26	(9.6)	4	30	(24.8)	2
University	120	(44.3)	1	13	(10.7)	4

Continued

Table 5.4. (Continued)

	United States			Caribbean		
	N	Percent	Rank	N	Percent	Rank
Married	4	(1.5)	6	7	(5.8)	6
Having children	3	(1.1)	7	8	(6.6)	5
Pursue career	44	(16.2)	3	18	(14.9)	3
Unemployed	—	—		7	(5.8)	6
Others	21	(7.7)	5	3	(2.5)	7
(total)	271	(100.0)		121	(100.0)	
Life in 5 yrs						
Working	75	(28.3)	1	55	(45.5)	1
Secondary school	4	(1.5)	7	13	(10.7)	3
University	68	(25.7)	2	8	(6.6)	4
Married	28	(10.6)	4	19	(15.7)	2
Having children	10	(3.8)	6	6	(3.0)	8
Pursue career	61	(23.0)	3	7	(5.8)	6
Unemployed	—	—		5	(4.1)	7
Others	19	(7.2)	5	8	(6.6)	4
(total)	265	(100.0)		121	(100.0)	

NOTE: Numbers in parentheses are percentages.
[c] — denotes no response to that category.

One's ability to establish wholesome linkages and networks in the community has been discussed in the sociological literature as an important dimension for understanding hopelessness and frustration. We have attempted to address this by including questionnaire items about youth engagement in sports, social activities, and clubs. Family living arrangements could be included with this group as well. Across the regions, youth were found to be marginally involved in formal social arrangements (see Tables 5.5 and 5.6).

Many respondents indicated that they were involved in some form of sports, although not necessarily organized team sports. Overall, they engaged in social and religious clubs to a lesser degree. Looking at Tables 5.3 and 5.4, which pertain to family living arrangements, the data suggest that compared to the U.S. sample where 43.7 percent responded that they live with a single mother, the Caribbean sample at 37.5 percent appears to be playing catch up. The East African sample remains comfortably behind at 9.7 percent (see Table 5.4). The fact that 9.7 percent of the East African sample responded that they live in households headed by their mother, compared to 60.5 percent who said that they reside with both parents, is consistent with the existing literature, which indicates that in non-Western societies, the prevalence of traditional values and attachments to family even in a changing world serves as a brake on the expansion of the urban dislocation in a society such as Tanzania. Globalization, which is responsible for

Table 5.5. Levels of Community Integration between United States and Caribbean Youth

	United States			Caribbean		
	Yes	No	Total N	Yes	No	Total N
Social Club	125 (39.6)	191 (60.4)	316 (100.0)	116 (48.7)	122 (51.3)	238 (100.0)
Religious club	96 (30.1)	223 (69.9)	319 (100.0)	106 (45.1)	129 (54.9)	235 (100.0)
Recreational club	92 (30.9)	206 (69.1)	298 (100.0)	80 (34.8)	150 (65.2)	230 (100.0)

NOTE: Numbers in parentheses are percentages.

Table 5.6. Levels of Community Integration between United States and Eastern African Youth

	United States			Africa		
	Yes	No	Total N	Yes	No	Total N
Social club	125 (39.6)	191 (60.4)	316 (100.0)	55 (44.4)	69 (55.6)	124 (100.0)
Religious club	96 (30.1)	223 (69.9)	319 (100.0)	59 (47.6)	65 (52.4)	124 (100.0)
Recreational club	92 (30.9)	206 (69.1)	298 (100.0)	47 (37.9)	77 (62.1)	124 (100.0)

NOTE: Numbers in parentheses are percentages.

economic hardship, cannot be singled out as the sole cause of family disruption and breakdown. However, it has contributed profoundly to the heavy burden on families, leading to increased domestic violence and forcing breadwinners to migrate elsewhere, even to foreign countries, in search of work.

Much has been said about the impact of mass communications and the media especially on youth populations. Unsurprisingly, television ownership is quite common across the regions. When this survey was conducted in 1994, television was just arriving at mainland Tanzania. That accounts for the huge television ownership differential reported between the East African sample and the others. It should also be pointed out that the televisions reported by the Tanzanian respondents were actually used as monitors to view videos. An astounding finding (see Tables 5.3 and 5.4) is the number of hours spent in front of the television. It is not so much the one- to two-hour category but the two to four hours and beyond that is so revealing. What should be noted is that accompanying the broadcasts are the unedited commercial advertisements that help develop youths' appetites for commodities and imported values.

The association between the television medium and youth powerlessness has already been established. Insofar as the type of programs viewed, not much difference was found across the regions. Whether one examines the United States, the Caribbean, or the East African samples, a consistent finding is the limited importance assigned by youth to news and information programs. If mitigating powerlessness is seen as crucial, then helping youth develop critical thinking about their condition and a better understanding about the need for social change would have to be seen as prerequisites. Toward that objective, appropriate news and information programming should be considered imperative.

Turning to youth perceptions of the problems that confront them (see Table 5.3 and 5.4), the data show that across the regions when asked to list problems from the most to the least serious, AIDS, street crime, drugs, unemployment, and the lack of guidance from adults appear to be very much on the minds of the youth. In the example of unemployment, we gather from the Caribbean and East African samples, where the prospects of school dropouts procuring government civil service jobs have markedly decreased with few alternatives, that the problem of unemployment has reached panic proportions. The fact that the lack of education appears as a problem for so many of the youth serves to fuel their thinking that they are not being adequately prepared to land decent jobs. This in turn reinforces their perception that the government is not doing enough to help them. While unemployment is a serious problem for the U.S. sample, it is slightly less so compared to the Caribbean or East Africa. This is best explained in terms of the level of economic development and the fact that there are more options available to youth who are in search of work.

We stumble across a contradiction when our examination shifts to where they see their lives two and five years into the future. Across the entire sample population, the respondents indicate strong optimism about working, pursuing a career, being enrolled in university, and even being married with a family. Their optimism could very well be real; nevertheless it points to their naiveté concerning the larger world and their place in it. As well, it might point to the respondents' naiveté about their country's preparedness or ability to accommodate their core needs and aspirations.

Overall, the data reported here indicate that contemporary urban youth in the diaspora are confused, are overcome by feelings of uneasiness, and lack direction. These are unambiguous indicators of powerlessness. Analyzing the Caribbean and East Africa against the U.S. backdrop provided us with a greater opportunity to assess the pace of change and urban dislocation taking place there.

With regard to our Caribbean sample, for the more cosmopolitan states of Trinidad and Tobago and St. Thomas, V.I., the pace is more rapid. But even in the cases of the tiny island states of St. Vincent and the Grenadines and Dominica, we are able to see that the game of catch up is well under way. Turning to East Africa, the differences are best understood by examining the internal region data. In that regard, we find that the urban dislocation in Kenya, a state that assumed a Western sociopolitical outlook immediately following its independence, has outpaced its more traditional, poorer neighbor, Tanzania. But as the pace of economic and cultural globalization gathers steam in that region of the world, it is predicted that the pace of Tanzania's urban crisis will soon parallel Kenya's.

The conditions that currently challenge the future generation are seen as resulting from the normal operation of globalization and market capitalism. The various states are not innocent bystanders. An obvious consequence of this is the persistence of powerlessness among the most vulnerable groups. Our survey data point to this generation's desire for a brighter future with improved living standards. But based on the youths' responses to survey items, it would appear that adults are no less confused than the youth about the state of affairs.

A quote by UNESCO at the beginning of this chapter sums up a crucial aim of this study, which is to listen to the future generation and to argue for their empowerment. Listening to the youth, it is hoped, will help us heed Mike Males' plea that we see them not as the "scapegoat generation," but as victims who aspire and deserve a better life.[4]

NOTES

1. Note: UNESCO NEWS 1985: 1–2, cited in C. K. Omari and L. P. Shaidi (eds.), *Social Problems in Eastern Africa* (Dar es Salaam: UDSM, 1991), 56.

2. "O" levels is the abbreviation for "ordinary levels" and is common to Anglophone and Caribbean and African countries where the education systems are still essentially tied to their former British colonial structure. The equivalent to "O" passes in the United States and St. Thomas, V.I., is the high school diploma.

3. Focus group with Trinidad and Tobago youth, Port of Spain, Trinidad, February 7, 1997.

4. Mike A. Males, *The Scapegoat Generation: America's War on Adolescents*. (Monroe, Maine: Common Courage Press, 1996).

6

The Dilemma of Moral Bankruptcy

Since the end of the Cold War, the world has undergone a sweeping ideological shift to the right on the issue of poverty and its victims, the powerless. Neoliberal policies and privatization are at the cutting edge of this shift and are being hoisted as the beacons of hope as we settle into the new millennium. Noam Chomsky captures this transformation in his monograph, "The Prosperous Few and the Restless Many." Throughout that work, Chomsky describes quite persuasively how the ideological pendulum is swinging toward the perspective that views the powerless as responsible for their miserable state, a state characterized by their expressions of frustration and hopelessness about the future.[1] The Soviet-led socialist alternative represented, at least symbolically, a sense of hope for the powerless and an opposition to capital and the prosperous few. There was evidence of this emerging sentiment of hope by the peasantry, the urban poor, and the powerless sparked during this period. In the Americas, we witnessed the rise of the Sandinistas in Nicaragua and a revolution in Grenada. On the African continent, several liberation struggles were taking place. But with the decline of the radical alternative, pressure appears to be mounting in every corner of the world against the poor and the powerless. This is the case whether our attention is drawn to the latest welfare reform measure in the United States, with its blatant disregard for the destabilization of families, or to urban policies in Kenya and neighboring Tanzania that call for the razing of squatter settlements and the harassment of petty traders and hawkers who are simply seeking to survive the uncertainties of daily life in the urban areas.

It should come as no surprise to find that absent from this jaded view about the powerless is any attempt to factor in the role of the state or its major functionaries. An indictment of the capitalist state does not gainsay the flagrant flaws experienced under socialism. For certain, those economies that were structured along the socialist model were a far cry from solving the problems of impoverishment and the material needs of the poor. Nevertheless, contrary to what conservatives would have us believe, the state under any system is not simply a helpless, or for that matter, an innocuous bystander in the process of minimizing rights and access to power for the citizenry. Rather, the state has options. It can commit to upholding the objectives of the true democratic state, foremost of which is providing the opportunity for all of its citizens to develop their fullest capacities. On the other hand, it can succumb to the narrow interests of those who happen to control capital within and without its borders. Unfortunately, the path chosen by far too many states in the developing and developed regions of the world that purport to be democratic has been the latter. We attempted to demonstrate this earlier in our examination of the United States, the Caribbean, and East Africa.

The development of empowered citizens, which we assume to be the objective of progressive black leaders, can be achieved only when moral bankruptcy, which is so pervasive at this historical juncture, is once and for all challenged. To counteract the backward activities of the state, the current leadership must be transformed and the organizations committed to preserving the interests of the disenfranchised must be emboldened. Because of their unique and internationally respected position as operatives that are, for the most part, distinct from the state and carry the potential for empowering the less fortunate, an assessment of nongovernmental organizations (NGOs) and community-based organizations (CBOs) is presented. But as we shall soon see, due to fiscal uncertainties and other limitations, NGOs and CBOs are experiencing tremendous difficulty living up to their potential as catalysts for change and advocates for the powerless.

To discuss moral bankruptcy is to discuss a dilemma that engulfs many developed and developing states today. Conceivably, it could be argued that bankruptcy in developing states is exacerbated by the presence of transnational corporations that transport new forms of corruption and in turn pollinate their host societies. Leaders of these states suffer from a lack of vision and ideas about how to stop the hemorrhage taking place most acutely in the urban districts. In a subordinate relationship with capital rather than the other way around, the state is incapable of carrying out its basic mission of meeting the material needs of all its citizens. Furthermore, in this construction, poor and working-class citizens are viewed as excess baggage, or, in other words, as people whose insatiable needs and constant demands on the state exceed their productive capacities. Along these same lines, distinctions between core and developing societies become negligible. In the core societies where heavy manufacturing has declined precipitously and is being replaced by tertiary sector industries, unskilled jobs at decent wages and with benefits are scarce in relation to demand. This dilemma constitutes the ongoing debate in the United States, where recent measures to restrict immigration are viewed as just another means of controlling labor. While these immigration policies may ultimately affect labor penetration by foreigners, the domestic demand for less-skilled jobs persists. This demand will persist as long as inner-city schools continue to fail children from economically deprived backgrounds, and the commitment to prepare people for newer roles in the labor economy or to create work is undermined.

Compared to the Caribbean and East Africa, the American state is in a better fiscal position to provide a modicum of relief to those in need and, in the process, nourish them with the false impression that they are better off compared to their counterparts in distant lands. But relief is quite often ephemeral and inconsistent. Differences exist among the 50 American states in terms of their welfare systems' administrative rules and procedures and the amount of the monthly allotment awarded to families and individuals. What is consistent is the indignity that applicants and beneficiaries have been forced to endure in order to negotiate the system. Because of corporate greed and corporations' ability to freely exercise their own brand of democracy, a name and institution that has become household to most Americans is Alan Greenspan, chairman of the Federal Reserve Bank, or America's national bank. Each time the feds are forced to raise the interest rate the government charges the nation's commercial banks—a common scenario that Americans have had to live with since the 1980s—and tax incentives, low interest mortgage loans, workers' wages, and stable employment levels are threatened. In this chapter, we wish to show that in the United States, the Caribbean, and East Africa, it is becoming apparent that leaders and heads of state are without a clue about how to remedy the crisis unraveling in their urban areas. If by chance they happen on a solution, the problems associated with its implementation are overwhelming.

For the greatest part, leaders from the Caribbean and East Africa continue to search for solutions to their problems from outside. In the Caribbean, most states belong to the 15-member CARICOM group, through which some attempt is being made to speak as a unified community. Nonetheless, there is maneuvering from time to time among the various pact members in pursuit of their own special interests [2] and favors from abroad. The recent "ship-rider" policy, also known as the "basic hot-pursuit" policy, is a case in point. In 1996, nine states—Dominica, Antigua and Barbuda, Belize, the Dominican Republic, Grenada, St. Kitts and Nevis, St. Vincent and the Grenadines, St. Lucia, and Trinidad and Tobago—rushed to negotiate agreements with the United States as a measure against drug trafficking in the region. The agreement permits the U.S. Coast Guard to follow suspected vessels into the other country's waters and to board and detain any suspicious vessels in those waters. Trinidad and Tobago went a step further by extending privilege to American aircraft to fly over its territory and to order suspicious aircraft traveling in its airspace to land there. Skeptical of the plan, several other states have either expressed reservation or are openly opposed on the grounds that it is tantamount to an invasion of their sovereignty and that it opens the door for further superpower penetration into their internal affairs.[3] Opposed are Jamaica, a major producer of marijuana; Haiti; and Barbados.

On May 12, 1997, President Clinton signed The Bridgetown Declaration, along with the 15 CARICOM member countries, promising them freer trade and receiving assurances of more help in fighting the scourge of illegal drugs. Here again, as evidenced at the December 1995 Miami Summit, no agreement was reached over the critical banana crop issue, which sought a guarantee that the United States would discontinue its efforts to overthrow an agreement guaranteeing Caribbean banana farmers a share of the European Union (EU) market or their entrance into NAFTA. In March of 1997, the WTO supported Washington's claim that preferences unfairly restrict American companies' access. But without preferential treatment, the island states will not be able to compete with companies like Chiquita Brands and Dole. In an effort to convey to the world the urgency of this issue for the region, former Prime Minister of St. Lucia, Vaughn Lewis, remarked at the Bridgetown meeting that "Bananas are to us what cars are to Detroit."[4] Here we find an instance where the leaders happen to have a clue about what they believe is needed to correct a situation that significantly contributes to their immediate problems but are without the clout to implement it. What the Caribbean nations want is to be able to negotiate independently with the EU against the United States. The problem is that the Clinton administration supports a policy whereby the EU would drop preferences and impose instead tariffs on bananas originating from outside the Caribbean. In that way, supposedly, the EU could use the proceeds to help the Caribbean nations diversify their exports.[5] Throughout the history of international relations, it is not the periphery[6] that dictates to the core, rather it is the other way around. If the United States reverses its position, the world can be assured that such a shift was determined not by the Caribbean leaders but by Washington.

LEADERS AND BANKRUPTCY

The United States

Unmistakably, the system of bankruptcy to which we refer rests heavily on the shoulders of leaders, official and unofficial. With few exceptions, leaders from the regions considered in the present study have demonstrated little resolve when it comes to taking a principled position concerning the protection of the interests and rights of their fellow citizens. They are, in other words, bankrupt. Leaders, we are reminded, come in different ideological molds. There are the conventionalists, who seek to uphold the status quo; nationalists, who advocate a position of cultural liberation for the race; and then there are radical leaders, who see a critical departure from the status quo and a transformation of the existing structural order as the only hope for the people. For black Americans this might be extended to include the accommodationist and the integrationist schools of thought. Booker T. Washington, who was born into slavery in 1856 and died in 1915, is credited with the rise of accommodationism. It emerged as the dominant school of thought after the collapse of Reconstruction in the South in 1877 and was an attempt to arrive at a rapprochement with white racism. As a school of thought, it built enormous trust around the resolve of white people to accept and respect industrious and successful blacks. Accommodationism is often considered a sheepish form of nationalism in that it recognizes the importance of establishing black institutions and uplifting the race. A chief limitation, however, is its heart-felt belief in the basic decency of white civil society and the failure to grasp the connection between politics and economics and the economic component of white racism. Integrationists, in their quest to create a racially harmonious society, do not see the need to challenge the economic system. Their assumption is that America is a democratic society committed to the basic principles set forth in its constitution.[7]

Currently there are more black elected officials than at any time in the history of black America. Drawing from 1993–1994 statistics, a total of 7,984 officials were calculated. This figure includes national, state, and county legislative leaders, law enforcement officials, and education officials. It is far more likely today than at an earlier period to find black mayors, school superintendents, principals, and even police chiefs in urban areas with significant black populations. As Basil Wilson and I argued in *The Struggle for Black Empowerment in New York City*, blacks' occupation of the oval offices in major cities is a tenuous indicator at best of the group's achievement of the empowerment objective. Newark, New Jersey's largest city, has enjoyed a black presence in the mayoral office beginning in the early 1970s. Minuscule changes notwithstanding, the material condition of average poor and working-class residents of Newark has not budged. Similarly, the presence of blacks in such roles as police chiefs, sergeants, and patrol officers has not affected the incidence of police misconduct against members of the black community or intimidated the powerful intransigent police unions. This is not meant as an indictment of these personnel or to suggest that blacks should not continue to quest for these important posts. It is intended to underscore the point that empowerment is not realized through the rudimentary manipulation of statistics or by playing the game of racial musical chairs. Rather, the litmus test of empowerment is met when a people become consciously aroused and prepared to change those structures that have historically served to subjugate them. In the United States, the system of institutional racism has ensured the denial of full privileges and rights for African Americans. As a numerical minority, African Americans have had to rely on the support of allies from outside the community in their struggle for rights and social change. Thus, although blacks were at the helm of the struggle for rights in the 1950s and 1960s, it was pressure from a multiracial- and multiethnic-based movement representing various classes that led to the passage of the landmark Civil Rights Bill in 1964 and the Voting Rights Act in 1965. In the black diaspora, each of the major leadership types mentioned above can be identified.

Prominent elected officials, leaders from the nation's oldest civil rights organizations, the National Association for the Advancement of Colored People

(NAACP) and the Urban League, and successful businessmen like California's Ward Connerly, a black member of that state's Board of Regents and ardent foe of affirmative action,[8] typify the conventional political model. Early in its history, however, the NAACP assumed the role as "warrior for the people." Its first director was the preeminent activist–scholar, W. E. B. DuBois, and from the first decade of the twentieth century through the 1960s, its legal defense office was credited with a number of victories. The historic Brown v. the Board of Education decision of 1954, in which the Supreme Court was forced to strike down the earlier separate but equal clause issued in Plessy v. Ferguson, was one of its most celebrated legal victories. The NAACP has managed to survive the test of time but not the test of a true warrior. Since the 1950s and 1960s civil rights movement, it has slipped into an abyss of nothingness, and most recently, leadership scandal. Membership has plummeted and few blacks today regard the NAACP as a serious liberating force in the black community.

Malcolm X's credentials placed him squarely in the radical–nationalist camp. Martin Luther King, for the greatest part of his activist life—but not including the latter stage—endorsed liberalism and integration as the logical conduit to change. King's shift to left of center[9] occurred toward the end of his life and appeared to have had little political effect on the lives of black people. In fact, the media did a splendid job of deemphasizing King's ideological shift, opting instead to maintain his image as the quintessential integrationist and loyalist to the free market system. This is borne out today in school districts around the country where Martin Luther King's birthday is honored. Children and the general population are so weaned on the last portion of King's "I Have A Dream" speech that they have missed its political implications. As well there is little familiarity with his other speeches that place him well beyond the platform of a dreamer. One example is his "Why I Oppose the War in Vietnam" speech, in which his patience with the American capitalist model to confront poverty and inequality was beginning to erode. On the other hand, what made Malcolm X such an extraordinary leader in the eyes of the black community was his ability to seize the opportunity for personal change. For one thing, his rhetoric against all whites had tempered and he was beginning to see the world quite differently. Unfortunately, in his case, as with King, the shift came about near the end of his life.[10]

In his seminal work, *The Crisis of the Negro Intellectual,* published in 1967, Harold Cruse was caustic in targeting black leaders and the black middle class for not measuring up and fulfilling their obligation to the community. Needless to say, the work was controversial. An unrepentant Cruse argued in 1992 that present day "liberal sponsored" black leaders are ideological holdovers from the 1960s and as such are reluctant to support the necessary race-specific public policies. I find it hard to disagree with Cruse that race-specific policies remain vital to black progress in the United States and that support is dependent on the younger generation through a process of intellectual and political maturation.[11]

Africa and East Africa

Since the decline of colonialism and the movement for independence in sub-Saharan Africa, we continue to witness this same variation. Julius Nyerere, Kwame Nkrumah, Sekou Toure, and Patrice Lumumba are among the radical–nationalist icons. But the masses have had to contend with the backwardness of Uganda's Idi Amin, UNITA's Jonas Sivimbi in Angola, Chief Mangosuthu Buthelezi, head of the Inkatha Movement and South Africa's Zulu people, Nigeria's late President General Sani Abacha, and the late dictator of Zaire, Mobutu Sese Seko, enemy number one of the people. Mobutu's estate at the time of his death was estimated to be somewhere in the vicinity of $5 billion. Hunger, disease, and all of the ills associated with poverty climbed during his rule of more than three decades. A name less prominent than those already presented but which warrants mention with this gang is Felix Houphouët-Boigny, the late president of the Ivory Coast. What catapulted him to international attention in the last decade was his construction of one of the world's largest and most spectacular Roman Catholic churches at an estimated cost of $150 million. Catholic pilgrims and other tourists from around the world pour in to see this spectacle in the jungle. What was the logic behind Houphouët-Boigny's decision, queried journalist Howard W. French, "in a country with one of the world's highest levels of indebtedness and huge unmet needs in such areas as education, housing, and simple health care?"[12] The salient questions are: How did any of these leaders come to rule in the first place? Was it the democratic choice of the people, or was it by fiat manipulated at the hands of foreign interests? In most cases, the answer is quite straightforward, especially when Africa's potential wealth in terms of natural resources, which are in high demand by foreigners, is taken into account. Coincidentally or perhaps not, when we consider the destabilization of governments and the overthrow of duly elected heads of state who promised to improve the condition of the powerless and defend their rights, the role of the American state is prominently featured. In Africa, for example, we can turn to the Congo, Angola, and Ghana. In the Caribbean, Guyana, Jamaica, and Grenada are called to mind.

In our examination of East Africa, a number of parallels between the states of Tanzania and Kenya were drawn. However, the pernicious politics of Moi in Kenya (inconsistencies that appeared even during the progressive Jomo Kenyatta's era) was not the experience of the Tanzanian people under Nyerere, whose record of human rights was fairer. Furthermore, Tanzanians have been spared this experience under Nyerere's successors, Ali Hassan Mwinyi and currently, Benjamin Mkapa. Following the death of Jomo Kenyatta in August 1978, independent Kenya's first elected president, leadership was transferred to his vice president, Daniel arap Moi. Moi's administration is alleged to be involved in corruption, electoral malpractice, fraud, and assassinations of his opponents including the February 1990 killing of Minister of Foreign Affairs Robert Ouko.

Moi was also charged with disrupting the Mwakenya Group, which was formed to oppose his reshuffling campaign and the strengthening of his privileges as president, and the Safina Party which was formed in 1995 by another prominent opponent, Muturi Kigano.[13] Moi succumbed to international pressure for reforms in the country, and subsequently the first multi-party elections were held in Kenya on December 29, 1992. Amid allegations that he had provoked ethnic violence to ensure his victory, Moi was reelected for a fourth term. Protests in the streets of Nairobi in 1997 concerned efforts by the masses and their leaders to repeal the colonial era laws that were inherited with independence. The British implemented these laws to contain the native population and to limit their rights and the possibility of serious political threat and opposition.

It would be inaccurate to assert that the Tanzanian state is exceptional or that it is free of skullduggery and other political inconsistencies. The harassment of Reverend Christopher Mtikila, who headed the Democratic Party, one of the country's newly formed political parties, is a case in point. Mtikila was detained and arrested several times on charges of sedition. In an interview this investigator conducted with Mtikila in August 1994, he defined himself as a nationalist who was unwilling to recognize the union with Zanzibar. As such, he continues to fly the original Tanganyika flag in his modest flat. He maintained that his harassment by the authorities was due to his criticism of the nation's most powerful minority group, the Asian Indians, and their economic success compared to Africans. Mtikila alleged that the Asian population, though absent from the political arena, has successfully used its economic clout to grease the hands of African leaders, which has allowed them to maintain their position of economic superiority. For this reason he supports the philosophy of "Tanzania for Black Tanzanians." The surge of inter-ethnic tension in Tanzanian civil society cannot be separated from the arrival of economic globalization and the subsequent decline in the material condition of the black masses. Multi-partyism is credited with paving the way for Mtikila and the opportunity to expose the system of ethnic privilege that is deeply rooted in the society. Reverend Mtikila was able to rally unprecedented numbers of supporters, many of them university students, at his speaking engagements throughout Dar es Salaam. It was not long before he became a thorn in the side of the ruling CCM party officials. With pressure exerted by the state, for example, a court injunction that silenced him from public speaking, and various measures to weaken his support base, Mtikila was unsuccessful in his efforts to shake CCM and seriously advance the cause of opposition politics in the nation. In 1995, the first multi-party general elections were held in Tanzania. However, CCM prevailed and former Minister of Science, Technology, and Higher Education Benjamin Mkapa was elected president.

Multi-partyism is an extremely important instrument of empowerment, and once gained, every effort must be expended to maintain it. For the people of Uganda, ridding themselves of Idi Amin was an enormous hurdle. Achieving multi-party status is yet another. Constituents who have been starved of their rights and the privilege of decision making under a dictatorship are vulnerable to manipulation by the benevolent liberator who professes nationalism and nation building but is reluctant to allow the masses the fullest exercise of their rights. President Yoweri K. Museveni, a proclaimed Marxist, has ruled Uganda since 1986. He claims that most African nations are not ready for a multi-party democracy as many of them require a thriving economy and a middle class that can form parties around issues other than ethnicity. These parties eventually become covers for tribal leaders seeking power for their ethnic group. So for him, African societies must be transformed and developed as a first step. Thus in Uganda, Mr. Museveni has banned all political parties with the exception of his own, the National Resistance Movement (NRM).[14] These leaders must be challenged. How they respond to that challenge will determine whether they are committed to a politic of liberation or a politic of greed.

The Caribbean

A similar assessment can be made of the Caribbean, where the pendulum swings from nationalists and radicals such as Eric Williams, the pan-Caribbean nationalist, and socialists Walter Rodney, Fidel Castro, and Cheddi Jagan to conventionalists like the late Prime Minister of Barbados Tom Adams, former Prime Minister of Dominica Dame Eugenie Charles, and the current stream of heads of state. This is unquestionably so in the case of two late tyrants, Eric Gairy of Grenada and Forbes Burnham of Guyana, both ardently supported by Washington. Given the tendency on the part of various leaders to vacillate, none of these ideological positions are firmly rooted. This is not the case for all, but too frequently this does occur and the impact for the constituents is severe. What we find in the Caribbean in general, and the anglophone Caribbean in particular, is that a history of denial of rights and subjugation was the rule rather than the exception during slavery and during the colonial period.[15] A left movement with the unmistakable objective to formulate a new political landscape, one that was radically opposed to conventionalism and upheld the empowerment objective, was on the horizon by the 1970s with the ascendance of Michael Manley and the People's National Party (PNP) in Jamaica, and Maurice Bishop and the New Jewel Movement in Grenada.[16] This was a momentous period for the left and Third World politics in general. Michael Manley referred to it as "a new international order for developing nations."[17] After two terms in office, between 1972 and 1980, Michael Manley's socialist experiment was voted out in the heat of the 1980 elections. The 1980 elections in Jamaica were a spectacle of political violence perpetrated by members of the two leading parties, the People's National Party and the Jamaica Labour Party.[18] More than 700 people were reported killed during that period of political unrest. After the storm, Edward Seaga, opposition leader of the conservative Jamaica Labour Party (JLP), succeeded Manley. Ironically, Seaga took office the very year that Ronald Reagan arrived at the Oval Office in Washington.

Mr. Reagan's first foreign visitor to the White House that year was none other than Edward Seaga. Michael Manley was returned to office for a third time in 1989 but was forced to step down in 1992 due to ill health.

Following three years of significant social and economic restructuring of the beleaguered Grenadian economy and social infrastructure, the New Jewel Movement succumbed to internal conflict and atrophied in 1983. Not to be dismissed was the background of allegations concerning U.S. interference throughout that revolution's brief history.[19] With the party-ordered assassination of Maurice Bishop in October 1983, the assassination of Walter Rodney in Guyana in 1980 at the hands of the state, and more recently, the deaths of Manley and Jagan (due to natural causes), no serious leaders of substance with their political portfolio and vision for change have emerged.

At its meetings with people across the region in 1992, the West Indian Commission focused on the tension between economic distress throughout the region and democratic governance. Participants at that meeting located the crisis of governance in the failure of Caribbean leaders and institutions to broaden and deepen participatory democracy in the region. Another consensus reached was that political leaders and institutions had failed to move beyond the formal trappings and structures of liberal democracy and to put into place people-centered policies and processes.[20] A most important observation of the commission was the growing sense of social and political cynicism, normlessness, and powerlessness among the youth in the region as a direct consequence of the crisis of governance. Consequently, youth come to see themselves as victims of the "credentials-inflation spiral" whereby qualifications for employment are consistently raised. Finding new strategies to allow youth greater involvement in decision making, particularly as it relates to issues of major concern to them, was seen as the only way to counter their victimization and entrapment.[21]

Earlier, we alluded to Walter Rodney's insightful observation that when the music is played in Paris, London, and New York, they dance in Abidjan, Accra, and Kinshasa. Although he was addressing Africa, Rodney could very well have been referring to Port of Spain, Roseau, Castries, and other major urban centers in the Caribbean and the diaspora as a whole. Thus, one of the greatest challenges facing blacks in the diaspora for the future will be to identify and support progressive leaders.

From this we are able to see that when progressive leaders in the diaspora have struggled to challenge the status quo, they have met stiff resistance and ultimately defeat. This resistance has come in the form of violence but also through the use of covert measures. In seminal articles, Ramphall (1996) and Deitz and Garcia (1996) make the point that during the Cold War the United States—preoccupied with the spread of communism, especially within its immediate hemisphere—moved swiftly against leftist movements it labeled Marxist–Leninist. At that time, it was willing to introduce various economic trade initiatives such as the Caribbean Basin Initiative (CBI) as palliative measures that would lure the small island nations toward minor trade arrangements with the United States and minimize the prospects of their gravitation to the left. But once the hostilities with the Soviets receded, signaling the end of the Cold War, the U.S. commitment to the Caribbean states began to wane.[22] This has increased feelings of intimidation on the part of the small island nations; some more so than others have been inclined to seek independent solutions to their problems where possible. In such an atmosphere, neoliberalism has come to be viewed by desperate leaders as a form of salvation rather than a spoiler.

There are those who argue that these societies have little choice other than to invite the multinationals on their own terms.[23] At the same time, others give praise to colonialism and modernization as the saviors of these otherwise backward societies. Historian Paul Johnson is one of those trumpeters. He offers a new form of colonialism, namely "altruistic colonialism," as the only way out for the poor nations of the world that find themselves trapped in the intractable misery of underdevelopment. These governments have crumbled and the most basic conditions for civilized life have all but disappeared. In Johnson's view, this altruistic colonialism is not only necessary in a practical sense, it is a moral imperative.[24]

A recent study by the Institute For Policy Studies (IPS) of the top 200 multinational corporations in the world examined the persistent role played by multinational corporations in developing countries. IPS's objective was to assail the myth that the transnationals are employing large numbers of the population in the Third World and are pivotal in helping to reduce the life-threatening conditions for the poor in these countries. It is to be expected that modernizationists and special interest groups would want to advance this misguided impression as evidence of their invaluable role in helping to make life more bearable for the poor in these countries. IPS data show that nothing could be further from the truth.[25] As the process of globalization escalates, affecting more and more workers from the core societies, the prospects for consciousness raising among labor are likely to increase, thereby providing the momentum needed to expose the inhumane practices of the multinationals.[26] The hope of the neolabor movement in America under the leadership of AFL-CIO boss Jim Sweeny is that these corporations will be forced to become more responsible and return lost jobs to the United States. However, not until a significant labor threat is felt will we begin to see a real dent in the level of corporate confidence about their ability to control these economies, expropriate earnings, and pick up their operations and leave at will.

From this discussion, it is dubious that the present and future leadership in the three regions we have examined—and there is sufficient cause to generalize to other regions of the world as well—will be capable of creating a truly democratic state that serves the interests of all citizens. In the meantime, excitement and hope have swelled around the role of nongovernmental entities as catalysts for change. The importance assigned to these entities is an inevitable reality of the efforts by people around the world to respond to global problems and to achieve some measure of global governance. It is all too easy to be swept up by a euphoric wave of false hope, especially when there is a void to be filled. For that reason, in the next section, we take a glance at the nongovernmental groups that have proliferated in order to gather preliminary answers to questions such as: Are they making a difference? To what degree have they too descended into the abyss of bankruptcy? The latter question is salient, given the basic fact that all groups and organizations in the modern world require resources of some sort in order to operate. A related question, therefore, is to what extent can these organizations maintain their credibility while in receipt of vital resources from a variety of donors that very often includes the state?

THE ROLE OF NGOS

Operating alongside the state, and quite frequently in conflict with it, are the community-based organizations and not-for-profit organizations better known internationally as nongovernmental organizations (NGOs). Theoretically, NGOs[27] are not part of the government and are voluntary nonprofitmaking, nonpartisan, and differ in size, statutes, fields of activity, methods of operation, and means and objectives. The term nongovernmental organization has appeared under a panoply of expressions and is used synonymously with such terms as the independent sector, private voluntary organizations, grassroots social change organizations, and nonstate actors. More important than their variegated usages are the roles they play and their potential for bringing about "global governance." Global governance refers to the condition whereby the experiences, views, and articulations of local people living in every village and hamlet on the globe can potentially influence international decision making. In other words, it advocates for the direct involvement by people who would otherwise be excluded in the affairs and decisions that directly impact their daily existence. One manifestation of this are international conferences that cover such topics as AIDS, the environment, women's issues, human rights, and habitats for humanity where local folk by way of their NGOs are able to participate on panels and voice their opinions.[28]

Progressive in outlook, NGOs provide an important alternative to state bankruptcy and in many instances offer the only thread of hope that sorely needed human services will be provided for the masses. They push and often embarrass governments and foreign diplomats to do their jobs and on a day-to-day basis, it is usually the NGOs that seem to have the capacity and the will to rally the cause for the linkage of democracy and peace. To carry out these roles, NGOs must secure and maintain their independence from the state apparatus—a basic condition for their credibility. From the perspective of the state, particularly where that state is structured to prioritize the interests of elites, it must use every means available to control the NGOs, which are seen as competitors and a potential threat to the imperatives of statehood. These imperatives include territorial hegemony, security, autonomy, legitimacy, and revenue.[29]

Since the end of the Cold War and the breakdown of ideological and social orthodoxy, the world has experienced an expansion of NGOs in developing as well as developed societies. The reluctance of many countries in the past to support these bodies in one way or the other evaporated and opened up new opportunities for communication and cooperation. Ng'ethe calculated that as recently as 1989, approximately 2,000 NGOs in the industrialized North were channeling financial and human resources, directly or indirectly, to some 10,000 to 20,000 NGOs in the South.[30] In France, 54,000 new associations have been established since 1987, and in Italy, 40 percent of all of these associations have been set up within the last 15 years. Since the start of the 1990s, approximately 10,000 NGOs have been established in Bangladesh, 21,000 in the Philippines, and 27,000 in Chile. A not-so-startling observation is that in post-Soviet Eastern Europe, these entities have taken on critical importance in people's lives.[31]

Chiefly, two types of NGOs are discussed: QUANGOS and DONGOS. QUANGOS are quasi-nongovernmental bodies that receive the bulk of their funding from public coffers. Among the best internationally known of these are the International Committee of the Red Cross and CARE. Organizations under this type believe they are independent and stress that so long as the support they receive comes unconditionally and that it is their priorities not the donors' that dominate, conflict can be minimized. But that is a far cry from reality. DONGOS, on the other hand, are donor-driven organizations whose resources tend to flow from outside the government by international organizations or private foundations and philanthropists. It is not uncommon for these same donors to mold NGOs to fit their own needs and special interests or to simply create their own NGOs when and if deemed necessary. Arguably, what could be determined a positive example of this is the United Nations' support of DONGOS that were responsible for mobilizing the population in the last elections in Cambodia and for the de-mining efforts in Afghanistan.[32]

It is very easy to overstate the role of NGOs in the manufacturing of empowerment, and for that reason it is necessary to carefully spell out their limitations. First of all, they vary in terms of mission. Some groups are strictly service oriented while others are service oriented but with a clear political agenda as seen in the case of human rights groups. It is fair to say that the latter category are in the minority and that most of them bear the potential for empowering their constituents. Contradicting the potentiality of NGOs are certain extrinsic and intrinsic limitations earlier alluded to that have to do with the politics of funding and their ideological outlook. Let us briefly examine the status of these organizations for each of the geographical settings in our study.

The United States and Community-Based Organizations

There are virtually scores of grassroots and voluntary type organizations functioning at the local community level in the United States today. They are responding to diverse needs such as housing, the environment, human rights, women's issues, health, recreation, and education needs, just to name a few. The bulk of these are service oriented, seeking to help residents negotiate their specific needs through the system. They might be classified quasi-private–voluntary, as a number of them may qualify for partial local or state government funding because of the specific programs they offer. Other groups, fewer in number, define themselves as independent grassroots groups that seek to mobilize and organize constituents to directly challenge the system for social change. Two such examples would be the Association for Community Organizing Now (ACORN) and the Industrial Areas Foundation (IAF), the renowned professional organizing outfit started by the late Saul Alinsky.[33] Securing funding poses a serious problem for the majority of these community-based groups, particularly for those that depend on some form of public support. Another factor is the contagion of tax referendums and propositions that have initiated in the state of California that point to the growing public concern about how their tax dollars should be spent. There is little doubt that American public opinion is not prepared to support overt social activism through the tax structure. As for those NGOs whose radical mission places them outside the purview of public funding, or for that matter, mainstream foundation donations, it is an even greater problem. They must creatively define new routes to funding, whether through constant fund-raising events, identifying progressive churches, or becoming the benefactor of some prominent closet radical. Sustaining themselves under these austere conditions is extremely difficult and consequently many atrophy.

The implication here is that groups that are in receipt of some form of public funding or mainstream foundation donations have bargained away their independence and credibility. In the United States, NGOs and donors operate under tight government-imposed restrictions. Foundations owe their prosperity to provisions of the tax laws that are subject to change. Also, they are forbidden to act in electoral and other political spheres and may not lobby the way special interest groups do.[34] If their purpose is to advocate for and mobilize their constituents to challenge the status quo, they can expect no assistance or have their support terminated. Using the example of public welfare programs, Frances Fox Piven and Richard Cloward demonstrated how these programs function as a measure of social control over the poor and working class by the state. They are heavily funded during periods of growing social unrest and disaffection but contracted once that unrest has subsided.[35] In a separate work, these same authors showed that negligence on the part of well-intentioned leaders of grassroots movements very often contribute to the demise of these groups. In examining several organizations, they found that frequently it was the leaders and not their constituents who mitigated the prospects of the group achieving higher ground. In many instances, during the height of insurgency, elites will invite the group's leaders to cease the protest, to formally air their grievances, and ultimately, to consider a truce. Symbolically, it would appear that the elites are responding to the organizations, but in actuality they are responding to the underlying force of insurgency.

Thus, the authors conclude that "By endeavoring to do what they cannot do (attempting to appease elites), organizers fail to do what they can do (achieve higher bargaining leverage)."[36]

With specific reference to the black community, we find a plethora of voluntary-type organizations that provide a service of some kind. The black church is prominently featured among these activities. Ideologically, the leadership is wedded to a combination of conventionalist–nationalist politics. They view the community's needs as best met through the delivery of services such as hot meals, neighborhood revitalization, housing, youth programs, health services, and so on. The need to directly challenge the economic system where the responsibility resides is not envisaged as important. From their perspective, the system is judged to be sound; rather it is the greed and racism that permeate the system and make it difficult for black people to have their material needs met. The leaders who make the most noise and attract the public's attention tend to have nationalist leanings. The United African Movement (UAM), formed by Reverend Al Sharpton and attorneys Alton Maddox and C. Vernon Mason in New York City in the 1980s, would qualify. UAM and its supporters have been out in the forefront leading marches and rallies against police misconduct and racist attacks on blacks by white supremacists in Howard Beach, Bensonhurst, and Crown-Heights, to mention a few. Sharing this same platform is the Nation of Islam (NOI), which, since the assassination of Malcom X in 1965, has suffered from factionalism. Nationalists, as we described earlier, tend to overidentify with the problem of race and the uplifting of the race at the expense of directly challenging the class structure and the system of capitalism that nourishes itself on the maintenance of class divisions and social inequities. Minister Louis Farrakhan, recognized as the leading and most controversial figure in the Muslim community, has not managed to come up with any earthshaking social policy recommendations to remedy the miserable state of black civil society. On October 15, 1995, more than a million black men from across the nation attended the Million Man March, a Farrakhan- and NOI-sponsored event held in the nation's capital. The event received full-day coverage by CNN. With worldwide media coverage and the rare opportunity to set forth a concrete agenda, the minister's best formulation was a two-hour address on religion and numerology with an underlying theme of spiritual atonement and the strengthening of black capitalism.[37]

In the late 1960s and early 1970s, it was radical nationalist groups such as the Black Panther Party and the Black Liberation Army whose philosophy was confrontational and who saw the transformation of the American political and economic structure as the only hope for black people. The Panthers' much celebrated school breakfast programs for inner-city public school children could not anticipate funding from public coffers. They had to rely on the shoestring support from the community and non-mainstream donors. Their political rhetoric, uncharacteristic of most present-day grassroots groups, failed to impress the FBI. With the eventual creation of that agency's counterintelligence project,

better known as Cointelpro, the Panthers and similar groups were ruthlessly
snuffed out of existence.

The Caribbean and NGOs

According to one analyst, the fundamental challenge for the Caribbean region
currently is how to revitalize its economies, which continue to struggle under the
burden of the recessionary inertia of the 1980s. This crisis has reduced levels of
income and increased levels of unemployment and underemployment and other
social ills to such an extent that the capacity of substantial segments of the population to acquire services in the market is weakened. As a consequence, we find
a growing demand for public services in such vital areas as education and health
at the very time that the governments have been forced to impose significant reductions in per capita spending in these very areas.[38] I agree with St. Cyr that promoting the transformation of the productive structure and clearing the way for
greater social equity are tasks that call for governmental action but also greater
participation from all the region's people. Encouraging local knowledge, skills,
and resources is the only way to ensure that the empowerment of the most vulnerable can be achieved. That is where NGOs enter as chief vehicles through
which social support services and poverty alleviation programs can be dispensed
to protect the truly disadvantaged while empowering them to take advantage of
new opportunities. In light of the new initiatives ushered in with economic globalization, donors have begun to shift their support from government sectors to the
nonprofit NGOs, which they perceive as more cost effective and possessing sub-
stantially greater flexibility for donor purposes. Hence, they are able to eschew
many of the pitfalls of the political process in these countries. This has led to the
proliferation of NGOs in the region, but accompanying it are newer constraints.

Maggie Huff-Rousselle's study of NGOs and the Caribbean provides further
evidence of the newer constraints imposed on these entities. In the Caribbean, the
majority of NGOs are bilateral and multilateral donor-dependent organizations
(DDOs). Some critics have blamed these policies and the values of donors for the
frequent failures of development projects.[39] Responsibility for this is also aimed
at the self-serving interest and incompetence of professionals who work directly
or indirectly for the donors. Based on interviews conducted with recipient clients,
Huff-Rousselle's study of DDOs found that the recipient clients had little direct
influence in the development of most of the organizations compared to the
donors.[40] Most of the staff at NGOs conveyed a sense of being powerless in their
own relationship with their donor agencies. Donors shape the portfolio of activities undertaken by donor-dependent organizations, and the project-oriented nature of donor assistance defines the internal structure of the DDOs.

This investigator's interviews with NGO leaders in Trinidad and Tobago, St.
Vincent, and Dominica[41] informed that the majority of these groups are organized
for service provision. They may receive small pensions from the government in

some cases, but generally, most depend on an assortment of donors for their funding. Due to the obscurity of groups classified as radical–activist, one finds that where they do exist in these and other Caribbean island countries, similar to the United States, they are alienated and find extreme difficulty sustaining themselves. In most of the island countries, a stratification exists among the NGOs based on their funding levels and the overall support they receive for their work. Some have more political clout than others, which may emanate from their leaders' past or present affiliation with the government or their social standing in the society. Consequently, it is more likely that they will be courted by the government and some of the most influential donor-granting agencies. A representative of St. Vincent de Paul in Port of Spain, Trinidad and Tobago, a small church-sponsored group that serves the indigent and performs various forms of community work, identified Service Volunteered for All (SERVOL) as one of the more privileged organizations in the country. SERVOL was founded in the early 1970s following the brief period of civil unrest and militancy better known as "The Black Power" movement in Trinidad and Tobago. Its mission was to organize and empower the youth who were and continue to be the nation's most troubled and misguided subpopulation and who were at the helm of the unrest in the streets in 1970. SERVOL offers an array of skill-based training services throughout the country that include carpentry, welding, plumbing and electrical installation, masonry, cultural projects, child care, baking, and home economics. In addition, the organization runs a residential teacher training center in the heart of Port of Spain that certifies for early childhood education and is validated by Oxford University in the U.K. in conjunction with the local Ministry of Education. Another of its highly acclaimed projects is Rebirth House, which is a center for recovering drug addicts.[42] In calculating the success of this NGO, it is necessary to factor in that its director, Gerard Pantin, a Roman Catholic priest, hails from a family of high social ranking. Within the context of Trinidad and Tobago society and the Caribbean as a whole, class and social standing are not to be taken lightly. Moreover, Pantin's brother, the late Anthony Pantin, was the nation's Roman Catholic Archbishop, and other family members have played key roles in government and the nation's political process. Seen in this context, we are better able to understand the comments by the less well-connected NGOs. SERVOL's government pensions have been guaranteed, but more so, the group has been successful in sustaining a respectable level of funding from religious and nonreligious donors over the years.

Finally, what we find with respect to Caribbean-based NGOs is that the donor regulations and reporting requirements are becoming more cumbersome and exceed the recipient agencies' capacity to comply. Most of those regulations, it is believed, serve the donors' purposes more so than the receiving organizations. It becomes even more complex when a single DDO has succeeded in diversifying funding and must comply with the different set of requirements imposed by the various donor agencies. This is yet another way by which donating agencies are able to exercise their control over the resources, decision making, implementation plans, and information and technology of the sponsored agencies.[43]

This, then, is an overview of the NGO situation in the Caribbean. Most of the island states in the region have an ample share of these groups. Despite its acclaimed work with youth and the many accolades it has received, including a commemorative award from the Nobel Committee for its outstanding work, SERVOL has not succeeded in reaching significant portions of Trinidad and Tobago's troubled youth population. Similar to ATOP, a government-supervised training program, it must contend with the problem of dropouts. Ad hoc interviews with youth revealed to me that for the average youth, these and other programs have had no direct impact on their lives. Judging from the double-digit unemployment in most Caribbean countries today amid increasing feelings of desperation by youth and the general population outlined in chapter 3, the efficacy of NGOs as potential agencies of social change and empowerment must be called into question.

East Africa and NGOs

In East Africa, NGOs operate in a variety of contexts that reflect the peculiar philosophies, histories, and development problems in each country. The period immediately following independence for the East African countries proved challenging for the new governments. At that time, formal self-help projects began to emerge. In Kenya, the term "Harambee" was popularized to describe these projects. The term was also used by various African American nationalists in the 1960s who sought to build black cultural pride and develop community-based programs. For the most part, these early nongovernmental groups, which were registered with the government, were not corrupt and provided much needed social services to poor and working-class people. By the late 1960s and early 1970s, the ujamaa policy in Tanzania was at its zenith. Because the state believed that it was living up to its basic responsibility to citizens, NGOs were seen as superfluous. But the climate was destined to change by the mid-1980s with the advent of liberalization policies.

As the post-independence woes accumulated, nongovernmental groups began to proliferate. Corruption and graft within governmental ranks in Tanzania and in Kenya were becoming the norm rather than the exception. Accompanying liberalization was the concern by international aid organizations and donors from the West to redirect monies from the public sectors to the nongovernmental groups who were believed to be more honest and trustworthy. This would not detract from their underlying interest to control and dominate these territories; it simply meant that a new strategy would be implemented. It was at this juncture of increased foreign attention that the transformation of NGOs in East Africa began to take place—that is, from "Harambee" to "big business." This is not to imply that all local groups were procuring donor money. What it does suggest is that the competition for resources was becoming the raison d'etre of many such groups.

But as we have already pointed out, local groups with radical political agendas to bring about structural change were least likely to be considered worthy candidates to receive donor support.

From the perspective of the governments, the nongovernmental groups were potential threats. After all, they had access to resources and were responsive in certain political ways to their donors. With the establishment of multi-party democracies in Kenya and Tanzania, the ruling parties of both states believed that some groups were merely fronts for instigating political instability. A campaign to reduce the autonomy of NGOs and to weed out certain of these entities has begun. New and stringent registration laws are being put into place alongside procedures to closely monitor their financial accounts. Not aiding the situation in Tanzania is the inter-NGO friction that is noted between the Tanzania Association of Nongovernmental Organizations (TANGO) and the Tanzanian Council of Social Development (TACOSODC), two bodies that claim to be NGO umbrella organizations and are engaged in a vehement struggle over control of donor resources into the country.[44]

The new wave of NGOs span all the traditional activities, for example, community mobilization, provision of services, family planning, youth, women, and research. Because there is still no significant coordination of NGO activities in Tanzania, allegations of corruption and the misuse of funds run high. Kenya has the most NGOs in the region (more than 600, of which 100 are international) and many donor agencies have their international regional headquarters located in Nairobi. While Kenya is able to boast that it is the only country in the region to have established (in 1989) a directorate to coordinate these organizations, according to Ndegwa (1993), it was put into place by the government chiefly to ensure that NGOs' activities are compatible with the national interests.[45]

Service-oriented nongovernmental groups seem to predominate in the two major countries in East Africa. As we have seen in the other regions, maverick groups with a clear mission to challenge the status quo are obscured and have not been successful.

CONCLUSION

We need not travel far to find the sources of powerlessness. Implicated are more than a handful of governments that have visionless, bankrupt leaders at the helm. There is also the long-standing problem of investment capital that has demonstrated little if any sensitivity to the host countries and their citizens. While grassroots movements and progressive nongovernmental organizations have been steadfast in their efforts to turn things around, their vulnerability has increased with the escalation of globalization, which in turn has reduced their potential as brokers of empowerment. This is the case in the United States, the Caribbean, and East Africa. When these groups are perceived as threats by the state, various methods are employed to undermine them. Sobering lessons have been learned in the case of the Black Panthers in urban America and progressive groups in Central America. In El Salvador, Guatemala, and other Central American countries an ideological break occurred during the 1970s between NGOs—many of which were church-based—and the governments. From the perspective of the NGOs, what was needed was a fundamental transformation of the societies as opposed to the continued push for modernization. Peter Sollis reminds us that it was "liberation theology" espoused by the Central American Roman Catholic Church that changed the way people perceived themselves, the state, and their roles in the state that was threatening to the existing powers. To counteract the mounting influence of the NGOs, the governments resorted to four strategies: legal restrictions, repression, cooptation, and the creation of competing NGO activity.[46]

Accompanying the new era of globalization has been a shift in the flow and direction of resources to governments. Presently, nearly 50 percent of U.S. assistance to the developing world is now channeled through nongovernmental groups. Western governments are turning to NGOs in lieu of direct allocations to governments in these countries because it is cost effective to do so, and importantly, the opportunity for their legitimate control and surveillance over the countries is maximized.[47] So NGOs gain in notoriety and acceptance but at what cost? For certain, it is the major international NGOs such as the International Committee of the Red Cross and CARE that receive the lion's share of these resources. They rely on contributions from governments of rich countries for most of their operating budgets to the tune of nearly 90 percent. Even the International Bank for Reconstruction and Development (The World Bank) has entered into the act. In 1993 alone, 30 percent of World Bank projects had provisions for NGOs' participation.[48] We should be careful not to imply that nongovernmental bodies should take the place of the state. The role of NGOs should be to pressure the state to live up to its responsibility to nationals and in the process provide relief. It should not be their objective to assume the responsibilities of the state. A similar clarification is due when discussing the matter of self-help and self-reliance. There too the same mistake is made: the assumption that as long as people are able to pull themselves up by their bootstraps, the state can continue to do whatever it chooses, which usually translates into attending the interests of the elite.

Commenting last year on the U.S. proposal for the African Growth and Opportunity Act, Ron Daniels, activist and director of the Center for Constitutional Rights, observed a contradiction. It concerned the president of Tanzania, who anointed the act as a profound measure of hope for the struggling countries on the continent. What Daniels found so contradictory was that the very country that became the beacon of hope and resistance for so many under the leadership of the venerable Julius Nyerere would now urge other African nations to support a measure that was clearly not in their best interests. Nelson Mandela is among the few African leaders who oppose the bill, calling it "unacceptable." Ironically, a majority of African American elected officials in the Congressional Black Congress support the measure. Daniels commented:

How ironic, tragic even, that as we prepare to enter a new century and millennium, Africa, the motherland, is so afflicted by poverty, underdevelopment, hunger, disease, corruption and debt that African leaders, out of desperation and expediency are in effect begging to be re-colonized. How ironic that the continent whose historical underdevelopment under slavery and colonialism with vast human and material resources that contributed mightily to the enrichment and development of Europe and America, must now turn to the former slave-masters and colonizers for a "bail-out."[49]

The central argument put forth in this book is that the prescription for change and solutions to the problems of urban diasporans should not assume a homogenized outlook. Recognition of the social and cultural peculiarities of the regions and territories will be required. Finding a way out of this quagmire and implementing hope with a new vision for the future, especially for the next generation, must become the hue and cry for progressives everywhere who seek real change. "Manufacturing Empowerment," the chapter to which we now turn, provides a snapshot for how this might be achieved.

NOTES

1. Noam Chomsky, *The Prosperous Few and the Restless Many* (Berkeley, Calif.: Odonian Press, 1995).

2. Carmen Deere, et al., *In the Shadows of the Sun: Caribbean Development Alternatives and U.S. Policy*. (Boulder, Colo.: Westview, 1990) (section on CARICOM, 137–140).

3. Larry Rother, "9 Caribbean Nations Open Waters to U.S. Drug Pursuit" in *The New York Times* (July 20, 1996), 2.; see also, Hilbourne Watson, "The Shiprider Solution and Post-Cold War Imperialism: Beyond Ontologies of State/Sovereignty in Caribbean–U.S. Relations" (An unpublished paper presented at the 23rd Annual Conference of the Caribbean Studies Association, St. John's, Antigua, 1998).

4. James Bennett, "Clinton in Caribbean: No Bananas Today," in *The New York Times* (May 11, 1997), 6.

5. Bennett, "Clinton in Caribbean," 6.

6. See Andre G. Frank, *Latin America: Underdevelopment or Revolution* (New York: Monthly Review Press, 1969); Immanuel Wallerstein, *The Modern-System* (Academic Press, 1974).

7. For a critique of the black middle-class position, see E. Franklin Frazier, *Black Bourgeoisie* (New York: Simon & Schuster, 1962); Clarence Lusane, *African Americans at the Crossroads* (Boston, Mass.: South End Press, 1994); Robert L. Allen, *Black Awakening in Capitalist America: An Analytic History* (New York: Anchor Books, 1990); Harold Cruse, *The Crisis of the Negro Intellectual* (New York: William Morrow, 1967).

8. For a candid discussion of racial identity and contradiction upon a prominent African American conservative, see Barry Bearak, "Questions of Race Run Deep for Foe of Preferences," in *The New York Times* (July 27, 1997).

9. Garrow discusses King's political shifting. See David J. Garrow, *The FBI and Martin Luther King, Jr.* (New York: Penguin, 1981); also, Michael C. Dawson, Riaz Khan, and John Baughman, "Black Discontent: The Final Report on the 1993–94 National Black Politics Study" (A Working Paper), University of Chicago Center for the Study of Race Politics and Culture, 1996.

10. See George Breitman, *The Last Year of Malcolm X* (New York: Pathfinder Press, 1967).

11. See Harold Cruse, "New Black Leadership Required," in *New Politics* (Vol. 11, No. 4, 1992), 43–47.

12. Howard W. French, "In Africa's Harsh Climate, Fruits of Democracy," in *The New York Times* (Jan. 4, 1998), 4.

13. The Europa World Yearbook, 1996 Data for Kenya (Vol. 2), 1821.

14. James C. McKinley Jr., "Uganda Leader Stands Tall in New African Order" in *New York Times* (June 15, 1997), 3.

15. Gordon Lewis, *The Growth of the Modern West Indies* (New York: Monthly Review, 1968); Franklin W. Knight, *The Caribbean: The Genesis of a Fragmented Nationalism* (New York: Oxford University Press, 1990).

16. Clive Y. Thomas, *The Poor and the Powerless: Economic Policy and Change in the Caribbean* (New York: Monthly Review Press, 1988).

17. Statement by Michael Manley cited in *The New York Times Obituaries* (Saturday March 8, 1997), 52.

18. Thomas, *The Poor and the Powerless*; see Obika Gray's excellent discussion of this in "Power and Identity Among the Urban Poor of Jamaica," in Charles Green (ed.), *Globalization and Survival in the Black Diaspora: The New Urban Challenge* (Albany, N.Y.: SUNY Press, 1997).

19. Maurice Bishop, *Forward Ever: The Years of the Grenadian Revolution, Speeches of Maurice Bishop* (Sydney, Australia: Pathfinder Press, 1982).

20. Selwyn Ryan, "The Decline of Good Governance in the Anglophone Caribbean" (a paper presented at the 20th CSA Conference, Willemstad, Curaçao, 1995), 3.

21. Ryan, "The Decline of Good Governance in the Anglophone Caribbean," 2.

22. James L. Dietz and Emilio Pantojas-Garcia, "Neo-liberal Policies and Caribbean Development: From the CBI to the North American Free Trade Agreement," in *21st Century Policy Review* (Vol. 2, No. 1–2, Spring 1994), 18–25; also, Davin Ramphall, "Rethinking Poverty and Development Policy in the Caribbean in the Age of Globalization," in *21st Century Policy Review,* 41–63.

23. Thomas Sowell, "Second Thoughts About the Third World," in *Harper* (November 1983); also, Peter L. Berger, *The Capitalist Revolution* (New York: Basic Books, 1986).

24. Paul Johnson, "Colonialism's Back—and Not a Moment Too Soon," in *The New York Times Magazine* (April 18, 1993), 22; Sowell, "Second Thoughts About the Third World," 34–42; Berger, *The Capitalist Revolution*.

25. Institute for Policy Studies, 1997; also, the National Labor Committee has been tracking the labor practices of leading manufacturing firms, among them, The Gap and the Disney Corp., for their use of child labor at slave wages; Professor Susan Eckstein of Boston University's Latin American Studies Association presented an informative talk and analysis on this subject at a forum on "New York and the World," The CUNY Graduate Center, October 23, 1997.

26. This consciousness is growing among labor in core societies. During the United Parcel Service strike in August 1997, a number of strikers and their supporters brought up the problems of Third World workers' wage structure and its impact on American workers.

27. The term NGO was originally defined in Resolution 288 (x) Feb. 27, 1950 at the UN Economic and Social Council (see Njuguna Ng'ethe, *In Search of NGOs* [Nairobi, Kenya: Univ. of Nairobi Institute for Developing Studies] [Occasional Paper, No. 58, 1989], 15–17).

28. Thomas G. Weiss and Leon Gordenker (eds.), *NGOs, The UN & Global Governance* (Boulder, Colo.: Lynne Rienner, 1996).

29. See Michael Bratton, "The Politics of Government–NGO Relations in Africa" in *World Development* (Vol. 17, No. 4, 1989), 569–587.

30. Njuguna Ng'ethe, *In Search of NGOs*.

31. Boutros Boutros-Gali, Foreword to Weiss and Gordenker, *NGOs, The UN & Global Governance*, 1996, 7–8; also Robert O. Keohane and Joseph S. Nye Jr., "Globalization: What's New? What's Not? (And So What?)." (*Foreign Policy*, Spring 2000, 116–117).

32. Weiss and Gordenker, *NGOs, The UN & Global Governance*, 21.

33. See Gary Delgado's historical review of the Association for Community Organizing Now: Gary Delgado, *Organizing the Movement: The Roots and Growth of ACORN* (Philadelphia: Temple University Press, 1986); IAF does mainly grassroots organizing consulting and training. For more, see Charles Green and Basil Wilson, *The Struggle for Black Empowerment in New York City: Beyond the Politics of Pigmentation* (New York: McGraw-Hill, 1992).

34. Weiss and Gordenker, *NGOs, The UN & Global Governance*, 34.

35. Frances F. Piven and Richard A. Cloward, *Regulating the Poor: The Functions of Public Welfare* (New York: Vintage, 1971).

36. Frances F. Piven and Richard A. Cloward, *Poor People's Movements: Why They Succeed, How They Fail* (New York: Vintage, 1979).

37. Marable critiques the Million Man March. See Manning Marable, *Speaking Truth to Power* (Boulder, Colo.: Westview, 1996), 139–145.

38. J. St. Cyr, "A Report on a Survey of the Potential of Non-Governmental Organizations As Partners in Development," UNECLAC, P.O.S. (Feb. 24, 1994), 15–16.

39. Maggie Huff-Rousselle, "Colonialism As An Organizational Development Strategy: Case Studies on Donor-Dependent Organizations in Haiti and the Commonwealth Caribbean," in *21st Century Policy Review* (Vol. 3, Nos. 1–2, 1996), 60.

40. Huff-Rousselle, *21st Century Policy Review*, 63–65, 67.

41. Interviews conducted in August 1993 with representatives from St. Vincent de Paul, the National Self-Help Commission, and The Ecumenical Church Loan Fund Committee of the Christian Council of Trinidad and Tobago (ECLOF), Port of Spain, Trinidad; Marion House in Kingstown, St. Vincent; Small Projects Assistance Team (SPAT), Roseau, Dominica.

42. "Supplement on Servol," in *Trinidad Guardian*, Sunday, October 1, 1995, 1–8; also, "Servol's Caring Touch," in *Express*, Sunday August 27, 1995, 13.

43. Huff-Rousselle, *21st Century Policy Review*, 71, 75.

44. For an in-depth discussion of the state's strategies to control NGOs, see Stephen N. Ndegwa's, "NGOs as Pluralistic Agents in Civil Society in Kenya" (A Working Paper, No. 491, Institute for Development Studies, University of Nairobi, 1993) (especially pages 11–33); data also gathered from an interview with Dr. Joe Lugalla, January 19, 1998.

45. Stephen N. Ndegwa, "NGOs as Pluralistic Agents in Civil Society in Kenya," 11–15.

46. Peter Sollis, "Partners in Development? The State, NGOs, and the UN in Central America," in Weiss and Gordenker, *NGOs, The UN & Global Governance*, 193.

47. Weiss and Gordenker, *NGOs, The UN & Global Governance*, 25.

48. Weiss and Gordenker, *NGOs, The UN & Global Governance*, 31.

49. Ron Daniels, "Cash Strapped African Leaders Beg To Be Re-Colonized," in *The Black World Today* (August 1, 1999), *http://www. tbwt.com/views/rd/rd.*

7

Manufacturing Empowerment
and Resisting Globalization

History informs us that to pull the plug and turn off the lights at the plant that manufactures powerlessness has never been an easy task. There is little reason to believe that it will change any time soon. Perhaps no one understood that better than ex-slave and abolitionist Frederick Douglass when he reminded us:

> If there is no struggle there is no progress. Those who profess freedom yet deprecate agitation are men who want crops without plowing up the ground; they want rain without thunder and lightning; they want the ocean without the awful roar of its many waters. Power concedes nothing without demand. It never did and it never will.

> Frederick Douglass [circa 1895].

For this chapter we return to the leading argument of this study, which is that efforts to empower urban blacks in the diaspora are unlikely to succeed if they fail to take into account cultural- and societal-specific concerns. In lieu of chronicling resistance movements to globalization in the various territories and regions, a useful alternative would be to explore some of the societal-specific solutions. To articulate these policy approaches, it will be necessary to integrate data that were previously presented in our discussion of the urban crisis in the three geographical settings alongside findings from the youth surveys.

A glance at the responses by youth across the diaspora to key survey items reported in chapter 5 lends credence to what many progressives have believed all along: that contrary to popular belief, the future generation is not made up of uncontrollable social misfits. Our survey data of youth revealed that the majority of them felt that they could take control of their present situation, that government should do more to help them, and that the police have a role to play in their communities but not as exploiters and abusers. Although the data show evidence of frustration and hopelessness among these young urban dwellers, the impression we are left with is that they are very much concerned about stability and with improving the quality of their lives. At the same time, we are cognizant that in the new global order, those who control capital have become even more sophisticated, technologically and politically, than in the past. Hence, a new quality of leadership will be required to mobilize the urban poor. Unfortunately, that quality of leadership is yet to arrive.

Two of the three regions explored in this study, namely the Caribbean and East Africa, are classified as developing regions. Development is not static, as regions and territories are classified along the development continuum on the basis of their high, medium, or low stage in human development. When the criteria of development are considered, that is to say, measures of GDP, the physical–social infrastructure, the extent of economic dependency, economic diversification, the level of technological advancement, and the legacy of colonialism, the Caribbean as a whole would qualify at the medium stage of development. But within the regions themselves, differences are to be found. This was noted among the territories in the Caribbean sample, for example, between Trinidad and Tobago and St. Thomas, V.I. at the higher end and St. Vincent and Dominica at the medium end of development. Similarly in the case of East Africa, it would be fair, though arguable by the calculations of some observers, to position Kenya at a slightly higher stage in the development process than its neighbor, Tanzania. However, the East African region as a whole would qualify at a lower stage of development compared to the Caribbean.

Development is an amorphous concept. As we have seen, whether we are addressing highly developed societies such as the United States, or the lesser developed societies of the Caribbean and East Africa, many of the same problems that afflict black urban dwellers are observed. In the following discussion, two developing regions plus North America, represented by the United States, are considered. Because we are not dealing with homogeneous societies, our aim is to move beyond the matter of commonalities and to address some of the societal-specific solutions. First we will examine the United States, followed by the Caribbean and East Africa.

The United States

For the United States, compared to the Caribbean and East Africa, race matters consume a major share of the discussion on urban policy issues and their solutions. Despite the expansion of the black middle class since the 1960s and passage of the civil rights legislation, national polls continue to show that blacks generally recognize racism to be the major obstacle to their achieving parity with whites and other groups, and why political and economic empowerment continues to elude them.[1]

The 1996 Texaco Oil Company case, which was the largest monetary settlement in a racial discrimination case in the nation's history at $140 million, corroborated claims by blacks in corporate America that race is a persistent factor in determining their ability to achieve and sustain parity with whites. In the Texaco case, senior white executives were captured on audiotape during a meeting disparaging nonwhite employees and threatening their prospects for mobility in the company. The tape was leaked by a disgruntled Texaco executive who attended that meeting.[2] Because the ugly head of racism will not disappear with the stroke of a pen, firm and consistent legislative measures remain necessary.

But history has revealed to us that it will take a far greater outpouring of sensitivity from members of the dominant racial group and the resolve of their progressive leaders to enforce the existing laws. Because these criteria have not been satisfied throughout the history of race and ethnic relations in the United States, racial and ethnic conflict continues to ebb and flow. What to do about the black problem preoccupied much of the attention of white civil society in the ante-bellum and post-bellum periods. Nearly a century and a half later, their concern is no less intense. In turn, how to survive the system of white supremacy has been the concern of blacks since their arrival at America's shores in chains right up to the present. Today, in the urban areas, the chains have been replaced by subtle racialisms and hostile, trigger-happy white police officers who live in the outer suburbs, far removed from the communities they patrol.

Appeals for affirmative action should not be interpreted as a retreat from the commitment to self-help. For too long, antagonists of affirmative action have played that mutually exclusive card. Ironically we find that card being played with greater zeal by black conservatives who are the products of the very policy they seek to discredit.[3] By all calculations, it appears that the conservatives now have the upper hand in the debate. White citizens will need to understand that to retreat now and push blacks back would be a regressive move for the cause of democracy. Clearly this was not what Alexis de Tocqueville predicted during his tour of post-Revolutionary America in the nineteenth century. Americans must be helped to see that it is not affirmative action that is hurting America; rather, it is the harsh, uncaring, and parsimonious tendencies of its economic system. Simply stated, unless as the result of some miraculous turnaround, white civil society is overcome by feelings of guilt and racism is forced to retreat, the need for this form of compensation for past and present discrimination will continue to be viewed as necessary by its black victims.[4]

In the opening chapter of this book, the United States was presented as the hub of world popular culture with cable television and the satellite dish serving as chief conduits. It is reported that over 90 percent of what is viewed by the American audience is domestically produced and that this is in stark contrast to what is understood to be the case in much of the developing world. In the Caribbean, for example, the ratio of foreign to domestic programming is just the reverse.[5] The impact of the media and commercial advertisement on African Americans and blacks in the Caribbean, and their youth subpopulations in particular, is astounding. The media has been criticized as an instrument of political distraction[6] in the African American community, but also as an instrument of economic destabilization to ensure that dollars exit the community.

To appreciate the media's dual functions of political distraction and economic destabilization, just consider the following statistics: Blacks constitute only 13 percent of the population yet 40 percent of all records and CDs sold in America are purchased by black teens. Fifty percent of all tickets to movie theaters in America are purchased by blacks between the ages of 12 and 24. Blacks drink 20 percent of all scotch whisky consumed in the country, and black professionals spend $16 billion annually at convention markets.[7] Madison Avenue and the other ad conglomerates are all too familiar with blacks' consumptive patterns and, importantly, that they are cultural trendsetters who other groups tend to emulate. On that basis alone, in 1990, these corporate giants spent $743 million on advertisements targeted specifically to black consumers; in 1996 that figure had risen to $865 million.[8] It is debilitating that blacks have not been able to stem this pattern and ensure that more of their hard-earned dollars remain in their own communities and contribute to their development. Due to poor leadership and disorganization in the black community, no serious offensive against the commercial media and materialism has flourished. So embedded are the values of materialism and consumerism in the socialization process of the black community that efforts to counter them appear insurmountable.

To temper blacks' materialistic and consumptive habits, some members of the community have proposed that the curriculum taught in schools should be infused with an African-centered content. Such an approach, it is believed, would assist in freeing young black minds, enabling them to become more conscious about their glorious past and their contribution to world culture.[9] This is a laudable idea, but because poor and working-class residents have not been successful at achieving full control of their school districts, implementing this curriculum has been mightily challenged by the various white-controlled education boards. Regrettably, this is what the black community's struggle for school decentralization and community control in the late 1960s has come to.

Violent crime in the inner cities all across America is reported to be on the decline. This is disputed by community activists who argue that the downturn is actually the effect of biased reporting methods used by official law enforcement agencies. Also cited is the hire of more police officers, aggressive policing, and the wave of new prison construction, which is creating an even greater incentive to find and lock up people.[10] These activists point out that the conditions that lead to crime have not been altered. We know these conditions all too well as unemployment, underemployment, classism, and the normal fluctuations and uncertainties of market capitalism.

But while crime and violent homicides are plummeting in New York City and other American cities, the incidence of police violence, mainly against young black males, continues to rise. In our youth surveys, an area of significant concern associated with the larger issue of hopelessness and frustration was their perceptions of the police. Surveys of youth from five major cities in five states pointed to their mistrust of law enforcement personnel. Some of the known causes are corruption within the police rank and file, racial profiling or stereotyping, and disrespect for the residents by predominantly white police officers. This persists despite efforts by the police brass over the years to integrate relevant ethnic content into the curriculum taught at many police academies. Enforcing residency laws for police officers in New York and other cities where these laws do not exist—a policy that residents have consistently advocated—should be implemented. That would not gainsay the need to examine the fundamental issue of the police culture itself and its penchant for violence. Arguably though, it would lay the groundwork for planning and implementing an effective community policing program. Furthermore, it would assure residents that their elected officials are accountable to them and their needs.

Drugs are a real issue for African American youth. Unlike their Caribbean counterparts who may play a role in the transshipment of drugs, urban youth in America tend to be engaged as users and retailers. Few will doubt that there is a great deal of work to be done by parents and community-based groups in the area of drug prevention and better supervision of young people. In the meantime, the state seems to be playing that old game of cat and mouse. Drug czars and the "Just Say No" policy that emerged during the Reagan years have become a mockery for drug pushers and young people. An aggressive education program to control demand and a more sensible interdiction policy are required. That there are more complex international initiatives yet to be adopted by the government cannot be overlooked.[11]

In June 2000 the U.S. Congress passed a bill granting $1.3 billion in aid to the Colombian government to fight drug trafficking and the coca plant production. Many Colombian and American critics do not see it as an effective antidrug bill. Instead they see it as another measure of victory for the Colombian military stronghold and the weapons industry. Growers of the coca crop and marijuana in developing countries see no reason to cease as long as the inequities between rich powerful nations and poor defenseless nations remain. It is these inequities that create havoc for poor farmers and campesinos in Latin America and the Caribbean and reduce their chances of making a decent livelihood. For most, the shift to drug cultivation is one sure means of feeding their families. The United States could take the lead by encouraging more equitable trade agreements between international bodies like the WTO and the drug-producing countries in the developing world that would implement a system of fairness and lead to more beneficial outcomes for the poor farmers. Of course, this will not happen without the application of pressure from the bottom.

Rising unemployment among inner-city youth is the other worrisome matter. A major effect of economic globalization on American labor has been the flight of industrial jobs out of the country entirely or to select locales within the country. Because black people populate the inner-city areas, they are the ones who have been unevenly affected by its disappearance. For blacks in the developing world, economic globalization has had the opposite effect. They have been the beneficiaries of low-paying assembly-type jobs that now traverse the globe[12] or in many instances, have no jobs at all due to structural adjustment policies. They have also suffered the effects of the downsizing of civil service government jobs where the majority of school dropouts were guaranteed employment.

While youth unemployment is a common concern for all young people between the ages of 15 and 24, the black rate is consistently higher than that of whites.[13] This finding is consistent with employment patterns for the general population. Contrary to popular understanding, there is a limit as to the number of low-paying service jobs available to young adults. Fast-food restaurants have become synonymous with part-time employment for youth. A commonly used expression by young employees to describe their jobs at these settings is to say that they "flip burgers." As families experience unemployment by the major breadwinner and as disposable family incomes decline, young people have felt an even greater need to help out at home and to maintain their material lifestyles. With the cost of higher education soaring and loan packages becoming more difficult to procure, urban and nonurban college students must find work to support themselves and maintain their fashion-conscious lifestyles.

Not adequately addressed is the competition among youth for jobs. Inner-city youth enrolled at local universities, those in regular attendance in high school, or those who just happen to have good networks must compete for sales, fast-food, and other positions that pay minimum wage without health benefits. The less fortunate and the school dropouts make up the bulk of the unemployed. In this area, the greatest responsibility lies with the government, most likely in partnership with the private sector for job creation, training, and support programs to guide young trainees along the way. Despite all of the rhetoric, this does not appear to be the will of either the state or the private sector. Persistent pressure at the grassroots level must be applied to force them to move in this direction.

Grassroots efforts will involve seeking out and supporting those politicians who appear to be leaning on the side of jobs over prisons and are willing to press for legislation that supports decent jobs at decent wages. The irony is that youth desire change and improvement in their lives no less than adults. That message came through clearly from the youth surveys. But there is also the issue of youths' lukewarm sense of trust for adults and the state. There is a great deal more that black people can do to improve their community, especially the small cadre of wealthy blacks, if they are effectively mobilized. In fact, earlier writers have been quite critical of the "black bourgeoisie" for their seeming invisibility in this important area.[14] Leaders must arm themselves with new strategies for mobilizing the community with emphasis placed on the youth. A key obstacle is the media and consumer culture that distracts the community from important political work. Efforts by organizers to appeal to the youth will require methods that have not been seriously contemplated in the past. Included might be writing in youth publications, working more creatively with local neighborhood organizations, appearing on cable television channels geared to young people, and using young artists, who through rap and drama might creatively convey alternative messages and values to other youth. One effort in this direction is the initiative by the former Nation of Islam Minister of Youth Conrad D. Mohammed, entitled Movement for Change. According to the minister, Movement for Change is conscious hip-hop activism for global empowerment, which attempts to take rap and hip-hop to a more political level.[15]

It has been said that it will take nothing short of a mass movement such as the Civil Rights Movement of the 1960s to turn things around for black people. To be more direct, action for change by a mere 13 percent of the American population will not be sufficient. For some strange reason the matter of allies has not received its fullest attention in the black community. One study found that in cities where there is racial and ethnic diversity, such as New York City, efforts by blacks for political empowerment are futile in the absence of support from other ethnic, racial, and issue-oriented groups.[16] Black people will have to convince poor and working-class members from other groups that their interests are shared. Moreover, they must convey that their suffering is not associated with the shortcomings of any one racial or ethnic group, but rather it is associated with the misdeeds of the American political economy. The misdeeds of American capital are historic and not easily dismissed with the creation of so-called "economic empowerment zones" throughout the nation's inner cities. These zones purport to address the problem of youth unemployment; however, the fact is that they are fraught with limitations. There is a limit in terms of the number of jobs that are made available in the neighborhoods, wages, and the extent to which the corporations can be regulated to ensure job security.

The Caribbean

An interesting observation is the extent to which many island residents from the Caribbean have come to perceive themselves as modernized people. We can credit this false identity to the proximity of the isles to the United States, the increased presence of transmigrants, and the inordinate penetration of foreign mass culture that has taken place. Because of this, the drive to build and develop their countries with the understanding that there is still a great deal of work left to be done has been compromised.

Another observation is that, notwithstanding the fact of their different development stages, in many respects the economic and social problems of the people of the Caribbean appear to overlap with those of the East Africans. Included among them are the problems of deagrarianization and the major effect of rural to urban migration. There is also the need for improved economic diversification to become less import oriented, and there is also the problem of youth unemployment.

Deagrarianization has resulted in the increased levels of food importation over the years. Thus policies that encourage reagrarianization will have particular significance for the people of the region. This hinges on the willingness of common folk to return to the land to feed themselves and develop their societies. One of the greatest ironies about development is that the more advanced economies in the world today are nations that were once functionally "developing" societies. They experienced the familiar stage of learning how to feed themselves prior to becoming great industrial and post-industrial powers. Suffering from self-imposed amnesia, these superpowers have been less than supportive of poorer nations' need to follow that same and very important development course. Precisely, they have encouraged policies of deagrarianization in these societies.[17]

Economic disequilibrium is at the root of the social dislocation we are witnessing in the region's urban districts. Whereas crime is reported as plummeting in the United States and its major cities, the reverse is true in the urban centers of the Caribbean. A major difference between the two regions along the issue of crime is seen in the policy response to the problem. In the United States, an expansion of low-wage service jobs has been accompanied by an increase in tax levy expenditures and bonds for the hire of more police officers and the construction of new prisons. But for the frail, debt-ridden economies of the Caribbean, where violent crimes are reportedly on the rise, a similar response has not occurred. So long as economic hardship persists, rising crime rates even in small island states like Dominica and St. Vincent and the Grenadines are to be expected. While debt cancellation would be the ideal policy, another approach would be for the financial institutions to permit countries to use a portion of the interest payments to finance social programs. For certain, these international bodies will require pressure at the diplomatic levels. However, pressure from grassroots efforts in these countries via social movements will be imperative.

Another reason debt relief is so essential is that it will free the various governments to begin to address the social needs of their urban areas. With these resources, job preparation for youth and a reevaluation and strengthening of the education curricula can begin to take place. Employment for youth and building hope for the future will require an appeal to their creative minds for jobs development. This might take the form of promoting and supporting home-grown artistic talents like calypso, steel pan, dance, and the creative arts that can be marketed outside the region and made to compete with imported culture. One such art form to emerge from the island of Jamaica is reggae music, which has a strong history of resistance. But it should be mentioned that similar to other art forms, reggae is not monolithic and the resistance message is joined and quite often dwarfed by dance hall music and the profane. Drug smuggling and trafficking is a major problem for the region compared to the United States. Resources recovered from debt cancellation could be diverted to address this problem.

Short-term work programs such as Trinidad and Tobago's controversial "10 Day" work policy should be revisited. This program was begun during the Eric Williams administration and is officially known as the Unemployment Relief Programme (URP). It amounts to nothing more than a temporary government make-work program that places the unemployed in jobs such as street cleaning, road repair, and similar works usually for a period of two weeks, from which the title "10 Day" is derived. Politicians have come to rely on this as an easy form of patronage that they can apply for and use to appease their unemployed constituents. But this has been at the expense of much-needed long-term training and planning for the nation's youth. If real alternatives can be presented to the youth, and they can be convinced that their government truly cares about their future and also that they have a real stake in the society, the prospects for a turnaround and empowerment may be realizable. This is where nongovernmental organizations can be of tremendous support, provided of course that their hands are not tied by the self-serving interests of donor agencies. Moreover, once this is able to take root throughout the country, another problem, that of urban primacy, can be better addressed.

An important survey finding was that youth are marginally integrated in local social arrangements such as religious, recreational, and social clubs. While several factors might help to explain this, not to consider the steadily growing consumer culture and the influential role of the foreign-based mass media, would be a serious oversight. A Caribbean Cultural Information Centre was proposed by the Assembly of Caribbean People (ACP), the brainchild of the Trinidad and Tobago Oil Field Workers Union (OWTU) that would serve as a media clearing house. It was ACP's belief that regional centers, which would be run by delegates representing the pan-Caribbean, could help neutralize the penetration by materialistic, dehumanizing values that emanate from outside the region. ACP's proposal was not intended as a call for media censorship; rather, its objective was to encourage critical thinking on the part of Caribbean people about the importance of indigenous culture and to help them determine for themselves which aspects of external mass culture they deem to be necessary or expendable.[18] It is this quality of mind, values, and outlook that will be required of poor and working-class people in order to challenge their powerlessness. Unfortunately, ACP's apparent slip into obscurity will mean that its important charge will have to be taken up by other enlightened organizations.

While many youth from the Caribbean sample indicated that the police have a role to play in the larger society and their immediate communities, similar to the U.S. sample, their responses underscored their mistrust of the police. Police officers in various island states, it should be pointed out, have been implicated in the drug trade and are known to be corrupt.[19] In a focus group conducted by this investigator with youth from Port of Spain, Trinidad, several youths mentioned that the police in their districts randomly stop and harass young people for no apparent reason. This contrasts with the U.S. case, where blacks are a minority and are patrolled by a majority white police force. Thus, in the absence of direct white racism, the issue of the police culture is uncovered as the obvious cause for police misconduct and brutality. Making members of the police force more responsive to the needs of residents is not an impossibility, but it will require the will of an organized people to bring that about. Unlike New York City and other urban areas in America, residency laws for police are not at issue for the Caribbean. What is needed are improved training and recruitment programs with competitive salaries for the police. That would help lessen their need to supplement their meager wages through involvement in illicit drugs and weapons smuggling.

Finally, solutions to the urban condition in the Caribbean cannot overlook the need for stronger interregional bodies such as CARICOM. Unification will encourage states to work together to pool their resources and identify their own approaches to problem solving.

East Africa

Turning to East Africa, population growth and the pressure for rural to urban migration, plus the problem of school dropouts who are without the prospect of employment, pose an immediate threat to the future of these societies and ultimately to the development and empowerment of their masses. Policies specifically designed to target these concerns must be explored in ways that are prepared to move beyond the confines of listless rhetoric. For starters, there is the need for policies to affect deagrarianization. That will mean applying pressure to the WTO to reconsider terms of trade that have led to the decline of commodity prices for tea, coffee, and sisal. It is doubtful that diplomats from East Africa and other African states are prepared to do what will be required to pressure the WTO. Their role appears to be defined more in terms of the perks—necessary to accommodate the high-fashion lifestyle of resident diplomats in New York, London, and Paris—than with advocating long-term change for their people back home.

To affect unemployment and the demand by young people for urban relocation, Mbilinyi and Omari (1996) have considered lengthening or staggering the school year to reduce the number of school dropouts looking for work.[20] Such policies, however, offer only temporary relief and should not exempt the state from its responsibility to address the future labor needs of the country.

East Africa suffers from the crisis of urban street children who are essentially nomads in search of food and shelter. It is more severe in this region than in the Caribbean. It is prevalent in Brazil and other Latin American countries and parts of Asia. In Brazil, police and citizen death squads have been unleashed to settle the problem of poverty and neglect.[21] This will require the forceful efforts by the NGOs but also the resolve of progressive leaders to set the tone that the victimization of these children will not be tolerated. Improved education and sensitive birth control methods are desperately needed to help stem the street children crisis that is so acute in Nairobi but steadily increasing in Dar es Salaam and in other Tanzanian cities as well.

As is the case elsewhere in the developing world, television and cable networks are becoming more sophisticated and are attracting larger audiences. East Africa is no exception. Our discussion in chapter 4 suggested that the development of this medium was taking place at a slower but more steady pace compared to the Caribbean. Tanzania, which in 1994 became the last country in the region to be wired for television and cable, highlights this point. There is an advantage to the slower pace. It can provide the necessary time to do consciousness-raising work, especially with the youth. Using Tanzania as an example, it means that creative local artists could be encouraged to promote their talents and gain employment.

Also, the argument could be made for the creation of a publicly owned network that would be directly responsible to the cultural needs of the society. This is mentioned because in many countries where state-owned networks continue to operate, they are a far cry from being people oriented. In fact, many state-owned networks see their role as competitors of the privately owned cable operations and, as such, race to see who can offer the best foreign programs. Moreover, we find that as a response to neoliberalism and privatization initiatives, many government-owned stations are being sold to private investors. Local artists need the opportunity to demonstrate their skills and to show that their work can be as entertaining and profitable as that which is now imported.

Here again, the resolve of determined and progressive groups will be essential in mounting the challenge against the opposition. That opposition comes mainly from western MNCs (multinational corporations), including Japan, who see the importance of seizing the opportunity and capturing what they can from the African market while increasing their cultural hegemony. The opposition also comes from local business elites who have controlling interests in some of the newly emerging cable companies. Recent political developments around the world have provided us the opportunity to see the operation of foreign media firsthand. They have begun to penetrate Russia and the newly formed republics that once constituted the Soviet Union as well as the People's Republic of China and Vietnam. It will be interesting to see if this same posturing will triumph in North Korea, one of the last and ailing bastions of traditional communism in the world today. Sensing North Korea's imminent collapse, one U.S.-based transnational, Coca Cola, is waiting patiently for the signal from Washington that North Korea is officially open to American business.

Compared to the United States or the Caribbean, crime in East Africa is less violent in nature and is usually committed out of desperation. Our survey data found that East African youth, like their diasporan counterparts, recognize the important role of the police. To a lesser degree, however, they share mixed feelings about the police and how they carry out their role as enforcers of the law. In Kenya, there is little doubt that the police serve as the eyes and ears of the state and are known to release undue force against youth and the urban poor. Kiosks are regularly ransacked and the "jua kali" (members of the informal sector) are harassed. More active of late, Tanzanian police have been carrying out actions similar to their Kenyan counterparts. In chapter 4 we noted Lugalla's description of the police harassment of the "machingas," the young male hawkers who operate along Congo Street in the Kariakoo district of Dar es Salaam. It is common practice for the police to steal their wares. The special trained Field Force Police Unit was unleashed against striking doctors at Muhimbili Medical Centre, the country's largest health facility, located in Dar es Salaam. Corruption is known to exist within the ranks of the police—triggered, as in the Caribbean, by their meager salaries and poor working conditions. Unlike their North American counterparts, they do not have the advantage of strong police unions. However, the new multi-party political system offers the opportunity for expressive democracy and the advance of demands by common folk. Once the residents and their leaders become mobilized around the issue of the police, the prospects of it swelling into a national movement for change will increase.

The "aid mentality" that has come to define so many of the African states and outpaces the Caribbean in terms of the amount of aid received will have to be balanced with a heightened emphasis on self-reliance. New and improved roles for regional and intercontinental alliances— beyond those that currently exist, such as the Organization of African Unity (OAU) and the Economic Cooperation of West African States (ECOWAS)—will have to be defined. To reiterate a point cited earlier by Tajudeen Abdul Raheem, General Secretary of the Global Pan African Movement, "The problem for Africa is not poverty. Africa is wealthy but it is the Africans who are poor." In Tanzania and Kenya, multi-party systems were recently introduced. Visionaries with the support of the people and nongovernmental agencies should seize this opportunity for constructive political mobilization. They can begin by helping people realize Dr. Raheem's perception of the problem, decide their own fate, and aggressively reclaim their lands and their cultures. From this, a new image of Africa and the empowerment of its people might stand a better chance of debuting on the world stage.

Modern Africa is contradicted by shades of traditionalism. Across the continent, identity is pegged to one's tribal or ethnic affiliation. Urban dwellers in Dar es Salaam and Nairobi are conscious of their ethnic roots—it is not uncommon to hear people proudly reference their ethnic origins. They know that they can visit their village homes at any time and connect with their people. In his study of social networks in Nairobi, Macharia (1989) found that for people operating in the informal sector, ethnicity and kinship ties with rural places of origin were the major basis for the network ties. Remittances are sent back to the village and once in the city, newcomers gravitate to relatives or other people from their ethnic community for support. Ethnic or tribal chiefs from the rural villages, usually elders, continue to wield influence even among members in the urban towns and cities. Policy engineers with recommendations for addressing the needs of urban folk would be wise to consult the various tribal chieftains for their advice and/or intervention.

Finally, the AIDS epidemic that has wreaked havoc all across the continent has been particularly destructive in East Africa. In fact, youth survey respondents ranked AIDS as the major social problem affecting their life chances (see appendix C). This problem is exacerbated by poverty, limited education, and powerlessness. Empowering the masses and reducing poverty are long-term measures, but they are the only assured measures to combat this scourge.

Toward a Universal Policy

Although our efforts thus far have been toward a rejection of the homogeniza-tion thesis, there is one policy that—if universally embraced by progressive leaders throughout the diaspora—could achieve many of the goals we have out-lined and simultaneously serve as a resistance to globalization. Even so, it would have to be tailored to the specific needs and structure of a given society. That policy is localization. Like globalization, localization is not a recent idea; however, it is experiencing a tremendous upsurge in various progressive circles. Helena Norberg-Hodge is one of its principal proponents.[22] Localization does not advocate the elimination of all trade but rather it seeks to boost the utiliza-tion of internal human and infrastructural resources that would strengthen and help diversify the frail economies of the developing South. Shifting to local-ization would not, as critics advance, lead to worsened economic conditions as a result of the North's forced cutback in trade. Instead, the shift toward smaller-scale and more localized production would benefit the North and South and allow for more meaningful work, such as manufacturing goods for northern markets. Finally, localized production would allow the South to keep more of its own resources and labor for itself.

With the development of interregional cooperation through organizations and the strengthening of existing bodies, decisions can be made about pooling re-sources for common investment in localized enterprises. The struggle in Mex-ico's poor southern state of Chiapas is a perfect example of a people who have determined that the only hope for them and their families is to engage in forceful resistance against the government for their rights to the land. Triggering their re-volt was the government's act in the 1980s following the drop in coffee, cattle, and corn prices, prohibiting small farmers' continued use of the land. However, the land was opened up to major private companies.[23]

Perhaps others may not be inspired in the same way as the Zapatistas of Chiapas, but the Zapatista movement has catapulted activists and leaders toward other forms of direct resistance to globalization in order to champion the case for localization policies. The Battle in Seattle in December 1999 over the annual WTO meetings, the anti-IMF/World Bank protest in Washington, D.C., in April 2000, and the Jubilee 2000 Campaign exemplify such action. Both movements drew scores of protesters representing NGOs and other grassroots entities from around the world. In the case of Seattle, between 60 and 80 thousand protesters from around the world who had begun mobilizing for many months prior gathered to demonstrate their resistance to WTO practices that affect people from developing countries most severely. It was en-couraging to note the participation by significant numbers of young people alongside middle-aged people. Unfortunately, the protesters did not draw heavily from the black diaspora and other communities of color. According to one analyst, their lim-ited participation might be explained by insufficient mobilization, and too, their reser-vations about consensus politics in the context of a majority white-led movement.[24]

Jubilee 2000 Campaign is an international Christian-based coalition that celebrates the two-thousandth anniversary of the birth of Christ. Its chief objective is to put into practice the teachings and leadership of Christ through a radical address of world poverty and the plight of Third World nations. Debt cancellation of developing nations is a central strategy of the Jubilee movement. In fact, over 17 million people around the globe signed the Jubilee 2000 petition to leaders of wealthy nations. Jubilee 2000/USA is a coalition of religious, social justice, and environmental groups that continues to exert pressure on the American government and its agencies, the IMF, and the World Bank for total cancellation of debt owed by poor countries by the end of this year. In fact, following pressure by Jubilee 2000/UK, the British government announced earlier this year that it will cancel 100 percent of bilateral debt owed by poor nations and pledged money to go to multilateral debt relief. Environmental protection and poverty reduction notwithstanding, Jubilee 2000/USA advocates for the empowerment of ordinary people in shaping the economic decisions of their government.[25]

In the final analysis, localization could also be defined as an expression of self-help or self-reliance. It can be shown to be effective even among poor and working-class inner-city youth from developed countries. Tapping their creative skills and talents could provide new paths to economic empowerment for themselves and their communities.

CONCLUSION

Optimistic in outlook, this chapter demonstrated how the prospects for manufacturing empowerment, as elusive and gargantuan as they may appear, are within the reach of poor and working-class people. But the matter of leaders who are without vision will have to be tackled. There is also the need to invigorate community-based, nongovernmental bodies, given their potential as democratizing and empowering entities. Much of the discussion centered on initiatives required of the victims and their leaders and also initiatives required by the state to make this happen. Mobilization with the objective of building new democratic political structures by, for, and of the people was not adequately discussed here. Nevertheless, we can assume that would be the next step once strategies are put into place.

Seeping through the lines is the ever-pressing need for an ongoing dialogue across the regions of the diaspora. This same position was called for in the conclusion to the recent volume, *Globalization and Survival in the Black Diaspora.*[26] There it was suggested that an alliance of blacks from the African continent, Europe, North America, the Caribbean, and Latin America could create an ongoing forum to begin to debate the ways and means of empowering persons of African descent and for challenging the new global order. In addition, there would be the opportunity for them to address the social and economic problems they commonly experience or that are specific to certain states and regions. Vital to this structure would be a special section devoted to the future generation and the specific areas in which youth would have direct input.

It is evident that many of the existing structures have not succeeded in initiating this level of dialogue and that parallel structures will be required. These existing structures—for example, the United Nations General Assembly, the Organization of African Unity, and CARICOM—will require face-lifts, new mission statements, and new blood at the helm. Certainly the Pan African Congress model deserves much credit for its pioneering work in this important arena. Toward this end, African Americans might be seen as having a unique role, given their history as political catalysts in the diaspora. This role was most visible during the Civil Rights and Black Power movements of the 1960s and early 1970s, but also during the anti-Apartheid struggle for South Africa. Interestingly, the cultural nationalist Marcus Garvey emigrated to New York City from Jamaica in 1917, where he established the Universal Negro Improvement Association, a "back to Africa" campaign that was international in scope. In addition, considering that the wealth of contemporary black culture emanates from "Black America," African American artists should be inspired to reexamine the symbolisms and genres that they project around the world with the objective of replacing these with politically constructive images and forms.

As the wrath of liberalization policies continues to punish the African poor, and as Africa's vast raw materials are seen as the basis for the recovery of the West, a rare opportunity is presented for progressive African Americans to link up with those political forces in Africa that oppose the Africa Trade and Development Bill. Jesse Jackson Jr. is one of the few members of Congress to oppose the Africa Trade Bill, also known as the Africa Recolonization Act. He has now altered that name to read Human Rights, Opportunity, Partnership and Empowerment for Africa Act (Hope for Africa Act). This alternative calls for debt cancellation, the restoration of the foreign aid budget line item for Africa, addressing the social needs of the African poor, enhancing educational opportunities for women, and battling the scourge of AIDS. The Hope legislation would provide preferential access to U.S. markets for a broad range of goods made in Africa by African workers and would ensure that these goods are produced in a manner that is consistent with internationally recognized labor, human rights, and environmental standards.[27]

There is reason to be optimistic about the future, but there is also reason to be cautious. The opportunity for full involvement in decision making over every aspect of their existence should be a right of all people in democratic societies. Unfortunately, this is not the case. Given the history of black subjugation throughout the world, empowerment is not something that can be taken for granted. To do so would be to trivialize the important message by Frederick Douglass that began this chapter, which he delivered more than a century ago.

NOTES

1. Michael C. Dawson, Riaz Khan, and John Baughman, "Black Discontent: The Final Report on the 1993–94 National Black Politics Study" (University of Chicago, Center for the Study of Race Politics and Culture, 1996); Andrew Hacker, *Two Nations: Black and White, Separate, Hostile, Unequal* (New York: Ballantine Books, 1992); Alphonso Pinkney, *The Myth of Black Progress* (Cambridge University Press, 1986); Joe R. Feagin, "Continuing Significance of Race: Anti-black Discrimination in Public Places" in Diana Kendall (ed.), *Race, Class and Gender in a Diverse Society* (Boston, Mass.: Allyn and Bacon, 1996); Bart Landry, *The New Black Middle Class* (Berkeley, Calif.: University of California Press, 1987).

2. Bean Counters. "What Went Wrong at Texaco: Dialogue" in *Emerge* (February 1997), 36–40.

3. Glen C. Loury, "Black Dignity and Self-Help" in Joseph G. Conti and Brad Stetson (eds.), *Challenging the Civil Rights Establishment: Profiles of a New Black Vanguard* (Westport, Conn.: Praeger, 1993).

4. Derrick Bell, *Faces at the Bottom of the Well: The Permanence of Racism* (New York: Basic Books, 1992).

5. A film by Christopher Laird and Anthony Hall, "And the Dish Ran Away with the Spoon" (Oley, Pa.: Bullfrog Films, 1992).

6. Although Parenti's analysis does not deal specifically with the black community, it is nonetheless relevant. See Michael Parenti, *Make Believe Media: The Politics of Entertainment* (New York: St. Martin's Press, 1992) (especially chapter 1, "Political Entertainment"); also, Noam Chomsky, *Turning the Tide* (Boston, Mass.: South End Press, 1985), 234–256; and *Manufacturing Consent: Noam Chomsky and the Media* (edited by Mark Achbar) (New York: Black Rose Books, 1994).

7. Tony Brown, black independent businessman and host of *Tony Brown's Journal* says, "If you took blacks out of America, Wall Street would collapse last week." See Tony Brown, *Black Lies, White Lies* (New York: William Morrow, 1995), 286.

8. Tony Chapelle, "Soul for Sale: Companies Are Taking Black Culture and Consumers To the Bank," in *Emerge* (January 1998), 42–48.

9. See Molefi Kete Asanti's statement on Afrocentricity, "Afrocentricity, Race and Reason," in *Race & Reason* (Autumn 1994, Vol. 1, No. 1), 20–22; also, Marcia Sutherland, *Black Authenticity: A Psychology for Liberating People of African Descent* (Chicago, Ill.: Third World Press, 1997).

10. Fox Butterfield, "Crime Keeps on Falling, but Prisons Keep on Filling," in *The New York Times* (Section 4, Week in Review, September 28, 1997), 1.

11. Ivelaw L. Griffith, *Drugs and Security in the Caribbean* (University Park, Pa.: Penn State University Press, 1997).

12. Stanley Aronowitz and William DiFazio, *The Jobless Future* (Minneapolis, Minn.: University of Minnesota Press, 1994).

13. These data on youth unemployment rates are from the Bureau of Labor Statistics and cited by Sklar. See Holly Sklar, *Chaos or Community? Seeking Solutions, Not Scapegoats for Bad Economics* (Boston, Mass.: South End Press, 1995), 13.

14. See E. Franklin Frazier, *The Black Bourgeoisie: The Rise of a New Middle Class in the United States*, 1957. Henry Louis Gates, Jr. and Cornel West, *The Future of the Race* (New York: Knopf, 1996).

15. Interview with Minister Conrad Muhammed in Harlem, N.Y., February 1999.

16. See Charles Green and Basil Wilson, *The Struggle for Black Empowerment in New York City: Beyond the Politics of Pigmentation* (New York: McGraw-Hill, 1992, paperback).

17. Various authors have pointed this out in their works. See, for example, Andrew Webster, *Introduction to the Sociology of Development* (London, U.K.: Macmillan, 1984, chapter 1); Mike Mason, *Development and Disorder: A History of the Third World Since 1945* (Toronto, Canada: Between the Lines Press, 1997); and Peter Worsley, *The Three Worlds: Culture and World Development* (London: Weidenfeld & Nicolson, 1984, chapter 1).

18. Charles Green, "Urbanism, Transnationalism, and the Caribbean: The Case of Trinidad and Tobago" in Green (ed.), *Globalization and Survival in the Black Diaspora: The New Urban Challenge* (Albany, N.Y.: SUNY Press, 1997),171–198.

19. Journalist Melvin Claxton discusses the role of the police and also political figures in the Caribbean drug trade. See his six-part series on drugs, violence, and crime in the Caribbean, *Daily News of the Virgin Islands*, March 1994.

20. Dorothy A. Mbilinyi and Cuthbert K. Omari, *Rural–Urban Migration and Poverty Alleviation In Tanzania* (Dar es Salaam: University of Dar es Salaam Press, 1996).

21. Irene Rizzini (ed.), *Children in Brazil Today* (Rio de Janeiro: Editora Universitâria Santa Ursula, 1994); also, Vania Penha-Lopes, "An Unsavory Union: Poverty, Racism, and the Murders of Street Youth in Brazil," in Green, *Globalization and Survival in the Black Diaspora.*

22. Helena Norberg-Hodge, "Shifting Direction: From Global Dependence to Local Interdependence," in Jerry Mander and Edward Goldsmith (eds.), *The Case Against the Global Economy* (San Francisco: The Sierra Club, 1996) 393–406.

23. Philip McMichael, *Development and Social Change: A Global Perspective* (Thousand Oaks, Calif.: Pine Forge Press, 1996), 235.

24. See: Barbara Epstein, "Not Your Parents' Protest," (*Dissent*, Spring 2000) 8-11; also "The Battle in Seattle: What Does it Mean for the Future?" (*As the South Goes: A Periodical from Project South*, Vol. 8, No. 1, Spring 2000) 1–5.

25. See David Bryden's report, "Jubilee 2000/USA Urges Making a Truly Meaningful New Years Resolution to Definitely Cancel the Crushing Burden of Debt," (*dbryden@j2000usa.org*, January, 2000).

26. Green, *Globalization and Survival in the Black Diaspora* (see the Conclusion).

27. Horace Campbell, "U.S. Partnership of Domination of Africa: Reflections on the Discussions over the Africa Growth and Opportunity Bill," International Committee of Black Radical Congress (Feb. 10, 1999), 6.

8

Conclusion

This book was as much a statement about the problems of development and urbanization as it was about race, ethnicity, and migration. Chiefly though, it was a statement about black people whose historical and ancestral roots embody wisdom, spiritual and cultural wealth, strong leadership, and courage but whose present state of affairs is in stark contrast to that rich and glorious past. Disappointing is the fact that blacks in the diaspora, including those on the African continent, are without a clear understanding about their rich and diverse cultural history. The legacy of slavery, colonialism, and white supremacy notwithstanding, it is the imposition of the globalized frontier that poses the latest threat to blacks in the new millennium. Victimization, it is discovered, comes not only at the hands of Europeans and the transnational firms they control but from within the ranks of the victims as well.

If there is a single observation to be made at this historical juncture it is that the more things change the more they seem to remain the same. What is cast as the "new global order" is, after all, not so new. In the background, the political and economic machinery of the world's most powerful nations and individuals is tediously serviced and lubricated each and every day to ensure the reproduction of powerlessness in its variegated forms and hegemony by the few. In the wake of universal antidotes such as neoliberalism, deregulation, privatization, structural adjustment, and the ever-so-free market, the fate of the urban poor is not contemplated. It is now up to those less fortunate souls to avail themselves of these and other incentives. In the new global order, their fate is in their own hands.

Powerlessness presents a clear and present danger for urban-bound blacks on the African continent and in the diaspora. Whether blacks control the political state (the Caribbean and East Africa) or not (the United States), the debilitating condition of powerlessness is evident. Powerlessness — as we have been arguing throughout this book — is the effect of economic and cultural globalization, but it is also the effect of politically bankrupt governments and visionless leaders.

Demographics and the debate over whether blacks constitute a minority or a majority in these societies appear to have little significance. Ruth Simms-Hamilton of the African Diasporic Research Project at Michigan State University discusses the need for studies on the diaspora that go beyond the observation that there is variation socially and culturally from one black society to another. She argues that needed now are theoretically integrated paradigms that offer an in-depth comparative-historical analysis.[1] The comparative approach that is operationalized in this study is one small step in that direction.

Continuing to operate is the inevitable issue of ideological divisions among and between blacks. These divisions have militated against the closing of ranks by blacks in the diaspora. The historic Pan African Congress appears to have lost ground. Although the United Nations is a useful institution, given its elitist top-down structure, its significance for those struggling countries in the diaspora seems more symbolic than substantive. Another limitation of the United Nations structure for the black cause is the absence of any African American voice. Activists during the 1960s, including Malcolm X, struggled to have the African American case for human rights brought before the United Nations General Assembly. There was also concern to have that international body reserve a permanent forum for African people living in the United States. Because these calls were seen as an embarrassment to the United States, they were snubbed.

We cannot begin to seriously debate the fate of black people in the new global frontier without taking a critical look at the youth who are the future generation. How we value our youth is an indication of our outlook on the future. Investment in youth must come to be valued in the same way that we invest in other aspects of long-term commitment. Falling short of that, what we are left with is an abomination. The antisocial behaviors observed by young people in the diaspora are symptomatic of their neglect and their response to it. It is not the youth who create the various consumer products from which their identities are derived. Neither are they the creators of the violent and obscene media they watch, nor the unemployment, homelessness, and economic recessions that shatter their families and their hopes and dreams for the future. Responsibility for these rest with adults.

Accepting the view put forth by the proponents of economic globalization that one day we will all be able to row our boats in the same direction—which implies that there is little need to concern ourselves with our cultural differences and the specific needs that arise from those differences—is reminiscent of the charge by convergent theorists during the immediate post–World War II period in America. Their objective was to shatter the left's insistence on demonstrating the real fact of class divisions and class conflict. They staged a masterful offensive that included the creation of consumer credit and showing average Americans that their material condition was improving at such a rate that they would soon converge with the upper classes. In simple language, the issue of class divisions and class conflict was becoming an anachronism. The interests of the poor, the working class, and the middle class were said to be indistinguishable.

Cultural homogenization, a byproduct of globalization, is credited with the shrinking of world cultures that is currently taking place. Findings from our youth survey point to an overlap of problems experienced by urban blacks across regions. What we have argued in the present study is that in spite of this, to consider the solutions to the problems as "faceless" would be incorrect. Undoubtedly, a generic approach would simplify matters but as we have seen, this approach has not always worked. Political, cultural, and social dimensions of a given society are inextricably linked to the nature of its problems and give specificity to urban-bound problems. Black people and their leaders throughout the diaspora must come to recognize the forces that connect them. At the same time, they must recognize their social and cultural differences and also that specific remedies will be needed to address their problems.

Resisting powerlessness is not an easy task, particularly when it is camouflaged as the latest in consumer products. This form of deception has proven successful as the masses are distracted more and more from the important work of critical thinking and consciousness raising. This was illustrated by a team of filmmakers, mentioned in chapter 3, that visited St. Lucia and several neighboring island states to examine the impact of foreign-based satellite television and other media on Caribbean people and their cultures. A relevant finding was that the people want this programming and are not supportive of policies that would threaten their daily diet of soap operas, situation comedies, police action movies, music videos, and so on that are imported mainly from North America. The very government officials who are at a loss for progressive responses to the bread-and-butter demands of their people are, however, anxious to coordinate their efforts with private cable operators to make sure that the public's media demands are met. Resistance will require commitment and sacrifice that too few people up to this point are prepared to make. Importantly, it will also mean identifying and working with allies inasmuch as many of these same problems are afflicting nonblack communities around the globe as well.

Understanding the importance of building unity and fostering dialogue among African Americans, a group of activists and scholars launched the Black Radical Congress as a precursor to forging alliances with others. At its initial meeting in Chicago in 1997, which brought together some of the brightest African American intellectuals and activists, the group drafted its preamble. Featured was its commitment to work for transformative politics that recognizes the contributions from the diverse ideological trends in the black community. These tendencies include revolutionary nationalism, radicalism, socialism, feminism, and conventionalism. The BRC's aim is to focus attention on the conditions of black poor and working-class people and is united against all forms of oppression including racism, imperialism, class exploitation, patriarchy, and homophobia. Finally, the BRC will not attempt to replace or displace existing organizations—rather it will mobilize them.[2] There are those who doubt that this strategy will work. What they fail to realize is that a strategy committed to respecting ideological differences, a prerequisite to meaningful dialogue about the current and future situation of the race, is a long-awaited step in the right direction. It is this quality of grassroots work that must germinate in every corner of the diaspora.

Our conservative survey of poor and working-class urban youth from the United States, the Caribbean, and East Africa failed to support the popularly held thesis about the state of hopelessness and limited aspirations for the future among urban youth. Young people in our study agreed that there is hope for a better life in spite of the frustration they feel. Powerlessness may serve as an obstacle to the free expression of hope, but it has not succeeded in eliminating it. Only through sustained resistance will change occur for the future generation. But resistance will require a positive working relationship between adults and youth. Youth in our survey believe that adults care about them, but this is contradicted by adults in government and law enforcement who consistently disregard them. Resistance will require the grooming and emergence of leaders who possess a clear vision for the future. It will also require ongoing dialogue between and among blacks in the diaspora through the creation of inter- and intraregional bodies around their common problems, their differences, and their specific solutions. Finally, resistance will mean developing the courage to confront the powerful.

There is reason to be optimistic about the future for blacks and other oppressed peoples of the world. Just when it appeared that the masses' desire for change was wiped out, the "Battle in Seattle" took place. The city of Seattle in Washington, as mentioned in Chapter 7, was the site of the World Trade Organization's annual meeting in December 1999. Protesters from around the world, including progressive nongovernmental organizations and labor, rose to express their objection to greed, ruthless exploitation, and environmental vulgarity by the multinationals. Particularly inspiring was the participation by significant numbers of young people that included high school youth and university students whose mobilization had begun months prior. Massive arrests and excessive force by the police and the National Guard helped to contain the insurgents. But a victory was scored as the protest movement grew more intense, causing a near shutdown of the city and a disruption of the meetings. Seattle was followed by anti-IMF and World Bank protests in Washington, D.C., in April 2000.

In the final analysis, pulling the plug at the manufacturing plant that reproduces powerlessness and resisting globalization is the only way forward. The fate of urban blacks everywhere is anchored to this process.

NOTES

1. Ruth Simms-Hamilton, "Toward a Paradigm for African Diaspora Studies," African Diaspora Research Project (Michigan State University, East Lansing, Michigan, 1990), 15.
2. The Black Radical Congress Mission Statement, 1998.

Appendix A

A Word about Methods

> We have only one means of demonstrating that one phenomenon is the cause
> of another: it is to compare the cases where they are simultaneously present or
> absent.
>
> É. Durkheim [1]

In basic social research methods we learn that the decision about which method
to use is seldom if ever a simple matter and, too, that this decision is heavily influenced by the study's objectives, the desired sample size, and the budget. Given
the objective of this study, which was to explore the similarities and differences
of the urban condition of blacks in the diaspora as well as the problem of their
powerlessness and its reproduction, the comparative method was considered the
logical choice. Comparison is, after all, a natural human exercise. We are constantly comparing our ideas, institutions, and people in relation to other ideas, institutions, and people.[2] Moreover, comparison is a universal tool in the social sciences and stands out as a quintessential approach for better understanding the
causes of observed social phenomena.[3]

Secondary sources combined with interviews were effective in the description
and analysis of the condition of powerlessness and urban dislocation for the regions and territories that were selected in this investigation. Once the decision
was made to include youth from each of the study regions to explore and compare their perceptions of their situation, their degree of hopelessness and relation
to the larger community, an additional method, namely the survey approach, was
considered.

Survey research is probably the best-known method available to social scientists interested in collecting original data for describing a population too large to
observe directly.[4] This is especially useful if the investigator is operating on a
limited budget, which was the case in this study. As with any other method,

problems are sure to arise. A problem that had to be resolved concerned the reluctance by some bureaucrats at schools and recreational programs in the United States to cooperate. These settings were identified as prime sources for subjects. Reflecting on the long history of invasiveness by journalists and others from outside the black community whose motives were often guided by the prospects of Pulitzers and personal gain than by any real concern for the plight of the residents, resistance by some bureaucrats was understandable.

Needless to say, this situation presented a real problem and reduced the prospects of obtaining a representative sample. Consequently, this meant having to rely on personal contacts who could guarantee the investigator access to the targeted population. These contacts included administrators at senior high schools, job training programs, public health projects that screen and treat youth, recreational programs that try to keep youth off the streets, teachers, and staff at church-based outreach groups who were sensitive about the need to protect their clients yet were supportive of this research project. They were all cognizant of the fact that researchers come in different packages. In Tanzania, researchers are required to procure a permit. Because time and budgetary constraints posed major concerns for this investigator, personal contacts in the country were tapped for their assistance in identifying respondents and administering the survey. Due to the sensitive nature of many survey items and the need to guarantee respondents' right to privacy, the use of actual names of schools, recreational facilities, and training programs with which the subjects were affiliated was avoided.

THE SUBJECTS

Effort was made to include a proportional number of males and females. All of the subjects were urban residents from poor and working-class backgrounds and were between the ages of 14 and 24. Most of them were still enrolled in secondary school, but some reported that they had dropped out of school. Others were enrolled in training programs, were unemployed, or were just hanging out on the streets. Homeless street youth and incarcerated persons were not included, as it was felt that their detachment from the day-to-day social experiences of community life would hinder the quality of their responses to a number of the survey items.

In sum, a total of 686 youth were asked to complete questionnaires. Forty-nine percent were males and 51 percent were females. The majority (47 percent) were between ages 14–15, 32 percent were between ages 16–18, and 21 percent were from the age group 19–24 years.

Three regions were selected for this comparison: North America (represented by the United States), the Caribbean, and East Africa with the United States serving as a backdrop against which the other two regions would be compared. As we pointed out in the first two chapters, the decision to do so was based on American cultural influence around the world and particularly the impact of African American cultural life on blacks across the diaspora. In each region, poor and working-class blacks are highly concentrated in the urban areas. Many of them have either lived in the urban areas for most of their lives or migrated there from the countryside with their families.

The United States

The questionnaire was administered to 323 inner-city youth from the United States. Three northeastern cities, one southern city, and one southwestern city were included. Among the northeastern localities were Newark, New Jersey, and the southeast section of Washington, D.C. New York City featured the districts of Bedford-Stuyvesant, Brooklyn, the southeast section of Jamaica, Queens, and the outer suburb of Nassau County on Long Island that included portions of Hempstead, Roosevelt, Freeport, and Rockville Centre. Nassau County, it should be noted, is a typical American suburb of mainly white residents who occupy single-family homes. In contrast, the black areas we identified in Nassau County stood out as inner-city eyesores against the backdrop of white middle-class suburbia because of their poor social and physical infrastructure.

Southerly was the city of Richmond, Virginia, and southwest was Central Los Angeles, California. In all of the urban areas surveyed, chronic joblessness, drug use and trafficking, poorly functioning local schools, and family and other social dislocations coexist with a declining physical infrastructure. It is worth noting that at least once during the last decade, these five cities appeared on the FBI's list as the nation's number one crime- and violence-prone city. Classic sociological case studies of the American urban scene have consistently relied on Chicago, Philadelphia, and even Boston.[5] It was the concern of this study to move beyond that model to include urban areas that have not benefited from that microscope but, due to radical structural changes in the political economy, now require similar attention.

The Caribbean

The questionnaire was administered to a total of 239 respondents from four Anglophone Caribbean cities: Port of Spain, Trinidad and Tobago (75 respondents), Kingstown, St. Vincent and the Grenadines (77 respondents), Roseau, Dominica (39 respondents), and Charlotte Amalie, St. Thomas, U.S. Virgin Islands (47 respondents). These countries were selected because of the escalating problems in their urban districts and the fact that they are consistently overlooked in the literature compared with countries such as Jamaica, Barbados, Puerto Rico, and the Dominican Republic. Another important rationale for their selection was the opportunity to explore the hypothesized differences between and within these island countries. It should be reiterated that the urban crisis is a regional crisis. It is apparent even in those territories where there is greater economic stability and prosperity. Examples are the Dutch colony of Curaçao, the British colony of the Cayman Islands, the Bahamas, and the U.S. Virgin Islands. But because of their unique economic situation, vis à vis others in the region, these territories were not included. An exception was made in the case of St. Thomas, U.S. Virgin Islands, which enjoys a more favorable economic and material existence compared with many of its closest neighbors. Due to the Virgin Islands' unique status as the only U.S. possession in the Anglophone Caribbean, the opportunity to include it in this study could not be bypassed. In any event, youth from the local high school, where a majority of the respondents originated, came from working-class backgrounds.

East Africa

Compared with West and South Africa, East Africa has received less attention in the literature despite the fact that urban problems in the eastern states have risen dramatically and are now considered to be proportional to the experiences of urban constituencies elsewhere on the continent. The neighboring countries of Tanzania and Kenya offered the opportunity to compare the development of the urban crisis and powerlessness in two societies that since independence developed at opposite ends of the political spectrum. Kenya became more Western in outlook while Tanzania struggled to maintain a sense of cultural and economic autonomy. One hundred and twenty-four respondents were identified from the central urban districts of these two East African countries. Seventy-one respondents came from Dar es Salaam, the former capital and most populous city of Tanzania. Fifty-three respondents came from Nairobi, Kenya's capital and largest city. Respondents from Dar es Salaam hailed from three districts: Temeke, Kinondoni, and Ilala.[6] Temeke District is the least developed of the three in terms of its physical infrastructure, the income-earning power of its residents, and the quality of social services available to them. Ilala District encompasses Buguruni, which is a residential area of mainly poor people and where unplanned squatter settlements such as Tandika and Mabatini are located. It also contains the Kariakoo area and the sprawling market where many residents, including the "machingas," engage in trade as a means of daily survival. Some middle- to low-income employees in government departments and factories also reside there. Finally, there is Kinondoni District, which contains Kawe, a partly planned area that accommodates middle- and high-income people. But the other end of Kawe, near the Lugalo army barracks, is an unplanned squatter settlement that accommodates the desperate poor who have been referred to in the Kiswahili language as "walalahoi." Kinondoni also encompasses the Manzese ward that is typical of the congested areas in Dar es Salaam where housing is mostly unplanned. A majority of the household heads from Manzese engage in petty informal businesses or are low-cadre working-class employees.

The Kenya sample was procured from four contiguous low-income housing development projects in the Eastlands District of the city: Uhuru, Jericho, Umoja, and Buru Buru Estates.

ABOUT THE QUESTIONNAIRE

The questionnaire consisted of 56 closed, mainly binary questions that solicited either a yes or no response. A more detailed questionnaire was preferable, but it was necessary to take into account the limited tolerance level of the targeted population for completing surveys, particularly lengthy questionnaires. Operating, too, were certain logistical matters such as the fact that subjects would be administered the forms in variegated settings that included the classroom, the basketball court, the street, or in many cases, in front of their housing project. For these and other reasons, an abbreviated questionnaire was designed.

Where possible, the principal investigator asked some respondents to participate in focus group sessions. These groups comprised no more than six subjects, ran for about one hour, and provided the participants the space to discuss at greater length select items asked of them on the questionnaire. Importantly, the focus groups allowed the investigator to gain further insight into youths' perceptions and feelings about their condition. With the exception of the Tanzanian survey, all of the questions were written in simple English and intelligible to subjects with primary school preparation. The items were developed by the principal investigator in consult with key informants from each of the study regions and were later standardized. Samples of question items were adapted from Public Opinion Quarterly and similar U.S. national surveys of youth.

Inordinate attention has been given in the literature to the question of youths' hopeless state and limited aspirations for the future as an explanation for their rebelliousness and antisocial behavior in general. Thus, survey items queried respondents' awareness of the serious nature of the problems confronting them, their perception of their government's ability to correct things, their own ability to control their environment, and their outlook for the future two to five years hence. This set of items is viewed as critical since it draws the state to center stage of the analysis in order to assess its role in the manufacture of powerlessness. Furthermore, it enables us to compare powerlessness among urban masses in sovereign black states with their counterparts in other states and regions where they are an oppressed minority with limited access to state power.

Another key survey concern was the extent of community integration, which was measured by their involvement in sports, social clubs, and familial and religious networks. Early sociological studies established the relationship between one's social attachments and bonding to community and the larger society and feelings of estrangement, frustration, and hopelessness. Durkheim, for example, believed that industrialization and the growth of cities weakened people's attachment to their local communities and led to their feelings of isolation and detachment. The result was self-destruction and various forms of antisocial behavior.[7]

Because high crime rates and violence in most urban areas throughout the diaspora are associated with youth, mostly males,[8] a set of survey items explored respondents' relationship to the criminal justice system and drug use. In light of the growing dissonance between youth in the urban areas and the police, a cluster of items centered on their view of the police and authority figures in general. Because the media—that is, television, videos, and the cinema—is viewed as a leading influential agency for violence and other forms of antisocial behavior among young people today, a set of items explored this area.

Likert scaling allows for a better interpretation of responses. Thus, some items including adult care, government help, police protection, and youth control were scaled as Likert questions that solicited a strongly agree, agree, no opinion, disagree, strongly disagree, do not know response. Because marginal differences were observed for certain of these categories and for convenience in reporting the findings, they were collapsed. "No opinion" was interpreted as ambivalence and consequently was collapsed with "strongly disagree" and "disagree" to form one category: "disagree." Similarly, "strongly agree" and "agree" were collapsed to form the single category, "agree." "Do not know" was dropped since fewer than one percent of all respondents bothered to select that category. Tables reported here include the numbers and percentages of those who responded to each category of the survey items.

LIMITATIONS

We have already mentioned the sampling limitations. The survey instrument was tested in the United States but not in the other regions, and that caused some problems. In Tanzania, one finds that the lingua franca at the central institutions of higher learning and government offices is English. Among average Tanzanians though, the mother tongue is Kiswahili. In Nairobi, some knowledge of English among common folk is far greater than in Tanzania. Thus, for the Tanzanian sample, the questionnaire was translated into Kiswahili. Any time one has to rely on translations, the risk of misinterpretation is present. If the translator is unfamiliar with the specific subculture of the sample population, the risk factor is increased. This presented a problem for the Tanzanian respondents and, as a result, some items were left blank or were incorrectly completed.

Finally, the survey data were gathered in 1994. Under normal circumstances, with the passage of time, the need to gather new data would be indicated. In this instance, however, the problem of urban dislocation throughout the black world has not abated. In fact, one observes that, especially in the regions and territories selected for this project, the problem has worsened.

NOTES

1. Émile Durkheim's *The Rule of Sociological Method* is cited in M. Dogan and D. Pelassy, *How to Compare Nations: Strategies in Comparative Politics.* 2nd ed. (Chatham, N.J.: Chatham House, 1990), 15.

2. Dogan and Pelassy, *How to Compare Nations*, 3; Rodney Stark, *Sociology.* 5th ed. (Belmont, Calif.: Wadsworth, 1996) (chapter 4, "Macro Sociology"),109.

3. Stark, *Sociology*, 16.

4. See Earl Babbie, *The Practice of Social Research.* 6th ed. (Belmont, Calif.: Wadsworth, 1992) (chapter 10 "Survey Research," 262–263).

5. Among the classic and contemporary works: W. E. B. Dubois, *The Philadelphia Negro: A Social Study* (New York: Schocken, 1967/1899); also Dubois, *Sociology and the Black Community* (Chicago, Ill.: University of Chicago Press, 1978); William F. Whyte, *Street Corner Society* (Chicago, Ill.: University of Chicago Press, 1943); Gerald Suttles, *The Social Order of the Slum* (Chicago, Ill.: University of Chicago Press, 1967); William Julius Wilson, *The Truly Disadvantaged* (Chicago, Ill.: University of Chicago Press, 1987); Elijah Anderson, *Streetwise: Race, Class and Change in an Urban Community* (Chicago, Ill.: University of Chicago Press, 1990).

6. Background information on each of these districts was extracted in part from Patrick Masanja's preliminary study on AIDS/Health Research in Tanzania (unpublished, Department of Sociology, University Dar es Salaam, 1993).

7. Émile Durkheim, 1964/1893; 1951/1897; *The Division of Labor in Society.* 2nd ed. (New York: Free Press); also, Ferdinand Toinnes, 1957/1887, *Community and Society.* C. P. Loomis, trans. and ed. (East Lansing, Mich.: Michigan State University Press).

8. Kenneth B. Clark, *Dark Ghetto* (New York: Harper & Row, 1965); Anderson, *Streetwise*; Wilson, *The Truly Disadvantaged*; Amos Wilson, *Black on Black Violence: The Psychodynamics of Black Self-Annihilation in the Service of White Domination* (New York: Afrikan World Infosytems, 1990).

Appendix B

Comparing Four Caribbean States

Appendix B. Comparing Four Caribbean States

POWERLESS-NESS	Trinidad & Tobago				St. Thomas				St. Vincent				Dominica			
	A[a)	D[b)	N[c)	T[d)	A	D	N	T	A	D	N	T	A	D	N	T
Adult care	46 (66.7)	9 (13.0)	14 (20.3)	69 (100.0)	32 (72.7)	4 (9.1)	8 (18.2)	44 (100.0)	47 (64.4)	13 (17.8)	13 (17.8)	73 (100.0)	22 (61.1)	6 (16.7)	8 (22.2)	36 (100.0)
Government help	60 (84.5)	2 (2.8)	9 (12.7)	71 (100.0)	43 (95.6)	1 (2.2)	1 (2.2)	45 (100.0)	73 (91.3)	3 (3.8)	4 (5.0)	80 (100.0)	36 (94.7)	1 (2.6)	1 (2.6)	38 (100.0)
Police protection	59 (85.5)	3 (4.3)	7 (10.1)	69 (100.0)	32 (82.1)	3 (7.7)	4 (10.3)	39 (100.0)	69 (88.5)	5 (6.4)	4 (5.1)	78 (100.0)	36 (94.7)	1 (2.6)	1 (2.6)	38 (100.0)
Police treatment	6 (15.8)	28 (73.7)	4 (10.5)	38 (100.0)	2 (9.5)	17 (81.0)	2 (9.5)	21 (100.0)	3 (7.3)	32 (78.0)	6 (14.6)	41 (100.0)	4 (20.0)	14 (70.0)	2 (10.0)	20 (100.0)
Fair trial	20 (43.5)	10 (21.7)	16 (34.8)	46 (100.0)	10 (34.5)	6 (20.7)	13 (44.8)	29 (100.0)	16 (33.2)	14 (29.2)	18 (37.5)	48 (100.0)	11 (50.0)	6 (27.3)	5 (22.7)	22 (100.0)
No youth control	18 (26.1)	39 (56.5)	12 (17.4)	69 (100.0)	6 (13.6)	35 (79.5)	3 (6.8)	44 (100.0)	8 (10.4)	67 (87.0)	2 (2.6)	77 (100.0)	4 (11.4)	27 (77.1)	4 (11.4)	35 (100.0)
Your ability to change	55 (83.3)	3 (4.5)	8 (12.1)	66 (100.0)	37 (82.2)	1 (2.2)	7 (15.6)	45 (100.0)	58 (77.3)	8 (10.7)	9 (12.0)	75 (100.0)	33 (86.8)	1 (2.6)	4 (10.5)	38 (100.0)

Continued

Appendix B. Comparing Four Caribbean States (cont.)

	Trinidad & Tobago			St. Thomas			St. Vincent			Dominica		
	Yes	No	T	Yes	No	T	Yes	No	T	Yes	No	T
COMMUNITY INTEGRATION												
Social club	34 (46.6)	39 (53.4)	73 (100.0)	23 (48.9)	24 (51.1)	47 (100.0)	40 (51.3)	38 (48.7)	78 (100.0)	18 (46.2)	21 (53.8)	39 (100.0)
Religious club	31 (43.1)	41 (56.9)	72 (100.0)	14 (30.4)	32 (69.6)	46 (100.0)	40 (51.9)	37 (48.1)	77 (100.0)	21 (53.8)	18 (46.2)	39 (100.0)
Recreational club	31 (44.3)	39 (55.7)	70 (100.0)	10 (21.7)	36 (78.3)	46 (100.0)	28 (37.8)	46 (62.2)	74 (100.0)	11 (28.2)	28 (71.8)	39 (100.0)
OTHER SOCIAL ISSUES												
Youth arrest	9 (12.0)	66 (88.0)	75 (100.0)	3 (6.5)	43 (93.5)	46 (100.0)	3 (3.7)	78 (96.3)	81 (100.0)	0 (0.0)	39 (100.0)	39 (100.0)
Arrest of friends	50 (76.9)	15 (23.1)	65 (100.0)	18 (48.6)	19 (51.4)	37 (100.0)	29 (42.0)	40 (58.0)	69 (100.0)	18 (52.9)	16 (47.1)	34 (100.0)
Drug use	12 (16.0)	63 (84.0)	75 (100.0)	6 (13.0)	40 (87.0)	46 (100.0)	13 (16.7)	65 (83.3)	78 (100.0)	7 (17.9)	32 (82.1)	39 (100.0)
Employment	16 (21.9)	57 (78.1)	73 (100.0)	15 (32.6)	31 (67.4)	46 (100.0)	18 (20.0)	64 (80.0)	80 (100.0)	6 (15.4)	33 (84.6)	39 (100.0)

Continued

Appendix B. Comparing Four Caribbean States (Cont.)

	Trinidad & Tobago			St. Thomas			St. Vincent			Dominica		
	N	%	Rank	N	%	Rank	N	%	Rank	N	%	Rank
MEDIA EXPOSURE												
Watch TV												
1–2 hrs	18	(25.0)		15	(31.9)		27	(36.0)		12	(32.4)	1
2–4 hrs	29	(40.3)		21	(44.7)		30	(40.0)		14	(37.8)	2
over 4 hrs	25	(34.7)		11	(23.4)		18	(24.0)		11	(29.7)	
(total)	72	(100.0)		47	(100.0)		75	(100.0)		37	(100.0)	
TV program												
Comedy	27	(48.2)	1	16	(40.0)	1	11	(19.3)	2	11	(34.4)	1
Drama	6	(10.7)	5	2	(5.0)	4	15	(26.3)	1	8	(25.0)	2
News	1	(1.8)	6	—	—		3	(10.5)	4	—	—	
Nature education	7	(12.5)	3	1	(2.5)	7	3	(5.3)	8	1	(3.1)	6
Police education	7	(12.5)	3	10	(25.0)	2	8	(14.0)	3	1	(3.1)	6
Soap operas	—	—		7	(17.5)	3	4	(7.0)	6	6	(18.8)	3
Sports	8	(14.3)	2	2	(5.0)	4	6	(10.5)	4	3	(9.4)	4
Talk shows	—	—		2	(5.0)	4	4	(7.0)	6	2	(6.3)	5
(total)	56	(100.0)		40	(100.0)		81	(100.0)		32	(100.0)	
YOUTH PROBLEMS												
AIDS	7	(11.7)	4	5	(12.2)	5	5	(7.5)	5	1	(3.1)	6
Street crime	6	(10.0)	5	11	(26.8)	1	1	(1.5)	7	2	(6.3)	4

Continued

Appendix B. Comparing Four Caribbean States (Cont.)

	Trinidad & Tobago			St. Thomas			St. Vincent			Dominica		
	N	%	Rank	N	%	Rank	N	%	Rank	N	%	Rank
Drugs	14	(23.3)	2	10	(24.4)	2	15	(22.4)	2	8	(25.0)	2
Lack of education	3	(5.0)	7	6	(14.6)	4	8	(11.9)	3	2	(6.3)	4
Poverty	—			1	(2.4)	6	1	(1.5)	7	—	—	
Suicide	1	(1.7)		—			1	(1.5)	7	—	—	
Unemployment	15	(25.0)	1	—			28	(41.8)	1	15	(46.9)	1
Poor government services	6	(10.0)	5	—			2	(3.0)	6	—		
Lack of guidance	8	(13.3)	3	8	(19.5)	3	6	(9.0)	4	4	(12.5)	3
(total)	60	(100.0)		41	(100.0)		67	(100.0)		32	(100.0)	
FAMILY LIFE												
Live with												
Both parents	35	(47.3)	1	17	(37.8)	2	26	(32.1)	2	13	(33.2)	2
Mother	24	(32.4)	2	24	(53.3)	1	27	(33.3)	1	15	(38.5)	1
Father	4	(5.4)	3	1	(2.2)	4	—	—		—	—	
Grandparents	3	(4.1)	5	1	(2.2)	4	3	(3.7)	4	6	(15.4)	3
Other relatives	4	(5.4)	3	2	(4.4)	3	18	(22.2)	3	2	(5.1)	4
Alone	1	(1.4)	7	—			1	(1.2)	7	1	(2.6)	6
Friends	—			—			1	(1.2)	7	—		
Partner	2	(2.7)	6	—			3	(3.7)	4	2	(5.1)	4
Spouse	1	(1.4)	7	—			2	(2.5)	6	—		
(total)	74	(100.0)		45	(100.0)		81	(100.0)		39	(100.0)	

Continued

183

Appendix B. Comparing Four Caribbean States (Cont.)

	Trinidad & Tobago			St. Thomas			St. Vincent			Dominica		
	N	%	Rank	N	%	Rank	N	%	Rank	N	%	Rank
FUTURE PROJECTS												
Life in 2 yrs												
Working	33	(50.0)	1	5	(11.4)	2	26	(35.6)	2	12	(36.4)	1
Secondary school	4	(6.1)	4	5	(11.4)	2	2	(2.7)	5	2	(6.1)	4
University	8	(12.1)	3	27	(61.4)	1	10	(13.7)	3	6	(18.2)	3
Married	1	(1.5)	6	1	(2.3)		2	(2.7)	5	—	—	
Having children	—	—		—	—		—	—		—	—	
Pursue career	18	(27.3)	2	3	(6.8)	4	28	(38.4)	1	11	(33.3)	2
Unemployed	2	(3.0)	5	—	—		3	(4.1)	4	—	—	
Others	—	—		3	(6.8)	4	2	(2.7)	5	2	(6.0)	5
(total)	66	(100.0)		44	(100.0)		81	(100.0)		33	(100.0)	
Life in 5 yrs												
Working	23	(37.7)	1	8	(20.0)	3	21	(30.0)	2	11	(37.9)	1
Secondary school	—	—		—	—		—	—		—	—	
University	6	(9.8)	4	13	(32.5)	1	9	(12.9)	3	4	(13.8)	4
Married	14	(23.0)	2	3	(7.5)	4	25	(35.7)	1	7	(24.1)	2
Having children	3	(4.9)	5	—	—		3	(4.3)	6	—	—	
Pursue career	12	(19.7)	3	14	(35.0)	2	8	(11.4)	4	5	(17.2)	3
Others	3	(4.9)	5	2	(5.0)	5	4	(5.7)	5	2	(6.9)	5
(total)	61	(100.0)		40	(100.0)		70	(100.0)		29	(100.0)	

NOTE: Numbers in parentheses are percentages.

a) A denotes two response categories: strongly agree and agree.
b) D denotes two response categories: strongly disagree and disagree.
c) N denotes no opinion category.
d) T denotes total number.
e) — denotes no response to that category.

Appendix C

Comparing Two Eastern African States

Appendix C. Comparing Two Eastern African States

	Kenya				Tanzania			
	A[a)]	D[b)]	N[c)]	T[d)]	Agree	D	N	N
POWERLESS-NESS								
Adult care	37	3	7	47	56	2	5	63
	(78.7)	(6.4)	(14.9)	(100.0)	(88.9)	(3.2)	(7.9)	(100.0)
Government	45	2	1	48	59	3	2	64
help	(93.8)	(4.2)	(2.1)	(100.0)	(92.2)	(4.7)	(3.1)	(100.0)
Police	43	2	2	47	68	1	0	69
protection	(91.5)	(4.3)	94.3)	(100.0)	(98.6)	(1.4)	(0.0)	(100.0)
Police	7	14	3	24	45	21	1	67
treatment	(29.2)	(58.3)	(12.5)	(100.0)	(67.2)	(31.3)	(1.5)	(100.0)
Fair trial	13	18	4	35	45	8	20	71
	(31.7)	(47.6)	(21.4)	(100.0)	(60.6)	(11.3)	(28.2)	(100.0)
No youth	13	18	4	35	43	6	3	52
control	(37.1)	(51.4)	(11.4)	(100.0)	(82.7)	(11.5)	(5.8)	(100.0)
Your ability	36	7	8	51	23	18	2	43
to change	(70.6)	(13.7)	(15.7)	(100.0)	(53.5)	(41.9)	(4.7)	(100.0)
	Yes	No	Total N		Yes	No	Total N	
COMMUNITY INTEGRATION								
Social club	39	14	53		16	55	71	
	(73.6)	(26.4)	(100.0)		(22.5)	(77.5)	(100.0)	
Religious	33	20	53		26	45	71	
club	(62.3)	(37.7)	(100.0)		(36.6)	(77.5)	(100.0)	
Recreational	26	27	53		21	50	71	
club	(49.1)	(50.9)	(100.0)		(29.6)	(70.4)	(100.0)	
OTHER SOCIAL ISSUES								
Youth arrest	14	37	51		3	68	71	
	(27.5)	(72.5)	(100.0)		(4.2)	(95.8)	(100.0)	
Arrest of	32	17	49		18	52	70	
friends	(65.3)	(34.7)	(100.0)		(25.7)	(74.3)	(100.0)	

Continued

Appendix C. Comparing Two Eastern African States (cont.)

	Kenya			Tanzania		
	Yes	No	Total N	Yes	No	Total N
Drug use	19	33	52	8	62	70
	(36.5)	(63.5)	(100.0)	(11.4)	(88.6)	(100.0)
Employment	11	42	53	5	66	71
	(20.8)	(79.2)	(100.0)	(7.0)	(93.0)	(100.0)
MEDIA EXPOSURE						
TV Watch						
1-2 hrs	19	(41.3)		5	(62.5)	
2-4 hrs	14	(30.4)		1	(12.5)	
over 4 hrs	13	(28.3)		2	(25.0)	
(total)	46	(100.0)		8	(100.0)	
TV program						
Comedy	13	(28.9)	1	2	(28.6)	2
Drama	2	(4.4)	5	3	(42.9)	1
News	2	(4.4)	5	—e	—	
Nature education	1	(2.2)	7	—	—	
Police education	10	(22.2)	2	—	—	
Soap operas	8	(17.8)	4	—	—	
Sports	9	(20.0)	3	2	(28.6)	2
Talk shows	—	—		——		
(total)	45	(100.0)		8	(100.0)	
YOUTH PROBLEMS						
AIDS	5	(10.2)	3	19	(27.1)	1
Street crime	5	(10.2)	3	1	(1.4)	8
Drugs	14	(28.6)	2	10	(14.3)	4
Lack of education	—	—		8	(11.4)	5
Poverty	2	(4.1)	7	13	(18.6)	2
Suicide	—	—		3	(4.3)	6
Unemployment	17	(34.7)	1	13	(18.6)	2

Continued

Appendix C. Comparing Two Eastern African States (cont.)

	Kenya			Tanzania		
	N	Percent	Rank	N	Percent	Rank
Poor government services	3	(6.1)	5	—	—	
Lack of guidance	3	(6.1)	5	3	(4.3)	6
(total)	49	(100.0)		70	(100.0)	
FAMILY LIFE						
Live with						
Both parents	36	(67.9)	1	39	(54.9)	1
Mother	7	(13.2)	2	5	(7.0)	3
Father	1	(1.9)	7	5	(7.0)	3
Grandparents	1	(1.9)	8	1	(1.4)	8
Other relatives	2	(3.8)	3	9	(12.7)	2
Alone	2	(3.8)	3	5	(7.0)	3
Friends	2	(3.8)	3	—	—	
Partner	2	(3.8)	3	5	(7.0)	3
Spouse	—	—		2	(2.8)	7
(total)	53	(100.0)		71	(100.0)	
FUTURE PROJECTIONS						
Life in 2 yrs						
Working	16	(31.4)	2	19	(27.1)	2
Secondary school	—	—		30	(42.9)	1
University	10	(19.6)	3	3	(4.3)	5
Married	—	—		7	(10.0)	3
Having children	1	(2.0)	6	7	(10.0)	3
Pursue career	17	(33.3)	1	1	(1.4)	7
Unemployed	5	(9.8)	4	2	(2.9)	6
Others	2	(3.9)	5	1	(1.4)	7
(total)	53	(100.0)		70	(100.0)	
Life in 5 yrs						
Working	28	(54.9)	1	27	(38.6)	1
Secondary school	1	(2.0)	6	12	(17.1)	3

Continued

Appendix C. Comparing Two Eastern African States (cont.)

	Kenya			Tanzania		
	N	Percent	Rank	N	Percent	Rank
University	1	(2.0)	6	7	(10.0)	4
Married	6	(11.8)	3	13	(18.6)	2
Having children	1	(2.0)	6	5	(7.1)	5
Pursue career	7	(13.7)	2	—	—	
Unemployed	4	(7.8)	4	1	(1.4)	7
Others	3	(5.9)	5	5	(7.1)	5
(total)	53	(100.0)		70	(100.0)	

NOTE: Numbers in parentheses are percentages.

a) A denotes two response categories: strongly agree and agree.

b) D denotes two response categories: strongly disagree and strongly disagree.

c) N denotes no opinions.

d) T denotes total numbers.

e) — denotes no response to that category.

Appendix D

Powerlessness and Other Social
Measures for the U.S. Youth

Appendix D. Powerlessness and Other Social Measures for the U.S. Youth

	United States			
	A[a]	D[b]	N	T
POWERLESS-NESS				
Adult care	243 (81.0)	14 (4.7)	43 (14.3)	300 (100.0)
Government help	261 (86.7)	10 (3.3)	30 (10.0)	301 (100.0)
Police protection	214 (71.3)	39 (13.0)	47 (15.7)	300 (100.0)
Police treatment	15 (10.1)	100 (67.6)	33 (22.3)	(100.0)
Fair trial	79.0 (31.9)	92.0 (37.1)	77.0 (31.0)	248.0 (100.0)
No youth control	67 (22.0)	202 (66.4)	35 (11.5)	304 (100.0)
Your ability to change	212 (69.5)	33 (10.8)	60 (19.7)	305 (100.0)
	Yes	No	Total N	
COMMUNITY INTEGRATION				
Social club	125 (39.6)	191 (60.4)	316 (100.0)	
Religious club	96 (30.1)	223 (69.9)	319 (100.0)	
Recreational club	92 (30.9)	206 (69.1)	298 (100.0)	
Youth arrest	66 (20.4)	257 (79.6)	323 (100.0)	
Arrest of friends	226 (72.4)	86 (27.6)	312 (100.0)	

Continued

Appendix D. Powerlessness and other Social Measures for the U.S. Youth (cont.)

	Yes	No	Total N
Drug use	85 (27.2)	228 (72.8)	313 (100.0)
Employment	108 (34.1)	209 (65.9)	317 (100.0)

	N	Percent	Rank
MEDIA EXPOSURE			
Watch TV			
1-2 hrs	69	(22.0)	
2-4 hrs	134	(42.7)	
over 4 hrs	111	(35.3)	
(total)	314	(100.0)	
TV program			
Comedy	123	(51.5)	1
Drama	10	(4.2)	6
News	5	(2.1)	8
Nature education	6	(2.5)	7
Police education	11	(4.6)	5
Soap operas	29	(12.1)	3
Sports	33	(13.8)	2
Talk shows	22	(9.2)	4
(total)	239	(100.0)	
YOUTH PROBLEMS			
AIDS	65	(26.0)	1
Street crime	32	(12.6)	5
Drugs	50	(19.6)	3
Lack of education	35	(13.8)	4
Poverty	5	(2.0)	6
Suicide	1	(0.4)	9
Unemployment	4	(1.6)	8
Poor government services	5	(2.0)	6
Lack of guidance	56	(22.0)	2
(total)	254	(100.0)	

Continued

Appendix D. Powerlessness and Other Social Measures for the U.S. Youth (cont.)

| | United States | | |
	N	Percent	Rank
FAMILY LIFE			
Live with			
Both parents	112	(36.0)	2
Mother	136	(43.7)	1
Father	10	(3.2)	5
Grandparents	19	(6.1)	3
Other relatives	14	(4.5)	4
Alone	6	(1.9)	6
Friends	6	(1.9)	6
Partner	5	(1.6)	8
Spouse	3	(1.0)	9
(total)	311	(100.0)	

	N	Percent	Rank
FUTURE PROJECTIONS			
Life in 2 yrs			
Working	53	(19.6)	2
Secondary school	26	(9.6)	4
University	120	(44.3)	1
Married	4	(1.5)	6
Having children	3	(1.1)	7
Pursue career	44	(16.2)	3
Unemployed	—[c]	—	
Others	21	(7.7)	5
(total)	271	(100.0)	
Life in 5 yrs			
Working	75	(28.3)	1
Secondary school	4	(1.5)	7
University	68	(25.7)	2
Married	28	(10.6)	4
Having children	10	(3.8)	6
Pursue career	61	(23.0)	3
Others	19	(7.2)	5
(total)	265	(100.0)	

NOTE: Numbers in parentheses are percentages.

a) Agree denotes two response categories: strongly agree and agree.

b) Disagree denotes two response categories: strongly disagree and disagree.

c) — denotes no response to that category.

Index

About the Author

Charles Green is professor and chairman in the Department of Sociology at Hunter College of the City University of New York. He also teaches in the Ph.D. program in sociology at the CUNY Graduate School and University Center. His published works have been in the areas of race and ethnic relations, urban politics, Caribbean migration, and comparative urban development issues. He is the coauthor of *The Struggle for Black Empowerment in New York City: Beyond the Politics of Pigmentation* and editor of *Globalization and Survival in the Black Diaspora: The New Urban Challenge.*